GOD DOESN'T NEED YOUR MONEY

God Isn't Collecting. Your Pastor Is.

By Reuben Armstrong

Copyright © 2026 by Reuben Armstrong
All rights reserved.

No part of this book may be reproduced or used in any manner without written permission of the copyright owner except for the use of quotations in a book review.

First Edition: April 2026

ISBN: 978-0-9798360-2-2

Published by Open Ledger Press

Contact: reubenarmstrong4907@gmail.com

IMPORTANT LEGAL NOTICE

This book represents the author's opinions, observations, and analysis based on documented sources and personal experience. It is not intended as legal, financial, tax, or professional advice. Readers should consult qualified professionals for guidance specific to their situations.

All opinions expressed are protected speech under the First Amendment. Net worth figures are sourced from publicly available financial reporting including Forbes, Celebrity Net Worth, and investigative journalism. Descriptions of institutional patterns are based on documented cases, journalistic investigations, and publicly available information — not accusations against any specific individual or organization unless explicitly stated with sourcing.

The author is not a licensed attorney, financial advisor, or mental health professional. Nothing in this book should be construed as professional advice in those fields.

Content Warning

This book contains detailed accounts of financial exploitation, emotional manipulation, and spiritual abuse within religious institutions.

If you are currently experiencing church hurt or religious trauma, please proceed with self-care. Some readers have reported that certain chapters triggered strong emotional responses. This is normal. Take breaks as needed.

Resources for support are provided in Appendix A.

Dedication

For everyone who knew something was wrong but was told the problem was them.

For every family bankrupted by seed faith while watching their pastor drive a Bentley.

For every woman trapped in the pastor's wife prison, serving without salary, suffering without voice.

For everyone who left and still hears the voice telling them they've betrayed God.

You didn't betray God. You protected yourself from people using God's name.

This book is for you.

You're not alone. You're not wrong. And you're finally free to say it.

How to Read This Book

This book documents a system. Its structure is intentional.

You are not required to read it linearly. Read based on where you are — not where you think you should be.

If you're still in a church and questioning: Start with Part 1 (The System) and Part 4 (The Extraction Tactics). These sections expose the structure and scripts that make manipulation feel spiritual.

If you've already left and need validation: Start with Part 5 (The Reckoning). These chapters focus on recovery, clarity, and rebuilding without surrendering your faith.

If you're researching for someone you love: Read the Introduction, Chapter 17 (Your Kids Are Hostages), and Appendix A (Practical Tools).

If you want the full picture: Read straight through. Each section builds on the last. The system only becomes fully visible when you see how theology, psychology, money, and control reinforce one another.

A note on evidence: Where specific dollar amounts or statistics are cited, sources are provided in References. Where patterns are described, they reflect documented, repeatable practices — not isolated incidents. All named individuals are public figures whose activities have been reported by multiple independent sources.

Read based on where you are. The system will reveal itself.

Table of Contents

◆ ◆ ◆

PART 4: THE EXTRACTION TACTICS 162

PART 5: THE RECKONING 196

Introduction

The Straw That Broke the Camel's Back

I am a believer in God.

Let me be clear about that from the beginning, because what follows might make you think I lost my faith. I didn't. I lost my faith in a system that uses God's name to operate systems that follow patterns of financial exploitation.

I grew up in church. Not casually. Not just Sunday mornings. I grew up IN church. I sang in the choir as a child. I directed the church choir as an adult. I was the drill team captain. I taught Sunday school. I went to Wednesday night prayer services. I knew the structure, the culture, the language, the playbook. I wasn't an outsider looking in. I was an insider looking around.

For years, I told myself what I was seeing wasn't what I thought it was. The financial pressure. The emotional manipulation. The lifestyle gap between pulpit and pew. I rationalized it. Justified it. Stayed silent about it.

Until the Sunday the pastor prophesied over me.

It was a typical service. High-energy worship. Emotional build-up. Then the pastor paused, looked directly at me, and said those words that make everyone in a charismatic church hold their breath:

"God is speaking to me about you." Everyone turned. This was the moment. The breakthrough. The word from God that would change everything.

He called me out by name. Publicly. In front of the whole congregation.

"God is telling me you're going through a lot right now. You're about to lose your house. But God says if you sow a seed of ten thousand dollars — right now, in obedience — He will bless you abundantly. Your house will be paid off in full." The congregation erupted. Shouting. Praising. Celebrating the prophetic word over my life.

I stood there, silent.

Because I didn't have a house. I lived in an apartment.

The prophet of God — the man who claimed to hear directly from heaven — didn't even know basic facts about my life.

But he knew exactly how much money he wanted from me: Ten thousand dollars.

I didn't correct him. Not publicly. What would I say? "Excuse me, pastor, but God must have given you the wrong address because I don't own a house"?

That would make me the problem. The one with insufficient faith. The one quenching the Spirit. The one causing division.

So I stood there. Nodded. Said "Amen" when I was supposed to. And walked out the moment service ended.

I was halfway to my car when I saw it.

The pastor, surrounded by his security team — yes, security team — walking through the parking lot like a celebrity. People waving. Smiling. Treating him like royalty.

He got into his Rolls-Royce.

His. Rolls-Royce.

I looked around the parking lot. The congregation that had just celebrated his "prophetic word" over me was getting into cars that shouldn't even be on the road. Rust. Duct tape. People who loved God, respected His work, gave faithfully — driving vehicles that were one breakdown away from the junkyard.

And the man who just told me God wanted my ten thousand dollars drove away in a Rolls-Royce.

That's when it hit me.

He was the one getting blessed. Not them. Not me. Him.

The prophecy followed patterns more consistent with sales tactics than divine revelation. A financial extraction attempt wrapped in spiritual language.

And I'd seen it work a thousand times before. I'd watched people give money they couldn't afford because a "word from the Lord" said they had to. I'd watched families go into debt funding building projects while the pastor upgraded from a Mercedes to a Bentley.

I'd watched it. Participated in it. Facilitated it.

And I'd called it ministry.

Walking to my car — my twelve-year-old sedan with the cracked windshield — I asked myself a question I'd been avoiding for years:

If God really wanted to bless me with a paid-off house, why would He require me to give ten thousand dollars I don't have to a man driving a Rolls-Royce?

And once I asked that question, a hundred others followed:

- Why do prophetic words always involve specific dollar amounts?
- Why does God's financial plan for my life require enriching someone else first?
- Why do people who give the most seem to struggle the most, while the people collecting the money live like executives?
- Why does questioning any of this get labeled as "touching God's anointed"?
- Why does the pastor need bodyguards?
- Why does blessing always flow upward — from congregation to pastor — never downward?
- Why does God's economy look exactly like a pyramid scheme?

I couldn't unhear those questions. And I couldn't un-see what I'd seen.

I didn't go back.

Not the next Sunday. Not ever.

People called. Texted. Asked what was wrong. Told me I was "going through something" and needed to come back to my "spiritual covering." The pastor sent word through intermediaries that he was "concerned" about my spiritual state. That I was "opening myself to attack" by leaving the house of God. That the blessing I walked away from would go to someone more obedient.

None of them asked why I left.

None of them wanted to know about the false prophecy. The Rolls-Royce. The ten thousand dollars. The pattern I'd finally recognized.

They just wanted me back in the seat. Back in the system. Back to compliance.

After I left, I started looking. Really looking. At the finances. The structure. The patterns. The playbook they all use.

I talked to other people who'd left. Hundreds of them. Their stories were different in details but identical in structure.

Financial pressure. Prophetic manipulation. Lifestyle contradictions. Questions forbidden. Dissent punished. And always, always, always — the money flows one direction. Up.

I found former staff members who described exactly how the system works. Former bookkeepers who saw where the money went. Former leaders who were taught the scripts for extracting offerings. Former members who lost homes, marriages, and savings chasing promises that never materialized.

And it runs on one fuel: The belief that God's blessing requires your money.

This book is the investigation I wish I'd read before I gave them my life.

It's what I would tell my younger self — the choir director, the Sunday school teacher, the faithful member who believed that questioning leadership was questioning God.

It's what I'm telling you now.

God doesn't need your money. He never did. The church that demands it does.

And God doesn't need a Rolls-Royce. But the pastor collecting your seed faith does.

Not because I researched from outside. Because I participated from inside.

I was there. I saw it. I enabled it. I stayed silent about it. Until I didn't.

If you're reading this and you're still in one of these churches, I know what you're thinking.

"This isn't my pastor. My church is different. This is bitter exaggeration." I thought that too. For years.

I defended my pastor. My church. My experience.

Until the evidence became undeniable.

So here's what I ask. Read this book and test what I'm saying against what you're experiencing. Not what you want to be true. What actually is true.

If your church is healthy, transparent, and genuinely serving people — you'll recognize the difference between what I describe and what you're part of.

But if what I describe sounds familiar. If you've felt that nagging sense that something's wrong but couldn't name it. If you've given money you couldn't afford because a prophetic word said you had to.

This book is for you.

This isn't an attack on Christianity, all churches, or all pastors. I'm still a believer. Many denominations — including mainline Protestant churches, Catholic parishes, and countless faithful congregations — operate with transparency, accountability, and genuine service. Many pastors are faithful, sacrificial servants doing honest, humble work.

This book targets a specific system: prosperity gospel theology and the financial extraction mechanisms it enables.

A system that uses religious framing in what critics describe as what would be called fraud in any other context.

A system that preys on people's desperation and calls it faith.

A system that makes prophets wealthy and congregants poor, then blames the congregants for lacking faith when the promised blessing doesn't arrive.

I still see that Rolls-Royce sometimes. In my mind. Driving away from a parking lot full of broken-down cars.

It's the image I can't shake. The moment I can't forget. The truth I can't unsee.

A man who claims to speak for God, demanding money from people who drive cars held together with prayer and duct tape, while he drives a vehicle that costs more than most of their annual income.

That's not ministry. That's not blessing. That follows patterns associated with confidence schemes in non-religious contexts.

And if you've experienced anything like what I'm describing, you already know it. You just might not have had permission to say it out loud yet.

Consider this your permission.

God doesn't need your money.

But the system that uses His name does.

The pages that follow will show you exactly how that system works.

And more importantly, how to recognize it, resist it, and walk away from it without walking away from God.

Because I learned something that Sunday in the parking lot.

Leaving the church that exploited me wasn't abandoning faith.

It was the most faithful thing I'd ever done.

Now let me show you why.

The $64 Billion Dollar Question

That day in the parking lot changed everything. But my story is just one of millions. To grasp the scope of what we're dealing with, look at the money.

"According to Giving USA and the National Study of Congregations' Economic Practices, U.S. religious congregations collectively receive tens of billions of dollars annually in donations commonly described as tithes and offerings."

Not to transparency. According to church transparency advocates and research on religious financial disclosure, most churches refuse to disclose detailed finances even to their own members.

So where does the money go?

Not to the poor.

It goes to real estate, payrolls, branding, and expansion — the machinery that keeps the donations coming. Churches spend enormous sums maintaining stages, screens, staff, and marketing pipelines designed to extract more money from the same people, week after week.

Meanwhile, the average American Christian gives far less than the preached 10 percent tithe, yet lives under constant pressure and guilt for "robbing God." Single parents choose between groceries and obedience. Seniors on fixed incomes are told their faith is measured by what they put in the offering plate. Medical bills don't pause for sermons.

At the top, the contrast is impossible to ignore.

Some megachurches operate on budgets in the tens of millions of dollars annually — complete with executive compensation packages, luxury vehicles, private travel, and lifestyle perks justified as "God's blessing." These organizations function with the scale and discipline of major corporations, while their members quietly take second jobs just to stay afloat.

And the most damning question isn't how much churches take in.

It's why so little ever reaches the people Jesus talked about most.

This book answers one question: If God needs nothing from you, why does the church demand it?

The answer will make you angry.

It should.

God needs nothing from you.

Your pastor does.

The building fund does.

The private jet does.

But God?

God never asked for it.

THIS BOOK IS NOT ABOUT LOSING FAITH.

It's about distinguishing God from the people who've built empires using God's name.

"Many New Testament scholars — including D. A. Carson, Craig Blomberg, and Andreas Köstenberger — note that the New Testament contains no explicit command requiring Christians to give a fixed 10 percent to a local church, emphasizing instead voluntary, proportional, and cheerful generosity."

It's about understanding that prosperity gospel follows patterns associated with financial exploitation — give to get rich only makes one person rich, the pastor collecting.

It's about exposing how churches operate like corporations, gangs, and cults — with manipulation, control, and extraction tactics refined over decades.

It's about naming what you've felt but couldn't articulate: something is deeply wrong.

A Note on Methodology

This book is based on firsthand experience inside church leadership, extensive interviews with current and former church members, publicly available financial data from tax filings and investigative journalism, and documented practices across multiple denominations and church sizes. Where specific dollar amounts or percentages are cited, sources are provided in the References section.

Where patterns are described, they represent observable trends documented across numerous contexts, not isolated incidents.

Who This Book Is For

If you've ever wondered why the pastor lives in a mansion while you struggle to pay rent — this book is for you.

If you gave sacrificially while watching church leadership live comfortably, travel freely, and never seem to "trust God" the way you were told to — this is for you.

If you volunteered 20 hours a week for free while paid staff collected salaries, benefits, and authority — and were told it was "service" — this is for you.

If you've felt guilty for questioning where the money goes — this is for you.

If you were told that leaving the church meant leaving God — this is for you.

If you stayed longer than you should have because your kids would lose their friends, your family would judge you, or your community would turn on you — this is for you.

Let's be honest.

The offering wasn't voluntary. It was extracted — through fear, shame, and spiritual pressure — using eternal consequences as leverage.

And if you tithed faithfully for years, believed the promises, obeyed the rules, and never saw the so-called "windows of heaven" open

This book is for you.

You weren't broken. You weren't faithless. You were managed by a system that monetized obedience and called it devotion.

WHAT YOU'LL LEARN

You'll learn how modern churches are structured like corporations — with executive leadership, brand strategy, growth targets, and revenue pipelines — while insisting they are "not about money."

You'll learn how tithing was transformed from a voluntary spiritual practice into a moral obligation, enforced through fear, shame, and selective scripture, where questioning finances is framed as rebellion and silence is called faith.

You'll learn where the money actually goes — how much is absorbed by salaries, facilities, marketing, and expansion — and why so little ever reaches the poor, the sick, or the people churches claim to prioritize most.

You'll learn how guilt is manufactured and maintained, keeping people giving long after doubt, debt, and burnout have set in.

You'll learn how unpaid volunteer labor quietly replaces paid work, saving institutions millions while being sold as "serving God."

You'll learn why leaving the church often comes with a social cost — lost friendships, fractured families, and vanished community — and how that penalty keeps people compliant long after belief has faded.

You'll learn how prosperity theology reshaped Christianity into a transactional system, where obedience is promised reward, suffering is blamed on the believer, and leadership is exempt from the rules they enforce.

You'll learn why pastors rarely model the financial faith they demand from members, and how luxury is spiritually justified at the top while sacrifice is demanded at the bottom.

Most importantly, you'll learn how to separate God from the institution using His name — without fear, guilt, or manipulation — and how to reclaim your conscience after years of spiritual pressure.

This isn't about destroying faith. It's about exposing a system.

And once you see it, you can't unsee it.

The Challenge

Read this book. Evaluate the evidence. Test the patterns against your own experience.

Then ask the questions you were trained not to ask:

- Where does the money actually go?
- Why won't leadership show detailed, transparent finances?
- Why do I feel guilty for having boundaries?
- Why does questioning feel like sin?
- Why is leaving so costly?

If everything I document is wrong, you'll know. If everything I document is true, you'll have a choice to make.

God doesn't need your money. But the system extracting it absolutely does.

And it's time someone said that out loud.

Let's begin.

A Necessary Acknowledgment: Not All Churches

Before we go any further, this needs to be said plainly.

This book documents a system of exploitation — not the entirety of American Christianity.

There are healthy churches. Many of them.

There are pastors who live modestly, operate transparently, serve their communities quietly, and never weaponize fear or guilt to fund their work. Failing to acknowledge that reality would be dishonest — and it would undermine everything that follows.

This book is not an attack on faith. It is an examination of what happens when faith is institutionalized, monetized, and shielded from accountability.

If you recognize none of what's described here, that doesn't invalidate the evidence. It may simply mean you were never trapped inside the system this book exposes.

But for those who were — For those who lived it — For those who paid for it

What Healthy Churches Look Like

I've seen churches that operate with genuine integrity. They exist. And they tend to share the same unmistakable traits.

Financial Transparency. Healthy churches publish detailed, line-item budgets that are accessible to every member. They don't hide finances behind vague summaries or closed-door meetings. They have independent financial oversight — not the pastor's spouse, siblings, or inner circle approving the pastor's compensation. Questions about money are welcomed, not spiritualized into accusations of rebellion.

Modest Leadership. Their pastors live at or below the economic level of their congregations. They drive reasonable cars, live in ordinary homes, and don't accumulate personal wealth through ministry. When finances tighten, leadership absorbs the impact first. Sacrifice flows downward, not upward.

Accountable Structure. They have real governance — elders, boards, or denominational oversight with actual authority. Pastors can be questioned, challenged, and if necessary, removed. "Touch not my anointed" is not a shield against accountability. Authority is earned, not demanded.

Voluntary Generosity. They teach generosity without manipulating it. No prophetic dollar amounts. No emotional countdowns. No promises that God will return your donation sevenfold. They understand that coerced giving isn't generosity — it's extraction.

Outward Focus. A meaningful portion of their budget — often 20–40 percent — goes directly to community service, aid, and missions, not just buildings, branding, or expanding payrolls. Success is measured by lives served, not seats filled.

Healthy Boundaries. They encourage members to have full lives outside the church. They don't demand total access to your time, energy, relationships, or identity. Not every friendship has to run through a ministry program. Not every absence is treated as backsliding. They celebrate when people thrive — even when that thriving happens elsewhere.

These churches don't need to control people to survive. They don't need secrecy to function. And they don't need fear to fund their mission.

Which makes the unhealthy ones impossible to excuse.

How Unhealthy Churches Reveal Themselves

Unhealthy churches don't usually announce themselves. They reveal themselves over time — through patterns, not scandals.

Financial Obscurity. Budgets are vague, partial, or inaccessible. Requests for detail are deflected with spiritual language: "Just trust leadership." Financial decisions happen behind closed doors. Oversight is internal, circular, and loyal to the pastor — not the people funding the operation.

Elevated Leadership. Pastors live far above the economic reality of their congregations. Luxury is reframed as blessing. Questioning compensation is labeled envy or rebellion. When money is tight, the sacrifice never starts at the top.

Unaccountable Authority. Governance exists on paper but not in practice. Boards answer to the pastor. Elders are selected for loyalty, not independence. Scripture like "touch not my anointed" is used to shut down scrutiny and protect power from consequences.

Manipulated Giving. Giving is no longer taught — it's engineered. Emotional music. Timed pressure. Prophetic amounts. Promises of supernatural return. Fear of loss replaces joy in generosity. What's framed as "obedience" feels suspiciously like coercion.

Inward Obsession. The budget prioritizes buildings, branding, and expansion while community aid remains symbolic. Success is measured by attendance, giving totals, and visibility — not by who is helped when no one is watching.

Boundary Erosion. Your time is never enough. Your availability is assumed. Your relationships are monitored. Outside commitments are subtly discouraged. Exhaustion is praised as faithfulness. Burnout is reframed as spiritual weakness.

Social Consequences for Dissent. Asking hard questions changes how you're treated. Access disappears. Influence evaporates. Friends grow distant. Leaving isn't just a choice — it's a penalty. The cost keeps people compliant long after belief erodes.

Spiritualized Guilt. Discomfort is labeled conviction. Doubt is framed as sin. Boundaries are called selfishness. And if the promises don't materialize, the failure is always yours — never the system.

Unhealthy churches don't survive because people are stupid. They survive because the pressure is subtle, constant, and wrapped in spiritual language.

And once you see the pattern, the confusion lifts.

What remains is clarity.

Why This Book Still Matters

The existence of healthy churches does not negate the need for this book. If anything, it makes it more urgent.

Consider the scale.

The prosperity gospel movement alone represents billions of dollars in annual revenue — according to investigative journalism by outlets including the Washington Post, Houston Chronicle, and the Trinity Foundation — and has shaped the theology, expectations, and financial practices of millions of families. Megachurch culture has normalized CEO-style pastoral leadership, brand-first ministry, and growth-at-all-costs thinking across denominations that once rejected those models outright.

For many readers, this book isn't a critique of one bad church. It's the first time they're seeing their entire experience named.

Many people reading these pages have never encountered a healthy church. They don't know transparency is possible. They don't know accountability can exist. They don't know generosity can be taught without pressure or fear. What they were taught — explicitly or implicitly — is that any church that doesn't demand total commitment isn't really following God.

That belief didn't come from nowhere. It was taught. And it was profitable.

So if you're part of a healthy church, this book isn't written against you.

But it may help you understand:

- Why your friend walked away and never came back
- Why your adult child refuses to attend even on Easter
- Why someone you respect flinches at the word church
- Why people who once believed deeply now want nothing to do with religious institutions at all.

From the outside, exploitative churches often look indistinguishable from healthy ones. Same language. Same music. Same scriptures. Same smiles.

The difference isn't always visible until the questions start.

This book exists because too many people were harmed quietly, blamed for noticing, and shamed for leaving.

And because silence — especially spiritual silence — has a cost.

That's why this book still matters.

The Difference Matters

From the outside, the difference between healthy and exploitative churches is rarely obvious.

Both hold worship services. Both quote Scripture. Both talk about community, faith, and God's love.

That's what makes the distinction so dangerous.

The difference doesn't show up in the branding or the sermons. It shows up in the details.

How does leadership respond when someone asks hard questions? Where does the money actually go? What happens when a member needs to leave? Is generosity invited — or demanded? Are people empowered — or managed?

Those answers reveal everything.

This book exists to make those differences unmistakable — to help people recognize exploitation when they encounter it, escape it when they're trapped inside it, and, if they still desire spiritual community, know that something healthier is possible.

I still believe in God. I believe authentic spiritual community exists. I've seen churches that live the values they preach — quietly, humbly, without coercion.

But I've also seen far too many that don't.

And the people harmed by those churches deserve more than silence. They deserve someone willing to name what happened to them — clearly, honestly, and without apology.

That's why this book exists.

If your church is healthy — genuinely healthy, not just claiming to be — thank you. The world needs more of what you're building.

For everyone else:

Read on.

The system always reveals itself — once you know what to look for.

PART 1: THE SYSTEM

Chapter 1: The God Business – When Churches Went Corporate

American Christianity didn't lose its faith. It found a business model. The shift wasn't announced. It happened gradually, pragmatically, with the best intentions.

Churches Are Corporations Disguised as Ministries

Here's what they don't tell you:

They track the same metrics as businesses:

- Customer acquisition cost (how much spent to get each new member)
- Lifetime value (how much each member gives over time)
- Retention rates (percentage who stay year over year)
- Conversion rates (visitors who become members)
- Average revenue per user

The Numbers They Track on You

You are not just a member. You are data.

Many churches now use internal tracking systems to monitor your behavior the same way corporations monitor customers. Not spiritually. Operationally.

They track:

- How often you show up
- How much you give — and whether it's increasing or declining
- How many hours you work for free
- Whether you're embedded in small groups
- Whether your "engagement" is trending up or slipping

You are scored. You are categorized. You are flagged.

When your numbers drop, alarms don't ring because someone's worried about your soul. They ring because retention is at risk.

That's when the text comes. The call. The coffee invite. The sudden "we've missed you."

Not because you're hurting. But because you're fading from the system.

This isn't pastoral care. It's churn management.

Your doubts aren't treated as pain — they're treated as leakage. Your burnout isn't concern — it's attrition. Your boundaries aren't respected — they're red flags.

And once you see it, everything snaps into focus.

Why concern only shows up after attendance drops. Why generosity is praised until it slows. Why distance triggers pursuit — but honesty triggers discipline.

Love arrives after the metrics change. Attention follows declining revenue potential.

That's not shepherding. That's surveillance — sanctified and spreadsheeted.

And the most disturbing part?

Most people never realize they're being watched until they try to leave and discover the system noticed before God ever did.

Pastors Are Evaluated Like CEOs

Pastors aren't evaluated on faithfulness. They're evaluated on performance.

Performance reviews are built around metrics like:

- Year-over-year budget growth
- Attendance increases
- Giving per capita
- New campus launches
- Social media reach and brand visibility

Hit the numbers, you're rewarded. Miss them, you're warned. Keep missing them, you're replaced.

Bonuses are tied to targets. Job security depends on growth. Salary increases track budget expansion.

This isn't spiritual leadership. It's executive management — with scripture as the compliance language.

That's why dissent is dangerous. That's why questions are disruptive. That's why transparency is treated like sabotage.

They didn't just silence you. They trained you to silence yourself — to second-guess your instincts, suppress doubt, and call discomfort "conviction."

Because when leadership is rewarded for growth, there's only one rational strategy:

Extract more from the people already inside — and recruit more people to extract from.

That's not a failure of character. It's a system doing exactly what it was designed to do.

When Growth Became the Only Metric That Mattered

In modern church culture, growth is treated as proof of God's favor. No growth means failure. Flat numbers mean decline. Decline means replacement.

Churches that don't grow are labeled stagnant. Pastors who don't produce numbers are quietly — or publicly — removed. Boards that question growth strategies are told they "lack vision" or are "resisting what God is doing."

And once growth becomes the standard, everything else disappears.

Every decision gets filtered through one question:

Will this increase attendance and giving?

Not: Is this spiritually healthy? Not: Does this serve people's actual needs? Not: Is this true, ethical, or sustainable? Not even: Is this what God wants?

Just: Will it grow the numbers?

When that becomes the metric, the outcome is predictable.

The Corporate Playbook They Use

This isn't accidental. It's borrowed — directly — from business.

- Donor cultivation — treating high givers like VIP clients with special access and influence

- Upselling funnels — moving people from attending → volunteering → tithing → leadership
- Loss prevention — intervening when someone shows signs of disengaging or leaving
- Brand management — controlling the narrative, suppressing criticism, protecting reputation
- Market segmentation — targeting demographics most likely to give, serve, and comply

This is standard practice in megachurches. It's common in corporate-style churches. And any system that prioritizes growth over people eventually adopts it.

Because once numbers are the goal, people become the resource.

Burnout becomes acceptable. Manipulation becomes strategic. Silence becomes spiritual. And exploitation becomes "leadership."

The tragedy isn't that churches use these systems.

It's that they call the results revival and anyone who questions them a threat to God's work.

They Hired Business Consultants to Teach Them

This didn't happen by accident.

Churches pay tens of thousands of dollars to business consultants whose job is to teach them how to extract more — more money, more labor, more compliance — from the same people.

These consultants don't teach theology. They teach tactics.

They sell sessions on things like:

- "How to increase giving by 30% in 90 days"
- "How to stop the back door" — keeping people from leaving
- "Donor retention in a post-Christian culture"
- "Maximizing volunteer engagement" without increasing payroll

These aren't ministry conferences. They're sales training events.

The language is spiritual. The strategy is commercial.

People are reduced to funnels. Faith is reduced to leverage. And guilt becomes the most reliable conversion tool.

And it works.

It works because you don't realize what's happening. You think the sermon was inspired. You think the appeal was spontaneous. You think the timing was spiritual.

You don't know the slide deck existed before the prayer. You don't know the giving goal was set before the altar call. You don't know the follow-up was triggered by your data.

Because the most effective system doesn't feel like exploitation.

It feels like conviction. It feels like obedience. It feels like love.

And by the time you realize what was sold

You were the product the entire time.

The corporate machinery now in place, the next question becomes: who fuels it?

Chapter 2: The Product Was Always You

YOU ARE THE REVENUE STREAM.

Not a member. Not a soul. Not a person being shepherded.

You are a revenue-generating unit with a measurable lifetime value.

Churches don't talk about it from the stage — but behind closed doors, your worth is calculated.

Here's how it works.

How Churches Calculate Your Value

- Average member gives $2,500 per year
- Average length of membership: 7 years

That puts your baseline lifetime value at $17,500.

That's just the starting number.

If they can get you to volunteer, your value increases. You're invested. You're exhausted. You're less likely to leave.

If they can get you to lead, it increases again. Now you're not just giving — you're recruiting. You're enforcing the culture. You're keeping others in line.

If they can get you into automatic withdrawal, your value spikes dramatically. No friction. No pause. No moment to reconsider. The money moves whether you're thriving or drowning.

This isn't spiritual formation. It's revenue optimization.

Your attendance isn't worship — it's engagement. Your giving isn't generosity — it's recurring income. Your service isn't calling — it's unpaid labor that stabilizes the model.

Discipleship asks what's best for people. This system asks how much can be extracted before they burn out or leave.

The Volunteer Labor Extraction

Megachurches don't survive on faith. They survive on unpaid labor worth millions.

Let's do the math they never put on the screen.

A Typical 2,000-Member Church

- 200 volunteers
- Working 10 hours a week each
- That's 2,000 hours of free labor every single week

At $15 an hour — a conservative baseline — that's:

- $30,000 a week in labor they don't pay for
- $1.56 million a year in wages they don't owe

That money doesn't disappear.

It just gets reallocated upward.

Where the Money Actually Goes

And the people keeping the lights on? The ones running kids' programs, parking cars, cleaning bathrooms, staffing cameras, managing live streams, holding the whole thing together?

They get a thank-you slide. A volunteer appreciation brunch. A sermon about "serving with joy."

Not wages. Not healthcare. Not retirement. Not rest.

They're told it's ministry. But it functions like extraction.

Free labor stabilizes the budget. Free labor inflates leadership compensation. Free labor fuels expansion.

And the most insidious part?

The harder you work, the more "committed" you look — and the harder it becomes to leave.

And once you see it, you can't unsee who's paying for the church to grow.

Churches Monetize Your Emotional Needs

Lonely? They offer small groups. (Show up every week. Bring others. Stay spiritually "connected." Keep giving so you don't drift out of good standing.)

Struggling? They offer recovery programs. (Facilitated by unpaid volunteers. Funded by your donations. Your pain becomes both content and currency.)

Need childcare? They offer kids' programs. (Staffed by volunteers — who you'll be quietly pressured to become once you're "plugged in.")

Looking for purpose? They offer serving opportunities. (Translation: we need free labor.)

None of this is accidental.

Every program solves a real need — and then attaches strings.

Belonging becomes conditional. Support becomes transactional. Care becomes contingent on compliance.

Most of these systems aren't designed to heal you. They're designed to keep you embedded.

Because dependency is the engine.

Dependency keeps you attending. Attendance keeps you visible. Visibility keeps you pressured. Pressure keeps you giving.

And every giver ends up subsidizing the very system extracting from them — with their money, their time, their labor, and eventually their silence.

That's why dissent is dangerous.

Questions interrupt the flow. Boundaries slow the machine. Honesty threatens the model.

So dissent gets renamed.

Concern becomes negativity. Accountability becomes division. Self-protection becomes rebellion.

Calling dissent "division" is how predatory systems protect themselves — by making the problem your character, not their structure.

Systems that do aren't offering help.

They're harvesting need — and calling it ministry.

And once you see how your emotions were turned into leverage, you realize the most valuable thing you ever brought to church wasn't your faith.

It was your unmet needs.

Automatic Withdrawal Is the Goal

Automatic giving isn't a convenience. It's the endgame.

Churches push it relentlessly because it does exactly what leadership needs it to do:

- It creates predictable, recurring revenue budgets can be built on
- It keeps money flowing even when you're angry, questioning, or doubting
- It continues after you stop attending
- And many people forget to cancel it when they finally leave

Automatic withdrawal removes friction. And friction is where conscience lives.

Once the money moves without action, you stop deciding to give. You just are giving — whether the church still serves you or not.

Charging inactive customers.

Any other organization doing this would call it retention leakage — or quiet churn monetization. Here, it's wrapped in worship language and defended as obedience.

Automatic giving isn't about generosity. It's about decoupling money from consent.

Because once consent is removed, the system doesn't need your belief, your presence, or your agreement.

It just needs your bank account to keep doing what it was designed to do long after you've emotionally checked out.

That's not faith.

The Financial Engineering

Nothing about this is accidental.

What's preached as doctrine functions as financial engineering.

- Pledge campaigns manufacture psychological commitment before cash ever changes hands
- "Faith promise" giving locks in future income you haven't earned yet
- "First fruits" theology demands payment before rent, food, or medical bills
- "Storehouse tithing" forbids giving anywhere except the local church

- Gross vs. net debates exist for one reason: to maximize extraction

Every theological argument just happens to land on the same conclusion:

Give more. Give sooner. Give only here. Give even when it hurts.

That's not coincidence. That's design.

Scripture becomes the wrapper. Money is the payload.

When You Needed Help, Where Was the Church?

Medical emergency? "We'll pray for you."

Car broke down? "God will provide."

Lost your job? "Have faith."

Can't pay rent? "Sow a seed for breakthrough."

But keep tithing. Keep volunteering. Keep showing up.

Because when crisis hits, the relationship flips.

You are no longer the beneficiary of ministry. You are the funding source.

The Math That Tells the Truth

Church collects from you: $380 per month Church spends helping you in crisis: $0

Church uses your story as a testimony: Yes (free marketing) Church asks you to give more anyway: Always

You gave $380/month for 18 months = $6,840

You received when you needed help: $0

You borrowed from a payday lender at 400% APR instead.

The church's response?

They turned your suffering into a sermon illustration.

This is not ministry. This is extraction.

And it continues as long as you believe serving them is serving God.

What Churches Actually Sell

Community. Belonging. Purpose. Hope. Access to God. Protection from spiritual harm. Meaning in suffering. Peace about the future.

And the price is never posted.

It wouldn't survive daylight.

The real cost is attendance, service, compliance, money — and silence when things don't add up.

The transaction is never stated explicitly because it would sound exactly like what it is:

Transactional. Business-like. Exploitative.

Instead, it's framed as mutual.

We serve God together. We build community together. We grow together.

But watch the flow.

Members give time, money, labor, loyalty, and emotional buy-in. Churches return programming, affirmation, and access — all of which cost far less than what's extracted.

The equation doesn't balance.

It's not supposed to.

This is extraction disguised as partnership.

And the more someone invests, the harder it becomes to walk away without losing everything.

Programming Dependency

Churches don't just offer Sunday services.

They build total life infrastructure:

Childcare. Youth programs. Marriage counseling. Career networking. Financial advice. Recovery groups. Social events. Volunteer ladders. Leadership pipelines.

Every life function absorbed increases exit cost.

Your kids' friends are there. Your support system is there. Your calendar revolves around church events. Your identity is tied to church roles.

This isn't community.

It's capture.

I spoke with a woman who wanted to leave her church after credible abuse allegations surfaced against the pastor.

She stayed two more years.

Why?

Her teenage daughter would lose her entire friend group. Her husband's business network was church-based. Their marriage group was their only social outlet. Their kids' sports teams were church leagues.

Leaving meant rebuilding everything.

That wasn't accidental.

Churches understand this dynamic perfectly.

Integration creates loyalty. Dependency creates compliance. High exit costs keep people silent.

This is the same strategy used by corporations that build closed ecosystems.

Churches call it discipleship. Businesses call it vendor lock-in.

The mechanism is identical.

And once you see it, the language stops mattering.

Because the outcome is the same:

People stay not because they're thriving, not because they're convinced, but because leaving would cost too much.

That's not faith formation.

That's structural coercion — wrapped in worship music and defended from the pulpit.

And the system will keep working as long as no one names it for what it is.

Emotional Surveillance

Healthy communities care about members. Extractive systems monitor them. In churches operating as businesses, emotional transparency becomes data collection. Small groups aren't just fellowship — they're intelligence gathering.

Leaders track who's struggling, who's questioning, who might leave. Not to help.

To intervene before departure. I've seen churches use database systems that flag members with declining attendance, reduced giving, or expressed doubts. These people get targeted for "pastoral care" — which often means pressure to stay, recommit, increase giving.

One former staff member described their church's "retention strategy": "We had software that tracked everything. Attendance patterns. Giving trends. Small group participation. Serving frequency. If someone's numbers dropped, an elder reached out. Not to ask what was wrong. To remind them of their commitments.

To question their faithfulness. To warn about spiritual danger." This is management disguised as ministry. The care isn't for the person. It's for the retention metric.

Control in church culture doesn't announce itself.

It speaks the language of love, protection, and spiritual authority. "I'm speaking into your life because I care about you." Translation: Submit to my authority. "You need covering to stay spiritually safe." Translation: You can't function independently. "God is calling you to serve more." Translation: We need your labor. "Your doubts are attacks from the enemy." Translation: Stop questioning. "Leaving would be abandoning God's plan for your life." Translation: Don't go.

Every one of these statements frames control as care. Dependence as safety. Compliance as spirituality. The person being controlled learns to interpret their own discomfort as spiritual immaturity rather than reasonable self-protection. This is how manipulation becomes internalized. The voice of control becomes your own inner critic.

You police yourself more effectively than any leader could.

Authority that can't be questioned isn't spiritual. It's tyrannical.

Labor Extraction

Churches run on free labor. Volunteers teach children's programs. Run sound systems. Lead worship teams. Organize events. Staff welcome booths. Manage social media. Design graphics. Clean facilities. Provide security. Coordinate logistics. Handle administrative tasks. The work is real. The compensation is not.

A megachurch might have 200 volunteers working 10-15 hours per week. That's 2,000+ hours of unpaid labor weekly. At minimum wage, that's $30,000 in saved costs per week. Over $1.5 million annually. Where does that money go? Not to the volunteers who make the church function. To salaries for senior leadership. To building expansions.

To marketing budgets. To pastor book advances and speaking fees. This isn't community participation. It's wealth extraction. The people doing the work don't benefit financially. The people benefiting financially often don't do the work.

And it's framed as spiritual." Serving is how we grow." Giving your time is worship." Sacrifice builds character." Meanwhile, the senior pastor's salary increases with church growth-growth made possible by that unpaid labor.

Here's what eventually becomes clear: The church wasn't selling access to God. It was selling you. Your time. Your money. Your labor. Your story. Your emotional vulnerability. Your need for belonging. Your fear of spiritual failure.

All of it was inventory. All of it was monetized.

God wasn't demanding your compliance. The system was. God wasn't extracting value from your suffering. Leadership was.

The product was always you. And realizing that changes everything.

Chapter 3: The Prosperity Exploitation – Faith as Transaction

◆◆◆

The Prosperity Gospel Is the Perfect Extraction System

PROSPERITY THEOLOGY GENERATES BILLIONS WHILE IMPOVERISHING BELIEVERS.

Here's the formula:

Tell people God wants them rich.

Convince them giving unlocks blessing.

Collect their money.

Keep it.

"Investigations by the Trinity Foundation and major media outlets, including John Oliver's 2015 HBO segment, indicate that the U.S. prosperity gospel industry generates billions of dollars annually, though precise totals are difficult to verify due to limited financial disclosure requirements."

Where does it go? Not to the people who gave it believing God would multiply it back.

The Wealth Concentration Is Obscene

Prosperity-gospel leaders preside over ministries that control **tens to hundreds of millions of dollars in assets**, including private aircraft, luxury real estate, media empires, and book revenues.

Investigative reporting by outlets such as *Forbes*, the *Washington Post*, and watchdog groups including the Trinity Foundation has documented lifestyles of extreme wealth among figures such as Kenneth Copeland, Jesse Duplantis, Creflo Dollar, Joel Osteen, Joyce Meyer, and T.D. Jakes — made possible through donor-funded ministries operating with minimal financial disclosure.

They teach: *"Give to get rich."*
They got rich.
Most donors did not.

The Mechanics of Extraction

STEP 1: Create the promise

"Sow a $1,000 seed, reap a $10,000 harvest" Give your way out of poverty" Faith activates financial miracles"

STEP 2: Demonstrate with testimony

Show the few who succeeded (or claim they did)

Hide the thousands who lost everything

Create FOMO (fear of missing out on blessing)

STEP 3: Close the loop

If it works — God blessed your faith

If it fails — You didn't believe hard enough

The system cannot lose. Only participants can lose.

The Real Revenue Numbers

A Hypothetical (But Common) Example

Consider a large prosperity-style megachurch operating at scale. The exact numbers vary by church, but the math below uses **conservative assumptions** to illustrate how quickly revenue accumulates.

Weekend services

- 5 weekend services
- 3,000 attendees per service
  = **15,000 total attendees**

If the average per-person "seed offering" is $25 (not $50):

- 15,000 × $25
  = **$375,000 per weekend**

Add recurring giving

- Automated tithes and midweek giving (conservative estimate):
  $150,000 per week

Weekly total

- $375,000 + $150,000
  = **$525,000 per week**

Annualized

- $525,000 × 52 weeks
  = **$27.3 million per year**

That money comes from people who are often told — explicitly or implicitly — that giving more will unlock personal blessing, breakthrough, or financial return.

Where the Money Actually Goes

Investigative reporting and documented cases show recurring patterns in churches operating at this scale:

- Executive-level senior pastor compensation packages
- Luxury real estate and high-end personal residences
- Private aircraft owned or controlled by ministries
- High-value vehicles justified as "tools for ministry"
- Travel labeled as ministry that mirrors executive leisure
- Branding, expansion, and institutional growth priorities

What donors are promised: blessing, increase, and divine return.
What many receive when they struggle: little to no direct financial relief.

Kenneth Copeland Defends His Private Jets

In a televised interview, Copeland defended his use of multiple private aircraft, arguing that flying commercial would expose him to a "demonic environment."

Investigative reporting has documented that Copeland's ministry has acquired and maintained private jets through donor-funded "seed faith" giving, while operating with limited financial transparency.

Although Copeland's exact net worth cannot be verified, his ministry controls assets valued in the tens of millions of dollars — funded by donations from followers, many of whom give sacrificially in the hope of financial blessing.

The Scriptural Manipulation

They use Malachi 3:10 constantly:

"Test me in this.. See if I will not throw open the floodgates of heaven and pour out so much blessing." Men aren't missing from church. They're awake.

What they don't mention:

- This is Old Testament ceremonial law, not New Testament teaching
- It was about agricultural offerings to support priests, not cash tomake pastors rich
- Jesus never taught "give money to get money"
- Paul worked a job while doing ministry — he didn't demand salary

They cherry-pick verses that mention prosperity, ignore everything about helping the poor, and build a theology where God is a slot machine and they control the payout.

The Psychological Warfare

Many prosperity preachers weaponize shame:

Can't pay rent?" You're not tithing in faith." Lost your job?" You must have unconfessed sin blocking blessing." Medical bills piling up?" Sow a seed for healing breakthrough." Struggling financially?" You're robbing God." The message is clear: Your poverty is your fault. Your lack of faith. Your spiritual deficiency.

Meanwhile, the pastor buying his third house blames YOUR faith for why you can't afford one.

The Bankruptcy Stories They Hide

Families who gave their rent money as "seed offerings" and got evicted.

People who donated their savings believing God would multiply it — then lost everything.

Elderly members who gave their retirement because the pastor said God would provide — now living in poverty.

Cancer patients who gave thousands for "healing offerings" while delaying medical treatment — and died.

You won't hear these testimonies. They're bad for business.

The Legal Loophole They Exploit

Churches don't have to disclose finances.

Pastors can pay themselves whatever they want.

No accountability. No oversight. No consequences.

A CEO making $2 million from a company with $27 million revenue would be scrutinized.

A pastor making $2 million from a church with $27 million revenue is "blessed by God."THE MLM COMPARISON IS EXACT

Multi-level marketing:

- Promise wealth through the system
- Showcase a small number of success stories
- Attribute failure to insufficient effort or faith
- Allow profits to flow upward
- According to Federal Trade Commission research, the overwhelming majority of participants — often more than 99 percent in analyzed models — lose money or earn nothing meaningful

Prosperity gospel:

- Promise wealth through giving
- Show a few testimonies
- Blame failures on insufficient faith
- Profit flows to the pastor

- 99% of givers stay broke

It's the same extraction pattern — just with religious branding.

They Sell Hope to Desperate People

Single mothers choosing between food and offering.

Unemployed workers giving their last dollars believing God will provide jobs.

Sick people sowing "healing seeds" instead of getting medical care.

Elderly believers giving retirement savings for "breakthrough." And when the breakthrough doesn't come?

The pastor is in a mansion. They're in crisis. And they're told it's their fault for not having enough faith.

You didn't betray God. You protected yourself from people using God's name.

The prosperity gospel doesn't fail people.

It works exactly as designed: funneling money from the poor and desperate to wealthy charismatic leaders who live like celebrities while teaching that God wants everyone rich.

If God wanted everyone rich through seed offerings, pastors would be broke and congregants would be wealthy.

The fact that it's the opposite proves who the system actually serves.

Prosperity theology is the most effective financial extraction system ever developed because it makes failure the participant's fault.

The theology has a built-in escape clause: if giving doesn't produce blessing, you didn't believe hard enough. You gave with doubt. You had unconfessed sin. You lacked faith.

The system cannot fail. Only you can fail the system.

Poverty as Spiritual Failure

Prosperity theology doesn't just promise wealth. It weaponizes poverty. If wealth indicates God's favor, poverty indicates God's displeasure. If financial breakthrough comes through faith, financial struggle reveals weak faith. If blessing follows obedience, lack reveals rebellion.

This theology makes systemic poverty an individual moral failure. Racism doesn't cause economic disparity. Wage stagnation doesn't. Healthcare costs don't. Lack of faith does. I watched a woman sob at the altar because she couldn't pay rent. The prayer team surrounded her, laying hands, commanding financial breakthrough.

They asked what sin might be blocking her blessing. Then suggested she wasn't tithing properly. Then encouraged her to sow a seed even though she couldn't pay rent. Nobody asked about her job. Her wages. Her rent increase. Her medical bills. The questions weren't about circumstances — they were about spiritual correctness.

Because if the problem is spiritual, the solution is giving more. And if giving more is the solution, the church consistently benefits. Meanwhile, the pastor preaching this theology lives in a gated community, drives luxury vehicles, and sends his kids to private schools. His wealth isn't evidence of exceptional faith.

It's evidence of who controls the revenue stream.

What prosperity theology actually sells: Not wealth. Hope. Not healing. Control. Not breakthrough. The illusion that suffering has a purchase price. People desperate for change are told change available-if they just believe hard enough and give consistently enough. That desperation becomes the product.

Many churches monetize hope, package it as theology, and sell it to people who can't afford to keep buying. The pastor in the Rolex isn't proof God blesses. He's proof the system extracts. Every dollar in that watch came from someone who believed giving would change their life. For most of them, it didn't.

For him, it bought luxury.

Chapter 4: The Cost of Staying – How Extraction Becomes Doctrine

◆ ◆ ◆

Marcus was a worship leader for seven years. Unpaid. Twenty hours per week minimum: Sunday morning services, Wednesday night rehearsals. Thursday song selection meetings, monthly leader training, plus random texts from the worship pastor needing "quick help" with arrangements.

He worked full-time as an accountant. Exhausted himself serving the church. Tithed 10% of his gross income-about $600 monthly. Gave additional offerings when the church had special campaigns. Then his wife got pregnant. Complications required bed rest. Medical bills piled up.

He asked the youth pastor if there was any way the church could provide a small stipend, even $200 a month, to help offset the financial strain. The youth pastor said the church didn't have a budget for that. But he reminded Marcus that serving was an act of worship, that God would provide, that financial pressure often preceded breakthrough.

Marcus quit the team two months later. Needed the time to take a second job. The youth pastor was hurt.

Said Marcus was "letting the team down." Suggested his priorities were "out of order." Reminded him that "where your treasure is, there your heart will be also." Meanwhile, that same youth pastor earned $65,000 annually, plus benefits, from the church budget.

The senior pastor made $180,000, plus housing allowance, car allowance, and book royalties. Marcus had given the church seven years of unpaid labor. The church couldn't give him $200 in his moment of need. That's when he realized: the extraction wasn't accidental. It was the model.

Exploitation Without Malice

Most people imagine exploitation requires bad people doing deliberately harmful things. It doesn't. Exploitation thrives wherever incentives reward extraction and punish independence. It doesn't need villains. It needs structures. The pastor probably believed he was helping Marcus grow spiritually by encouraging sacrifice.

The senior pastor probably believed his salary was appropriate for his education and responsibility. The church board probably believed their financial policies were standard and biblical. None of them needed to be evil. They just needed to participate in a system where leaders benefit financially while volunteers absorb costs.

Where power concentrates at the top while accountability diffuses at the bottom. Where questioning is discouraged and loyalty is monetized. Good intentions don't prevent harm when structures incentive extraction.

SACRIFICE FLOWS DOWN, REWARD FLOWS UP

Watch where the costs land and where the benefits accumulate. Members sacrifice time, money, energy. Leadership receives salaries, authority, visibility. Members absorb financial strain to tithe. Pastors receive housing allowances, book advances, conference speaking fees. Volunteers work unpaid. Staff get health insurance and retirement plans.

The disparity is explained through spiritual framing. Leaders carry more responsibility. Their calling requires compensation. Their sacrifice is different because it's full-time. But notice: members' sacrifice is expected and praised. Leaders' comfort is justified and protected. Members are told to give until it hurts.

Leaders determine how much is "enough" for themselves — and it's always comfortable. That's not partnership. That's extraction dressed as spiritual maturity.

Silence Through Social Consequence

People learn silence by watching what happens to those who speak. Someone questions financial transparency? They get labeled divisive. Someone asks why the pastor needs a luxury car? They get accused of envy. Someone requests accountability for leadership decisions? They get reminded about respecting God's anointed.

The consequences aren't always formal. Often they're social. Relationships cool. Invitations stop. Status diminishes. The questioner becomes suspect. This is how institutions enforce compliance without explicit rules. The pattern teaches itself. People see what happens to dissenters and decide silence is safer.

Eventually, self-censorship becomes automatic. People stop questioning because questioning has been associated with punishment so thoroughly that the impulse itself generates anxiety. The church doesn't need to threaten anyone directly. The culture does the work.

Eventually, some people see it clearly: God was not demanding burnout. The system was. God was not requiring financial strain. Leadership was. God was not punishing boundaries. The church was. God was not monetizing dependency. The church was. That distinction-between God and the systems claiming to represent God-is everything.

When you realize God never asked you to be exhausted, broke, and silent. When you understand that extraction isn't discipleship. When you see that leaving isn't betrayal but self-preservation. Everything changes. The power the church held over you evaporates. Not because you rejected God.

Because you finally distinguished God from the people who were selling God. God doesn't need the church to survive. But the church needs you to believe God does. And once you stop accepting that false teaching, you're free.

We've seen how the system operates — the corporate structures, the metrics, the financial engineering. But a system only works if it has fuel. The next section examines where that fuel comes from: the specific populations these churches target and the methods they use to acquire and retain them. Some of what follows may be difficult to read. It should be.

PART 2: THE EXPLOITATION

Chapter 5: The Missing Men – Why Churches Lose Half Their Audience

◆◆◆

The Gender Gap Nobody Wants to Discuss The ratio was impossible to ignore. I counted during a Wednesday night service at a 2,000-member church in Atlanta. Seventy-three women. Nineteen men. And twelve of those men were on stage — pastors, worship leaders, tech crew. That left seven men in the congregation. Seven. Out of a room of eighty-plus adults.

Let that sit for a moment.

This wasn't an anomaly. According to Pew Research Center data and the Hartford Institute for Religion Research, women consistently outnumber men in American congregations, with many churches reporting 60-65% female attendance — some significantly higher. The Barna Group's extensive surveys confirm this pattern across denominations. Sunday morning looks like a sea of women, with men scattered like punctuation marks in a long paragraph. The question nobody asks publicly: Why?

Why do women flood into churches while men stay away? According to the Bureau of Labor Statistics and multiple studies on religious volunteerism, women volunteer in religious organizations at significantly higher rates than men — some research shows rates 1.5 to 2 times higher. Women also give more consistently across income levels, according to the Women's Philanthropy Institute. Why do they serve more sacrificially and stay more loyal — even when leadership is problematic?

And definitely not to the pastors who've built empires on this dynamic. Because what looks like devotion is often something else entirely.

Research on gender socialization suggests women are often encouraged from childhood to seek help, admit vulnerability, ask for guidance, value relationships, and defer to authority when uncertain. According to a 2019 Pew Research Center study on gender and religion, women consistently report higher levels of religious commitment across virtually every measure. Men, by contrast, are often socialized toward self-reliance and emotional stoicism —

patterns documented in decades of psychological research. These are tendencies, not absolutes, and many individuals defy these patterns entirely.

Deferring to authority is emasculating. Emotional dependence is shameful. Churches market to the first group and repel the second. Not intentionally-though some are quite intentional about it — but structurally. The entire product is designed for people who've been taught that needing help is virtuous.

I spoke with a man who stopped attending church after years of regular participation. "Every sermon assumed I was broken and needed fixing," he said. "Every message was about submission, obedience, following leadership. I'm a grown man. I don't need a father figure.

I need equals who challenge me to think." He wasn't angry. He was bored. And he wasn't coming back. Meanwhile, his wife still attends. Volunteers in three ministries. Rarely misses a service. "She gets something from it I don't," he said. "I can't figure out what." I could.

Walk into any megachurch and observe the women in the front rows. They're not just attendees. They're devoted. Eyes locked on the pastor. Laughing at his jokes. Nodding at his points. Taking notes. Some visibly emotional. Some mouthing "yes" and "amen" throughout the sermon. The energy isn't religious.

It's romantic. Not always sexual-though sometimes it absolutely is — but romantic in the broader sense. The pastor provides what many husbands don't: attention, emotional availability, spiritual authority, confidence, vision, purpose. He remembers their names. Asks about their week. Prays over their struggles.

Provides certainty in chaos. Offers meaning in mundane life. Tells them they're valued, seen, important. For women in marriages where husbands are emotionally unavailable, checked out, or simply focused on work and kids, the pastor fills a void. He becomes the man who cares. The man who listens.

The man who makes them feel spiritually significant. This isn't accidental. Pastors cultivate this dynamic. Some consciously, some unconsciously, but the pattern is unmistakable. I've watched pastors work a sanctuary and the pews. The way they make eye contact. The way they touch shoulders and hold hands during prayer.

The way they remember details from previous conversations. The way they create intimacy through vulnerability-sharing struggles, admitting weakness, crying on stage.

It's not ministry. It's emotional affair infrastructure. One woman told me she'd been attending her church for eight years, volunteering twenty hours a week, before she realized she was obsessed with her pastor. "I thought about him constantly," she said. "Not sexually. But I wanted his approval.

I wanted him to notice my work. I wanted to be special to him. When he praised me, I felt high for days. When he ignored me, I felt devastated." She eventually left after realizing she'd structured her entire life around impressing a man who barely knew her name.

But the church had already extracted eight years of unpaid labor, consistent tithing, and emotional devotion. From the church's perspective, the system worked perfectly.

Charismatic churches add another layer: spiritual power as sex appeal. The pastor doesn't just have wisdom. He has "anointing." He doesn't just preach. He "flows in the Spirit." He doesn't just lead. He's "chosen by God." This framing makes attraction feel holy.

Strip away the spiritual vocabulary and you're left with: "I'm attracted to this man's confidence and authority, and the system has taught me to interpret that attraction as divine." Some pastors are aware of this dynamic and carefully maintain appropriate boundaries.

They limit private interactions with female congregants. Involve their wives visibly. Dress down the spiritual authority rhetoric. Create structural accountability. Others weaponize it — cultivating mystique instead.

They speak in prophetic language that creates dependence — "God told me to tell you." They offer private prayer sessions. They develop inner circles of trusted women. Then they test boundaries with increasingly personal conversations and touch. Any discomfort gets framed as spiritual attack or lack of faith.

The result is a church full of women competing for a powerful man's attention, all of it framed as spiritual devotion. Meanwhile, men watch this dynamic and check out. They see what's happening, even if they can't articulate it. And they want no part of it.

Here's what women won't say publicly but admit privately: many prefer male pastors. Not all women. Not even most. But enough that female pastors consistently face attendance challenges that male pastors don't. I've spoken with female lead pastors who've described the difficulty.

Women question their authority in ways they never would with men. Women leave when decisions get controversial. Women form competing power structures. Women gossip and undermine in ways that make leadership nearly impossible." Men might disagree with me," one female pastor said," but they do it to my face and then move on.

Women smile, say they'll pray about it, and then spend months creating coalitions to oppose me."

But the result is clear: churches with male senior pastors attract more women, retain them longer, and extract more volunteer labor and financial giving from them. Which means male pastors have a structural incentive to maintain the gender imbalance. The business model depends on it.

Manufactured Dependence

Testimonies showcase transformation through submission: "I was lost until I submitted to this church's teaching." "I was broken until I let leadership speak into my life." "I was confused until I stopped trusting myself and trusted God through my pastor." Small groups program emotional dependence: Share your struggles.

Be vulnerable. Trust us with your pain. We'll pray for you. We'll check on you. We'll make sure you're okay. This sounds like community. It functions as control. Because once someone's entire support system is church-based, leaving becomes impossible. Where will they go? Who will they talk to?

Who will pray for them in crisis? Research in social psychology suggests that women, on average, tend to prioritize relational connections and community belonging — making some more susceptible to institutional dependence. Men, who are often socialized toward independence and self-sufficiency, may resist such dependence more readily. These are tendencies, not rules — but the pattern helps explain why many churches end up with congregations where women feel unable to leave while men never fully engage.

The demographic churches love most: single women over 30. They volunteer at the highest rates. Give the most consistently. Attend everything. Serve without complaint. Stay loyal through leadership failures. And desperately seek the belonging and purpose that society tells them should come from marriage.

Churches provide a substitute: serve the church as bride of Christ. Find purpose in ministry. Build your identity around church community. Your singleness isn't failure — it's freedom to serve. The theology is beautiful. The application is exploitative.

I know women who've given twenty years of unpaid labor to churches that promised community and purpose, only to realize they've been used. They're now in their fifties, still single, with no savings (because they tithed sacrificially), no marketable skills outside church work, and profound resentment.

But the church got two decades of free administration, childcare, hospitality, and emotional labor.

From the church's perspective, the pipeline worked exactly as designed.

Churches claim they want more men. They host men's conferences. They preach about biblical manhood. They create men's ministries. But structurally, they don't want men. They want male leadership and female labor. Men ask questions that threaten authority. Men demand financial transparency. Men resist emotional manipulation.

Men, on average, don't volunteer at rates that make free programming sustainable. Men don't give as consistently according to philanthropy research. Many women — shaped by cultural expectations around relationships and service — fill these roles. From an institutional perspective, this creates a dynamic where women become the backbone of church labor: often devoted, often unpaid, and less likely to demand systemic change. This isn't a statement about individual women's capabilities or choices — it's an observation about how institutions exploit gendered patterns.

So churches market to women's vulnerabilities-need for community, desire for purpose, search for spiritual authority, longing for belonging — and extract maximum value while preaching male headship. The contradiction is intentional.

Men don't avoid church because they're spiritually deficient. They avoid it because they recognize the dynamic. The emotional manipulation. The manufactured dependence. The authority structure that demands submission without accountability. The celebrity pastor system that concentrates power and rewards compliance.

The financial opacity. The volunteer labor extraction. Many men see what's being sold and decide they don't need it — or they're less likely to find the relational trade-offs worthwhile. Many women, having been shaped by different cultural messages about the importance of community and spiritual guidance, may calculate that the trade is worth it — trading some autonomy for belonging, independence for purpose, questions for acceptance. These are generalizations that don't apply to everyone, but they help explain the stark demographic patterns.

Neither choice is wrong. But only one is profitable for institutions. And churches have built billion-dollar empires on that one choice.

There's one more piece to this puzzle: the pastor's wife. She's simultaneously the most important and most irrelevant person in the church. Important because her presence legitimizes the pastor's authority and deflects accusations of inappropriate relationships with female congregants.

Irrelevant because she has no real power and is expected to smile, support, and stay silent. The pastor's wife is the ultimate church volunteer: unpaid, overworked, always on display, never allowed to fail or complain.

She's supposed to be attractive enough to reflect well on her husband but not so attractive as to threaten female congregants. Involved enough to seem engaged but not so involved she develops independent authority. Spiritual enough to lead women's ministry but not so spiritual she questions male leadership. She's a prop.

And every woman in the congregation is watching her, either aspiring to be her or competing with her. This dynamic reinforces the gender hierarchy while creating plausible deniability about the pastor's relationships with other women." How could he be inappropriate?

"His wife is right there!" But proximity isn't protection. And many pastors' wives are the loneliest women in the building — surrounded by hundreds of people, none of whom they can actually trust.

Here's what churches never examine: What would happen if women stopped volunteering? The entire operation would collapse. Immediately. Children's ministry? Gone. Women run it. Hospitality and events? Gone. Women organize everything. Administration? Gone. Women handle it unpaid or underpaid. Small group coordination? Gone.

Women lead most groups. Worship teams? Decimated. Women fill most spots. Giving? Down 60-70%. Women give most consistently. Churches could survive without men. They'd just have smaller budgets and less leadership testosterone. Churches cannot survive without women. Which raises the obvious question: Why don't women demand better?

Why don't they demand financial transparency, equal pay for equal work, leadership positions, accountability for male pastors, protection from exploitation? Because churches have convinced them that demanding anything is unspiritual. That submission is virtue. That sacrifice is sanctified. That questioning authority is rebellion against God.

And because many women have nowhere else to go, church becomes their community, their purpose, their identity. Walking away means rebuilding everything from scratch. So they stay. They volunteer. They give. They hope. **And churches continue profiting from that hope.**

Imagine a church that said to women: "Your labor has value. Your questions are welcome. Your autonomy is sacred. Your boundaries matter. Your submission is not required. Your presence is appreciated, not exploited." That church would revolutionize Christianity. It would also have trouble sustaining the megachurch model.

Because respect costs more than exploitation. Equality requires sharing power. Transparency threatens revenue. Accountability limits growth. The business model requires inequality. Which is why churches preach male headship while depending entirely on female labor. Why they celebrate women's service while limiting women's authority.

Why they market to women's vulnerabilities while preaching women's submission. Why they need women more than they respect them.

It's not weakness. It's not naivete. It's not desperation for male attention. It's hope. Hope that serving will lead to belonging. Hope that devotion will lead to purpose. Hope that sacrifice will lead to significance.

Hope that submission will lead to safety. Hope that if they just believe hard enough, serve long enough, give sacrificially enough, the promise will be fulfilled. Churches know this. They market to it. They monetize it. They build empires on it. Because hope is renewable. Hope doesn't quit.

Hope keeps showing up, keeps volunteering, keeps giving, keeps believing-even when the return never comes. And as long as women keep hoping, churches keep extracting.

God doesn't prefer women's devotion over men's skepticism. God doesn't require women to be vulnerable and men to be stoic. The divine doesn't demand women's unpaid labor to fund male pastors' salaries. God doesn't benefit from gender imbalance in churches. But institutions do.

And until women recognize the difference between serving God and serving systems that exploit God's name, the gender gap will persist. Not because women are weak. Because churches have made women's socialized traits-vulnerability, community-seeking, authority-deferring, relationship-prioritizing-the currency of institutional survival.

And they're willing to dress that exploitation in biblical language for as long as women accept it.

The gender gap in churches isn't a mystery. It's by design. Churches attract people who've been socialized to seek authority, value community over autonomy, and equate vulnerability with spirituality. In American culture, that's overwhelmingly women.

Men don't stay away because they're spiritually deficient or intimidated by strong women or uncomfortable with emotion. They stay away because they recognize a system designed to extract devotion in exchange for belonging — and they've been socialized to reject that trade.

Women recognize the same system but have been socialized to believe the trade is worthwhile, even virtuous. Both responses are rational given gender socialization. But only one is profitable. And churches have built billion-dollar businesses on that one response. The question isn't why women come to church.

What are churches really selling them? And what's the cost of buying in?

The answer matters because it reveals the transaction at the heart of gendered church marketing. Women aren't being served — they're being sold an identity that requires ongoing church participation to maintain. The cost isn't just financial, though tithing extracts plenty. The real cost is autonomy: the freedom to define virtue, community, and spirituality on their own terms.

If you've wondered why your church seems designed for women but led exclusively by men, now you know. The missing men aren't a mystery. They're a market segment the church decided wasn't worth the investment.

Chapter 6: The Youth Group Pipeline – How Churches Groom the Next Generation

◆ ◆ ◆

They start young. That's the strategy. I watched a youth pastor give his annual "commitment talk" to a room of seventy teenagers. The message was simple: your faith needs to be your own now. Not your parents' faith. Yours. And to prove it's yours, you need to make three commitments tonight.

First: Attend youth group every Wednesday. No excuses. Sports, homework, family obligations-none of that matters more than God. Second: Bring friends. Each of you should commit to inviting at least one unchurched friend per month. That's your mission field. Third: Start tithing.

Even if it's just five dollars from your allowance or part-time job. God honors faithfulness, and you need to learn early that everything you have belongs to Him. The teenagers nodded. Took notes. Some cried. When the altar call came, forty-three of them walked forward to pledge these commitments publicly. I did the math later.

Seventy teens, attending weekly for a year, each bringing one friend monthly. That's potential growth of 840 new contacts. Teens who start tithing at fifteen continue through college, career, marriage, parenthood. Lifetime value per convert: potentially hundreds of thousands of dollars. The youth pastor's salary was $52,000 annually.

If he converted just ten teens into lifelong tithers earning median income, he'd generate $2-3 million over their lifetimes. From the church's perspective, investing in youth ministry isn't charity. It's customer acquisition.

And the product they're acquiring is children who've been trained since adolescence to equate faithfulness with financial giving, to prioritize church over family, and to recruit aggressively. This isn't youth ministry. It's multi-level marketing with Jesus branding.

Youth group isn't youth group anymore. It's a sophisticated retention and recruitment operation designed to capture children before they develop critical thinking skills. The programming is intentional:

Ages 12-14: Emotional Bonding

Middle school youth group focuses on fun, belonging, and identity formation. Games, pizza, silly competitions. The message is subtle: church is where you belong. These are your people. Outside the church, you're alone. Kids at this age are desperate for belonging. Their brains are wired for peer bonding.

Youth groups exploit that developmental stage by creating artificial community that dissolves if they leave. I've watched kids sobbing because they had to miss youth group for a family vacation. Not because they'd miss God. Because they'd miss their friends.

The church had successfully replaced family bonding with institutional bonding.

Ages 15-16: Ideological Commitment

High school youth group shifts to theology — or what passes for it." Why do you believe?" Is your faith real?" What makes Christianity true?" But these aren't actual explorations. They're inoculation sessions. Present simplified objections to Christianity, provide easy rebuttals, declare victory.

Kids think they've wrestled with doubt when they've actually been handed apologetics talking points. The real goal: prevent genuine questioning later. When they encounter sophisticated critiques in college, they'll assume they've already heard and defeated those arguments. They'll dismiss rather than engage.

Ages 17-18: Institutional Loyalty

Senior year youth group prepares kids for the transition. The messaging intensifies: Find a church at college immediately. Don't drift. Stay connected. Your faith will die without community. Translation: Don't stop giving. Don't stop attending. Don't stop recruiting. Churches track college freshmen closely.

If a kid stops attending church in the first semester, someone reaches out. A leader. A youth pastor. Sometimes the senior pastor himself." We're praying for you. Just checking in.

How's your walk with God?" Not: "How are you?" Or "How's the transition?" Always: "How's your walk?" Which means "Are you still in the system?"

Sexual Purity as Control Mechanism

The youth group obsession with sexual purity isn't about morality. It's about control. Teenagers have two primary drives: social belonging and sexual exploration. Youth groups weaponize both. The purity messaging creates shame around normal adolescent development. Attraction becomes sin. Masturbation becomes addiction. Dating becomes dangerous. Any sexual thought requires repentance. This serves multiple purposes:

First: Creates perpetual guilt. Teenagers who feel constantly guilty are easier to control. They believe they're broken, need fixing, require authority to stay on track.

Second: Prevents external relationships. If dating outside the church is spiritually dangerous, teens only date within the church. Which means their romantic lives become dependent on church membership.

Third: Establishes church as moral authority. If teens can't trust their own bodies and desires, they must rely on church teaching for everything. Church becomes the arbiter of right and wrong, normal and abnormal. I've spoken with dozens of adults who spent their teen years in purity culture. The damage is profound.

Sexual dysfunction. Relationship problems. Inability to trust their own judgment. Years of therapy trying to undo messages absorbed from ages thirteen to eighteen. But from the church's perspective? Those messages worked. Most of them are still attending. Still giving. Still recruiting.

The trauma was collateral damage in successful customer retention.

Isolation as Strategy

Youth groups don't supplement family life. They replace it. Wednesday night youth group. Friday night events. Saturday service projects. Sunday morning and evening services. Weekly small groups. Monthly retreats. Annual mission trips. A committed youth group kid spends 15-20 hours per week on church activities. That's a part-time job.

Unpaid, obviously. This schedule is deliberately overwhelming. It prevents teenagers from developing friendships outside church. It limits time with family. It makes leaving costly — not just socially but practically. Where will they spend their time? Who will they hang out with?

Parents often celebrate this involvement." At least they're not getting into trouble." Better than them hanging with the wrong crowd." What they don't see: the church is the wrong crowd. Just better branded.

Your anger isn't sin. It's your psyche saying: This should not have happened to you.

I watched a sixteen-year-old girl have a breakdown because she wanted to quit youth group to focus on school. Her parents supported her decision. The youth pastor did not. He pulled her aside. Told her Satan was attacking her faith. Said she was choosing the world over God. Suggested her priorities were out of order.

Warned that walking away always starts with small compromises. She stayed. Failed two classes that semester because she couldn't manage the workload. But she stayed. Which meant she kept attending. Kept giving. Kept recruiting. The youth pastor got a bonus that year for growth metrics.

Youth mission trips are genius business strategy disguised as service. Here's how they work: Teenagers pay $1,500- $3,000 to spend a week building something in a "developing country." They fundraise through car washes, bake sales, appeals to family friends.

The total raised often exceeds the trip cost-excess goes to "ministry support"(the church's general fund). The actual construction work could be done cheaper and better by local labor. But that's not the point.

The point is bonding teenagers to the church through shared experience, emotional manipulation, and poverty tourism. The formula is predictable:

Day 1-2: Culture shock. Everything is different, scary, uncomfortable.

Day 3-4: Emotional breakthrough. Kids see poverty they've never witnessed. Feel guilty about their privilege. Cry during evening devotions.

Day 5-6: Savior complex activation. They're helping! Building! Making a difference! They matter!

Day 7: Emotional commitment ceremony. Pledge to never forget this experience. Promise to stay committed to missions. Dedicate lives to service. Then they go home, post Instagram photos with poor children (#blessed

#missions #changed), and become fiercely loyal to the church that gave them that experience. The cost-benefit is incredible.

Spend $2,000 per teenager, gain a lifelong donor who feels personally invested in the church's mission work. They'll give thousands over decades, and they'll recruit others into the same system. I spoke with a man who went on four mission trips as a teenager.

He's now thirty-eight, hasn't attended church in fifteen years, and is still angry." We built the same schoolhouse three times," he told me." Three different trips, three years apart, same village. Each time they told us the previous structure had problems.

Looking back, I think they just tore it down between groups so they could keep bringing kids back." He spent $10,000 as a teenager-money his parents fundraised-building infrastructure that may never have been used.

But the church gained his loyalty for a decade, his parents' giving for two decades, and his siblings who followed the same path. The schoolhouse didn't matter. The bond did.

Conferences as Conversion Events

Youth conferences are emotional manipulation at industrial scale. Pack 5,000 teenagers into an arena. Blast contemporary worship for ninety minutes. Strobe lights, smoke machines, stadium sound. Peak the emotional energy until kids are crying, hands raised, completely overwhelmed. Then bring out the speaker. He doesn't teach. He performs.

Paces the stage. Voice rising and falling. Tells stories designed to provoke tears. Delivers ultimatums disguised as invitations." How many of you are tired of living lukewarm? How many are ready to go all in? How many want to stop pretending and get real with God?" Every hand goes up.

Social pressure and emotional overwhelm make resistance impossible." If you're serious, I want you to come down front right now. Don't wait. Don't think about it. Just come." Hundreds flood forward. Crying. Shaking. Convinced they've had a genuine spiritual encounter.

What actually happened: manufactured emotional crisis resolved through public commitment. It's the same technique used by timeshare presentations, cult recruitment, and high-pressure sales environments. The teenager goes home changed. More committed. More devoted. More willing to give, serve, recruit. The church counts it as a win.

But talk to these same kids ten years later. Many describe it as manipulation. They felt pressured. Emotionally coerced. Caught up in something they didn't understand. By then, though, the church has already extracted value. And there's a new crop of teenagers at next year's conference.

Youth groups don't just recruit members. They recruit future leaders. The progression is systematic:

Age 16: Join the youth leadership team. Help with middle school ministry.

Age 18: Become a small group leader. Responsible for 8-10 younger teens.

Age 19-22: College intern. Work part-time for the church, often for minimal pay or "stipend." Age 23-25: Full-time staff. Youth pastor. Worship leader. Administrative role. By age twenty-five, someone who entered youth group at twelve has spent half their life in the church system. They have no outside skills.

No other professional network. No identity apart from ministry. They're completely captured. And they're cheap labor. Youth pastors typically make $35,000- $50,000. They work 60-hour weeks. They're always on call.

They have no boundaries between work and personal life because "ministry is a calling, not a job." They also reproduce the system. Having been recruited young, they recruit young. Having been emotionally manipulated, they emotionally manipulate.

Having sacrificed education, career options, and life experience, they encourage the next generation to do the same. One former youth pastor told me: "I was twenty-four, making $38,000 a year, working seventy hours a week, and I'd convinced myself I was doing God's work.

I had no training in adolescent psychology, no understanding of trauma, no education beyond a Bible college degree. But I was responsible for the spiritual development of eighty teenagers." He burned out at twenty-eight. Left ministry. Spent five years deprogramming.

But the church had already gotten six years of cheap labor and whatever institutional loyalty he'd created

in those eighty kids. He was replaceable. They typically are.

According to former youth pastors and church leadership interviews, many churches set baptism targets for youth pastors. Ten baptisms this quarter.

Twenty this year. Growth percentage measured against last year's numbers. This creates obvious incentives. Youth pastors push kids toward baptism before they're ready.

Some as young as six or seven-too young to understand the commitment but old enough to count toward metrics. I've watched youth pastors baptize kids who clearly didn't want to be baptized. Parents pressuring. Peers watching.

Youth pastor framing it as "taking your faith public." The kid goes under water terrified, comes up confused, and everyone celebrates. It counts as a conversion. Gets reported in the church newsletter. Adds to the youth pastor's performance review. Never mind that the kid will likely deconstruct in their twenties.

The church got the photo op, the celebration, and ten more years of loyalty from the family. What's particularly insidious: baptism creates sunk cost fallacy. Once someone's been publicly baptized, leaving feels like betrayal. They've made their commitment public. Everyone knows. Walking away means admitting they were wrong.

Churches leverage this psychology." Remember your baptism." You made a commitment." Don't turn back now." It's not spiritual guidance. It's retention strategy using childhood decisions kids weren't ready to make.

Youth group only works because parents cooperate. Parents want their kids in church for understandable reasons: community, moral framework, safe environment, something to keep them busy.

What many don't realize: they're outsourcing spiritual formation to people with institutional incentives that conflict with their children's wellbeing. Youth pastors aren't primarily concerned with healthy development.

They're concerned with retention metrics, baptism numbers, and pipeline feeding into adult ministry. If a teenager's mental health suffers from purity messaging, but they stay in church, that's a win. If a teenager's academic performance drops from over-commitment, but they remain active, that's a win.

If a teenager develops anxiety from constant guilt and shame, but they continue tithing, that's a win. Parents see their kids engaged and assume it's positive. They don't see the mechanisms underneath-the emotional manipulation, the social pressure, the ideological control, the financial pipeline being established.

By the time parents realize something's wrong, their kids are often already captured. College-age, working in ministry, identity fully formed around church. I've spoken with parents who've expressed regret. "I thought I was keeping them safe.

I didn't realize I was handing them over to a system that would use them." But most parents rarely question it. Their kids grow up, stay in church, raise kids in the same system. The pipeline perpetuates.

Here's a pattern nobody discusses: churches encourage teenagers to attend Christian colleges. Youth pastors promote specific schools. Bring college recruiters to youth events. Frame attending secular university as spiritually dangerous. Christian colleges are often wildly expensive- $30,000- $50,000 per year.

Students graduate with $100,000+ in debt. But they've been steeped in church culture for four more years. They often meet spouses there. Their entire social network is Christian. Their degree may have limited marketable value outside Christian organizations. They're trapped.

With that much debt, they can't afford to leave the system. If they deconstruct, they lose community, career options, and often marriage (spouses who remain committed to the faith). So they stay. Work in ministry for poverty wages. Continue giving to churches despite barely surviving financially. The church benefits from this debt.

It creates dependence. It prevents exit. It ensures compliance. And it all started with a youth pastor encouraging them toward a Christian college at seventeen, when they had no concept of financial consequences.

Youth group isn't about spiritual formation. It's about customer acquisition and lifetime value maximization. The earlier churches capture someone, the longer they can extract value. A teenager who starts tithing at fifteen and remains committed for life represents $200,000- $500,000 in giving at median income levels.

A teenager who brings friends into the system multiplies that value exponentially. A teenager who goes into ministry becomes a recruiter, generating value through others for decades. This isn't about saving souls. It's about building pipelines. And the product being developed isn't mature Christians.

It's compliant donors who've been trained since adolescence to:

- Prioritize church over family

- Equate faithfulness with financial giving
- Recruit aggressively
- Submit to authority without question
- Suppress doubt and critical thinking
- Feel guilty for normal human desires and needs

That's not discipleship. That's indoctrination.

What would youth ministry look like if churches genuinely cared about teenagers' wellbeing over institutional growth? It would encourage critical thinking, not suppress it. It would promote healthy sexuality, not shame normal development. It would protect family time, not compete with it.

It would prepare kids for life outside church, not create dependence on it. It would celebrate questions, not provide prefabricated answers. It would acknowledge complexity, not offer false certainty. But that version of youth ministry doesn't serve the church.

That version produces adults who think independently, question authority, prioritize wellbeing over duty, and see church as optional rather than mandatory. That version doesn't generate predictable revenue or sustainable growth.

So churches build youth groups that program compliance, manufacture guilt, create dependence, and establish giving patterns early. Because the goal isn't raising healthy adults. The goal is raising lifelong donors.

I've talked to dozens of people who grew up in intensive youth group culture. Now in their twenties and thirties, many describe it as damaging. Sexual shame that required therapy to overcome. Anxiety from constant guilt and spiritual performance pressure. Inability to make decisions without external validation.

Broken relationships with family who they learned to deprioritize. Lost educational and career opportunities from overcommitment to church. Financial strain from tithing habits established in adolescence. One woman told me: "I gave my entire teenage experience to that church. Every Wednesday, Friday, Saturday, Sunday. I missed family events.

Stopped doing activities I loved. Lost touch with school friends. All because I thought God required it." I'm thirty-two now and I've spent the last five years trying to figure out who I am apart from church. I don't know I enjoy. I don't know what I believe.

I don't know how to make friends outside that context." They took my adolescence and used it to build their church. And I let them because I thought I was serving God." That's not a unique story. That's the pattern. And churches know it. They see the turnover. They see the deconstruction. They see the pain.

But as long as the pipeline produces enough new recruits to offset the losses, the system works. The cost to individual children acceptable collateral damage in successful institutional growth.

Youth ministry isn't outreach. It's not even discipleship. It's customer acquisition for a business model that depends on capturing people young, programming loyalty early, and extracting value for decades.

Every youth event, every mission trip, every conference, every small group-it's all infrastructure for long-term revenue generation. The youth pastor genuinely caring about kids? Maybe. Some probably do. But genuine care doesn't change structural incentives. The system doesn't need malicious intent.

It just needs people willing to participate in pipelines that groom children into lifelong donors. And as long as parents cooperate, teenagers are vulnerable, and churches profit-the youth group pipeline will keep running.

Do the math on a successful youth ministry:

Investment: $80,000/year (youth pastor salary + programming budget)

Output: 20 teenagers captured into lifelong giving patterns

Average lifetime giving per convert: $250,000 (conservative)

Total return: $5,000,000

ROI: 6,250%

From a business perspective, youth ministry isn't expense. It's the highest-return investment a church can make. And that's why they do it. Not because they love teenagers. Because teenagers are the most profitable long-term asset a church can acquire. The divine doesn't require your children's devotion. But the church building million-dollar budgets absolutely does. And they're willing to call that recruitment "discipleship" for as long as parents buy it.

This is what the youth group pipeline reveals: children aren't being discipled — they're being developed as revenue sources. The emotional bonds, the identity formation, the community belonging — all of it serves the institution's financial sustainability more than the child's spiritual growth.

If your teenager is deeply involved in youth group, they're not just finding faith. They're being shaped into a lifelong contributor. The question isn't whether youth ministry helps kids — some of it genuinely does. The question is whether the help is the goal or the hook.

Chapter 7: Safer on the Streets – Why Church Operates Like a Gang

◆◆◆

I had the conversation with a former drug dealer turned youth advocate. We were discussing manipulation tactics, loyalty enforcement, and territorial control. He stopped mid-sentence. "Wait," he said. "Are you talking about churches or the streets?" I was talking about churches. But his confusion was understandable.

Because the operational structures are nearly identical. Street organizations and religious institutions use the same playbook: recruit vulnerable people, create artificial family structures, demand absolute loyalty, punish dissent, extract resources, expand territory, and maintain power through fear mixed with belonging. The difference?

Street organizations are honest about what they are. Churches pretend they're something holy. But strip away the religious language, and you're looking at the same system. Same incentives. Same tactics. Same harm. The uncomfortable question nobody wants to ask: Are you safer on the streets or in the church?

The answer isn't as obvious as it should be.

Street organizations target:

Young people looking for belonging

People from broken families seeking structure

Individuals in poverty needing resources

Those seeking protection in dangerous environments

People wanting respect and status they can't get elsewhere

Churches target:

Young people looking for belonging

People from broken families seeking structure

Individuals in poverty needing resources

Those seeking protection from spiritual danger

People wanting purpose and meaning they can't find elsewhere

See the pattern? Both systems recruit people at their most vulnerable. Both promise what's missing: family, purpose, protection, belonging, significance.

A gang member told me: **"They got me at thirteen. My dad was gone. My mom worked three jobs. The older homies paid attention to me. Remembered my name. Asked about my day."**

"Made me feel like I mattered. By the time I understood what I'd gotten into, I was already in too deep."

A former church member told me almost identical words: **"They got me at fourteen. My parents were divorcing. I was lost. The youth pastor paid attention to me. Remembered my name. Asked about my struggle**

Made me feel like I mattered. By the time I realized what the church really was, I'd already built my entire life around it." Different context. Same mechanism. Same exploitation of vulnerability.

Street initiation might involve:

Being "jumped in"(beaten by members to prove toughness)

Committing a crime to prove loyalty

Public declaration of allegiance

Taking on a new name or identity

Getting marked (tattoos, brands)

Church initiation might involve:

Being "called out" in front of congregation

Public baptism to prove commitment

Altar call confession of allegiance

Taking on new identity (" born again,"" new creation")

Getting marked (baptized, sometimes literally tattooed with scripture)

Both are designed to create point-of-no-return moments. Public commitments that make leaving psychologically costly. Identity transformations that separate you from your old life. The difference is that gang initiations are recognized as coercive. Church initiations are celebrated as spiritual.

But a fourteen-year-old being pressured to get baptized in front of 500 people isn't making a free choice any more than a fourteen-year-old being jumped into a gang. Both are children being manipulated into commitments they don't fully understand, with consequences they can't predict.

Street organizations use family language intentionally:

"Homeboy,"" brother,"" sister"" We're family here"" Blood in, blood out"" Family for life" Leadership as father figures

"Brother,"" sister "in Christ

"Church family" Once saved, always saved"(or eternal damnation if you leave)

"Family of God" Pastor as spiritual father

This isn't accidental. Calling it "family" makes demands feel natural rather than coercive. Family language transforms "obey me" into "trust your family." It makes questioning feel like betrayal. It makes leaving feel like abandoning people who love you.

But real families don't require loyalty tests. Real families allow disagreement. Real families don't punish independence. Real families don't demand financial contributions to prove you belong. These aren't families. They're organizations using family language to manufacture obligation.

A gang uses "family" to keep soldiers working for leadership. A church uses "family" to keep members working for the institution. Both call it love. Both punish you if you leave.

This isn't bitterness. This is clarity.

Street organizations control territory:

- Claim neighborhoods as theirs
- Mark boundaries (graffiti, colors, symbols)
- Discourage members from leaving the area
- View other organizations as threats
- Expand by taking over new territory

Churches control territory:

- Claim neighborhoods through "church planting"
- Mark boundaries (signs, buildings, visible presence)
- Discourage members from attending other churches
- View other denominations as competition or heresy
- Expand by opening new campuses and "reaching" new areas

I watched two megachurches go to war over a suburban neighborhood. Both launched satellite campuses within two miles of each other. Both sent mailers to every house. Both ran billboards attacking each other's theology. Both preached sermons about "false teachers," clearly referencing the other church.

One pastor told his congregation, **"If you visit that church, you're putting your soul in danger. They preach a different gospel."**

The other pastor responded, **"Some people would rather have entertainment than truth. We'll be here when they realize their mistake."**

This wasn't spiritual concern.

It was a territorial dispute. Both churches were fighting over the same donor base, the same pool of volunteers, the same market share. The language was religious. The motivation was expansion. The tactics were straight out of gang warfare — just without the violence.

Though sometimes there *is* violence. Churches split over territorial disputes. Members attack each other. Families divide. Communities fracture. All while both sides claim God is on their side.

Street organizations have clear hierarchy:

- Founders or original leaders at the top
- Shot-callers making decisions
- Soldiers doing the work
- New recruits at the bottom
- Rank earned through loyalty and service

Churches have clear hierarchy:

- Senior pastor at the top
- Executive or associate pastors in leadership
- Staff and volunteer leaders doing the work
- New members at the bottom

- Influence earned through service and giving

In both systems, access to power requires proving yourself. You start at the bottom. You serve. You sacrifice. You demonstrate loyalty. Eventually, if you're useful enough, you get promoted. But the real power stays concentrated at the top. In gangs, shot callers make the money while soldiers take the risks.

In churches, senior pastors make six figures while volunteers work for free. In gangs, getting out is dangerous because you know too much. In churches, getting out is dangerous because you know too much-about finances, about scandals, about leadership failures.

Both systems protect themselves by making departure costly and by ensuring those who leave can't damage the organization without damaging themselves.

How street organizations enforce loyalty:

- Surveillance (members watch each other)
- Snitches face consequences
- "Checking in" systems (prove you're still committed)
- Public punishment for violations
- Violence or threats for betrayal

How churches enforce loyalty:

- Surveillance (small groups, accountability partners)
- Those who question face social consequences
- Attendance tracking (prove you're still committed)
- Public "church discipline" for violations
- Spiritual threats for leaving ("losing your salvation," opening yourself to demons)

The mechanisms are parallel. Both systems know that loyalty cannot be assumed — it must be continuously monitored and reinforced. Small groups aren't just fellowship. They're intelligence gathering. Someone notices if you miss. Someone asks why. Someone reports back to leadership if you express doubts.

Accountability partners aren't just support. They're oversight. You're assigned someone to confess struggles to, but that person often reports patterns to leadership. I spoke with a man who was in a church accountability partnership.

His partner asked about his marriage. He admitted he and his wife were struggling.

Within a week, the pastor called him in for a meeting. His "accountability partner" had reported the conversation. "I thought I was talking to a friend," he said. "Turns out I was talking to an informant." In gangs, they call these people snitches.

In churches, they call them "concerned brothers." Same function. Different language.

Street organizations extract money through:

- Required contributions from members
- "Taxes" on illegal activity in their territory
- Protection money from businesses
- Forced labor (members work for the organization)
- Consequences for not contributing

Churches extract money through:

- Required tithes ("10% belongs to God")
- Offerings, special campaigns, and building funds
- Expectations that members support church-affiliated businesses
- Volunteer labor (free work presented as service)
- Spiritual consequences for not giving

Here's what's remarkable: street organizations are more transparent about the extraction." You owe us X percent." Clear. Churches frame it as spiritual duty." God requires this." The consequences aren't physical — they're worse. Eternal. Supernatural.

You're not just extracting resources from the organization. You're **"robbing God."**

Analysis of sermon transcripts and firsthand observation show that pastors commonly preach Malachi 3:10:

"Bring the whole tithe into the storehouse.

Test me in this," says the LORD Almighty, "and see if I will not throw open the floodgates of heaven."

They typically emphasize the blessing. They rarely mention the verse immediately before it:

"Will a man rob God? Yet you rob me.
But you ask, 'How do we rob you?'
In tithes and offerings."

The implication is clear: if you're not tithing, you're a thief. A thief stealing from God Himself.

That's more coercive than any street tax. At least gangs admit they're taking your money. Churches convince you that giving it was your idea.

Leaving a gang might cost you:

- Physical safety (retaliation)
- Your reputation (labeled a traitor)
- Your community (cut off from most people you know)
- Your identity (you were someone — now you're nothing)
- Sometimes, your life
- **Leaving a church might cost you:**
- Social safety (isolation, shunning)
- Your reputation (labeled backslidden, deceived, rebellious)
- Your community (cut off from most people you know)
- Your identity (you were saved — now you're lost)
- Threats to your eternal life

Notice: church consequences can actually be worse. A gang might hurt you physically. A church threatens your soul eternally. A gang might kill you once. A church teaches you'll burn forever. A gang threatens your body. A church threatens your children-if you don't raise them right, they'll go to hell too. I've spoken with people who left gangs and people who left churches. The gang leavers talk about fear of violence, but eventual relief.

The church leavers talk about decades of guilt, nightmares about hell, broken families, and psychological damage that required years of therapy. One woman told me: "My gang-affiliated cousin got out after five years. He was scared for a while, but he moved cities and rebuilt his life.

He's good now." I left my church after twenty years. It's been eight years since I left. I still have panic attacks. I still wake up terrified I'm going to hell. I lost my parents, my siblings, my friends. Everyone.

And I still don't know if I made the right choice because they convinced me that doubting them was Satan." Which system was more dangerous?

Street organizations offer protection:

"Pay us, and we'll keep you safe from other gangs."(They're often creating the danger they're protecting you from)

Churches offer protection:

"Stay with us, and we'll keep you safe from spiritual danger."(They're often creating the fear they're protecting you from) Both are classic protection rackets. Street gangs create violent environments, then offer safety for a price.

Churches create spiritual terror, then offer salvation for compliance." You need us to be safe "is a misrepresentation in both contexts. You need them because they've created a system where not having them feels dangerous. But the danger is manufactured. The protection is conditional. And the cost is your autonomy.

Here's where people push back: "But churches don't commit violence!" Don't they?

Physical violence: Some do. Abuse scandals, beatings justified as "discipline," exorcisms that cause harm, faith healing that leads to deaths.

Psychological violence: Absolutely. Trauma from purity culture. Anxiety from constant guilt. Depression from failure to "measure up." PTSD from spiritual abuse. Suicidal ideation from rejection.

Economic violence: Undeniable. Predatory giving expectations. Financial manipulation. Families bankrupted by special offerings. People unable to leave because the church has their money.

Social violence: Systematic. Shunning. Reputation destruction. Family separation. Community exile. The violence isn't physical most of the time. But violence isn't just punches. Violence is any action that causes harm while preventing escape. By that definition, churches commit violence constantly. They harm people psychologically, financially, and socially — and make leaving so costly that people stay despite the harm. That's violence.

Just harder to photograph than a black eye.

Street organization leaders often:

- Live luxuriously while members struggle
- Make money from members' labor
- Have affairs with members' women

- Break the rules they enforce on others
- Protect themselves from consequences

Church leaders often:

- Live luxuriously while members struggle
- Make money from members' labor
- Have affairs with members' wives/daughters
- Break the rules they enforce on others
- Protect themselves from consequences

The pattern is identical because the incentive structure is identical. When you concentrate power without accountability, corruption is inevitable. Doesn't matter if you call the leader "shot caller" or "pastor." Doesn't matter if the organization sells drugs or faith. Power without transparency corrupts. Always. The difference: we expect street leaders to be corrupt. We act shocked when pastors are. But we shouldn't be. The systems create the same outcomes.

Street organizations use coded language:

Street terms for activities that sound innocent to outsiders Inside jokes that identify members Phrases with double meanings Communication that excludes non-members

"Spiritual warfare,"" seed faith,"" covering,"" anointing" Inside theological jokes and references Phrases that mean something different to members Communication that excludes non-believers Both create in-group/out-group dynamics through language.

If you don't understand the code, you don't belong. If you understand it, you're part of something exclusive. The language simultaneously creates community and isolation. It bonds insiders while alienating outsiders. It makes members feel special — they're part of something others don't understand.

But it also prevents clear communication. When everything is coded, accountability becomes impossible. does "God told me" mean? How do you verify it? What does "seed faith offering" actually mean? Who audits where it goes? What does "spiritual covering" actually mean? Who enforces its boundaries?

The vagueness is protective — for leadership.

Street organizations trap families:

- Father in the gang, son follows
- Siblings recruit siblings
- Generations stay in the same organization
- Kids grow up knowing nothing else
- Leaving means abandoning a family legacy

Churches trap families:

- Father in the church, son follows
- Siblings recruit siblings
- Generations attend the same church
- Kids grow up knowing nothing else
- Leaving means abandoning a family legacy

This is how systems perpetuate without force. When your identity is tied to an organization, when your family has been in it for generations, when leaving means betraying most people you love-you stay. Not because you want to. Because exit has become unthinkable. I know a man whose family has attended the same church for four generations.

He stopped believing in his twenties but kept attending until his forties. Why?" My grandfather helped build that building. My father was an elder. My siblings all go there. My mom would die if I left.

So I sit there every Sunday, pretending." He's trapped in a system he doesn't believe in, maintained by family loyalty and social obligation. That's not faith. That's generational captivity. And churches depend on it.

Every organization engaged in harmful practices claims they're different." We're not like those other gangs. We're about community, respect, protecting our neighborhood." We're not like those other churches.

We're about authentic relationship, biblical truth, genuine worship." Same defensive posture. Same inability to see themselves clearly. Because once you're inside, the system looks noble. The exploitation looks like sacrifice. The control looks like care. The extraction looks like stewardship.

It's only from outside that you see it clearly. And the system is designed to keep you inside.

If you described church operations without using religious language, most people would recognize them as predatory." We recruit vulnerable people by promising belonging. We perform public initiation rituals. We demand 10% of income. We use surveillance to ensure compliance. We punish people who question leadership.

We threaten consequences for leaving. We separate members from outside relationships. We call it family but enforce it through fear." Is that a gang or a church? The answer: both. The structure is identical. The tactics are parallel. The harm is comparable. The only difference is legitimacy.

Society recognizes one as criminal in law and protects the other as sacred. But sacred doesn't mean safe. And religious doesn't mean righteous.

Would you let your teenager join an organization that:

- Recruits them at their most vulnerable
- Performs public initiation rituals they can't take back
- Teaches them to prioritize the organization over family
- Demands financial contributions
- Monitors their behavior constantly
- Punishes questioning
- Makes leaving socially catastrophic
- Uses family language to manufacture loyalty
- Concentrates power in leadership without accountability
- Protects that leadership from consequences

If I described it that way, you'd call it a gang. But I just described youth group. And you probably sent your kid there yesterday.

Here's what makes churches potentially more dangerous than street organizations:

Street organizations are honest about what they are. They don't pretend to be something noble. You know what you're joining. The exploitation is visible.

Churches operate under moral cover. They claim divine authority. They frame extraction as virtue. They call control "spiritual covering." They brand manipulation as "discipleship." Street organizations have external accountability. Police watch them. Society condemns them. Law enforcement investigates them.

Churches operate with legal protection. Tax-exempt status. Religious freedom shields. Society defers to them. Investigations are rare and resisted.

Street organization members often know they're being exploited. They make calculations: the benefits outweigh the costs, or I can't escape safely, or I'll get out eventually.

Church members often don't realize they're being exploited. They think it's normal. Spiritual. Necessary. They frame their own exploitation as growth. Their trauma as transformation. That's more dangerous. At least gang members know they're in a gang. Church members think they're in a family.

So which is safer-the streets or the church? Physically: the church, usually. Psychologically: depends on the church. Financially: depends on the church. Socially: depends on what happens when you try to leave. But here's the real answer: Neither should be exploiting you in the first place. The fact that we're comparing churches to gangs at all should be alarming.

The fact that the comparison is accurate should be devastating.

Systems reveal themselves through their structure, not their stated purpose. Strip away religious language. Remove the moral framing. Look at the actual operations.

What you see is a hierarchical organization that recruits vulnerable people, demands loyalty and resources, punishes dissent, prevents exit, and concentrates wealth and power at the top. Call that a gang, and society condemns it. Call it a church, and society protects it. But the structure is the same. The harm is the same.

The exploitation is the same. The divine requires nothing from organizations that operate like gangs. But churches that profit from exploitation need you to keep believing they're different. They're not.

You can:

Stay and pretend the parallels don't exist. Convince yourself your church is different. Ignore the structure. Focus on the good feelings. Keep participating.

Leave and face the consequences. Social exile. Family rejection. Identity crisis. But freedom to think clearly, live autonomously, and stop funding exploitation.

Stay and fight to change it. Demand transparency. Require accountability. Challenge the hierarchy. Redistribute power. Watch yourself get labeled divisive and eventually forced out anyway. Most people choose option one. Because it's easiest. Because exit is costly. Because seeing clearly requires admitting you've been used.

But the structure doesn't change just because you refuse to see it. The exploitation doesn't stop just because you call it holy. And your participation doesn't become righteous just because someone put God's name on it.

I'm not saying churches are gangs. I'm saying churches operate using the same structural mechanisms as gangs-recruitment, initiation, loyalty enforcement, territorial control, financial extraction, hierarchy, coded language, and exit penalties.

I'm saying those mechanisms produce similar outcomes-concentrated power, unaccountable leadership, exploited membership, and people too afraid to leave. I'm saying we give churches a pass on behaviors we'd condemn anywhere else, simply because they use religious language.

And I'm saying that pass is killing people. Not physically, usually. But spiritually, psychologically, financially, socially-churches are causing significant harm to lives while claiming to save them. No deity requires your unconditional loyalty to churches that operate like criminal organizations.

God doesn't benefit from systems that look identical to gangs when you remove the vocabulary. God doesn't require you to accept exploitation just because someone dressed it in scripture. But the institutions profiting from that exploitation absolutely need you to keep believing otherwise. The streets might be dangerous.

But at least you know what you're walking into. Can you say the same about your church?

Chapter 8: The Miracle Marketplace – When Healing Becomes Business

The girl's name was Emma. Seven years old. Leukemia. Treatable-according to the oncologist, she had an 85% survival rate with chemotherapy (standard medical prognosis for childhood leukemia). Her parents chose faith healing instead. They'd attended a healing crusade three months after her diagnosis.

The evangelist-a man who traveled in a tour bus with his face airbrushed on the side-laid hands on Emma during the altar call. He declared her healed. Told her parents that seeking medical treatment would show lack of faith and reverse God's miracle. "If you truly believe," he said, "you won't need doctors.

"God's healing is complete." The parents believed. They canceled the chemo appointments. They stopped returning the oncologist's calls. They praised God and waited for the miracle to manifest physically. Emma died six months later. In pain. Confused about why God wasn't healing her.

Asking her parents if she didn't have enough faith.

The faith healer never followed up. Never checked if she was healed. Never refunded the $2,000 "seed offering" her parents gave that night — money they could have used for treatment.

He was in another city by then, performing the same show, collecting the same offerings, making the same promises. Emma's funeral was on a Tuesday. The faith healer held a crusade that Thursday. Told another crowd that he'd seen hundreds healed that week. Never mentioned the seven-year-old who died believing she just needed more faith.

This isn't an isolated story. It's a business model. And it's killing people.

Faith healing isn't about healing. It's about revenue. The business model is perfect: sell a product that can't be proven to work, can't be held accountable when

it fails, and targets people at their most desperate and vulnerable.

The pitch: God will heal you if you have enough faith.

The price: Substantial offering (suggested amount varies, always substantial).

The guarantee: None. If it doesn't work, you lacked faith.

The refund policy: There isn't one.

The follow-up: Rarely happens. It's a remarkably effective extraction system. The product is invisible. The results are unfalsifiable. The liability is transferred to the customer. And it's all protected by religious freedom. A terminal cancer diagnosis is a market opportunity.

A parent's desperation to save their child is a revenue stream. Chronic pain is customer acquisition. financial analysts and investigative journalism reports report the faith healing industry generates hundreds of millions annually. Not from healings-from hope. Because hope renewable.

Even when the healing never comes, people keep hoping, keep giving, keep believing that next time will be different. And faith healers keep collecting.

Faith healing services follow predictable scripts. Because they're performances, not genuine supernatural events.

Act 1: Build the Energy

Worship music for 45-60 minutes. Repetitive choruses. Key changes designed to trigger emotional release. Lights dim, then brighten at crescendos. Crowd singing, hands raised, emotions heightened. This isn't worship. It's preparation. Get people emotionally elevated, defenses lowered, critical thinking suspended. Create an environment where suggestion becomes reality.

Act 2: Establish Authority

The healer takes the stage. Shares testimonies from previous crusades. Shows videos of people walking, seeing, hearing for the first time. References scripture about faith and healing. Positions himself as conduit for God's power. The testimonies are always from other cities. The videos are never verified. The scripture is always taken out of context. But the crowd is primed to believe.

Act 3: The Demonstration

This is where the show gets technical. Because "miracles" require methods.

The Leg Lengthening Trick:

A classic. The healer has someone sit down, extend their legs. He manipulates their posture, rotates their hips, and "proves" one leg is shorter. Then, holding both feet, he subtly pulls on the "short" leg while relaxing the "long" one. The legs "even out." The crowd gasps. It's a miracle! It's actually basic geometry and body mechanics. Any chiropractor could explain it. But the audience doesn't know chiropractors. They know what they just saw looked miraculous.

The Planted Testimonies:

Some people in wheelchairs aren't actually disabled. They're paid. Or they're church members instructed to sit in wheelchairs for the demonstration. The healer calls them forward, prays dramatically, they stand and walk. The crowd erupts.

I've spoken with someone who was paid $200 to sit in a wheelchair at a healing service and then stand up when called forward. "They told me I was helping people believe," he said. "That my 'testimony' would increase faith in the room and that would help real miracles happen." He was helping people believe lies.

And he was part of a revenue operation that collected $50,000 that night from a crowd who believed they'd witnessed genuine miracles.

The Psychological Healing:

Some people do experience relief during healing services. Not because of divine intervention-because of psychological and physiological responses to suggestion, expectation, and emotional arousal. Psychosomatic symptoms can temporarily improve through belief and expectation. Chronic pain can be modulated by emotional states. Functional disorders can respond to intense belief. This isn't miraculous. It's documented psychology.

But faith healers claim it as proof of supernatural power and use it to justify asking for money.

Act 4: The Offering

After the demonstration comes the appeal. The healer explains that healing is linked to giving. That seed faith requires sowing financial seeds. That God honors those who give sacrificially. The suggested amounts are substantial. $100, $500, $1,000. For people facing medical bankruptcy, it's catastrophic.

But they've just witnessed "miracles." They're emotionally elevated. They're desperate. They give. The buckets overflow. The healer praises their faith. Assures them their breakthrough is coming. Most people never get healed. But they've already paid. And the healer is in another city next week.

"There are documented cases in the United States where children have died after parents chose prayer over medical care, even for treatable conditions such as urinary tract blockages, pneumonia, and appendicitis. In several cases, parents cited faith healing as their reason for refusing treatment, and subsequent reporting and legal action confirmed the outcomes."

A diabetic woman died after a healer told her to stop taking insulin." If you're healed, you don't need medicine." She believed him. Her blood sugar killed her.

A man with cancer refused chemotherapy after a healing service. He died eighteen months later, having spent his final time raising money for the healer's ministry.

A woman with a treatable heart condition died after being told her symptoms were "spiritual attack" and that seeking medical care would show doubt. The faith healers faced no legal consequences. Religious freedom protected them. The families were blamed for insufficient faith or "opening doors to the enemy." The deaths were treated as spiritual failures, not medical negligence. And the healers continued touring, collecting offerings, making promises, leaving bodies behind.

Why don't faith healers face legal consequences? Or practicing medicine without a license? Or negligent homicide? Religious freedom. Courts have consistently ruled that religious practices, including faith healing, are protected. Even when they kill. Parents can be charged — and some have been-for medical neglect when their children die.

But the faith healers who convinced them to refuse treatment? Protected. The church that taught them that medicine shows lack of faith? Protected. The system that created the ideology that killed their child? Protected. It's legal to sell fake healing as long as you call it religion.

It's legal to convince people to refuse life-saving treatment as long as you frame it as faith. It's legal to collect money for non-existent services as long as you claim divine intervention. A financial advisor who promised guaranteed returns and delivered nothing would be prosecuted for fraud.

A doctor who performed fake procedures would lose their license and face criminal charges. A pharmaceutical company that sold pills proven to be useless would face billions in fines. But a faith healer who promises healing, delivers nothing, and collects millions faces no consequences. Because it's religion. And religion gets a pass.

Faith healers use documented techniques that create the appearance of healing without any actual healing occurring:

The Temperature Check:

"I'm feeling heat coming from your body-that's the Holy Spirit healing you right now!" It's body temperature. most people has it. But in a heightened emotional state, being told you're feeling something makes you feel it.

The Pain Scale Manipulation:

"On a scale of 1-10, how much pain are you in?" Eight." Now how much?" Maybe. six?" Praise God! You're being healed!" The pain hasn't changed. The person's awareness and expectation have. Attention to pain and emotional state affect pain perception. This isn't healing. It's psychology.

The Vague Prophecy:

"Someone here has back pain. The Lord is healing backs tonight!" In any crowd over 50 people, someone has back pain. It's one of the most common ailments. The healer isn't prophetic. He's playing odds. When someone responds, he prays over them, they report feeling better (expectation + adrenaline), and the crowd believes they witnessed a miracle.

The Delayed Manifestation:

"You're healed, but it might take time to manifest physically. Keep believing." Translation: You're not actually healed, but I need you to keep believing so you don't ask for your money back. When the healing never manifests, it's the believer's fault. They stopped believing. They allowed doubt. They didn't stand in faith. The healer is never wrong. The theology is never questioned. The scam continues.

The blame shifts downward.

When the miracle fails, responsibility is quietly reassigned to the believer: insufficient faith, hidden sin, negative words, doubt, or disobedience. The promise is never questioned; the person is. Illness becomes evidence of spiritual failure. Death is reframed as mystery or "God's timing." There is no audit, no apology, no accountability.

The healer moves on. The stage lights reset. Another city. Another service. Another offering.

Medical bills remain. Bodies deteriorate. Families grieve. And the system continues unchanged — because it was never designed to measure outcomes, only revenue. Success is counted in attendance and giving, not recoveries. Losses are absorbed privately, while wins are advertised publicly.

In this model, healing is optional. Payment is not.

That's the tell.

The sick person is blamed." You didn't have enough faith." You're harboring secret sin." You're not speaking the healing into existence correctly." The enemy has a foothold in your life." Never: "The healer misled them." Never: "Faith healing doesn't work." Never: "The follows patterns associated with financial exploitation." The theology is designed to prevent accountability.

If healing fails, it's always the believer's failure, never the system's. This creates profound shame. People believe their illness is their fault. That their lack of healing proves spiritual deficiency. That they're disappointing God.

I've spoken with people who were terminally ill and felt guilty about dying. They believed their death would disappoint their church, prove they lacked faith, harm the faith of others. They died believing they were spiritual failures rather than victims of a predatory system that sold them false promises. That shame keeps people silent.

They don't warn others. They don't speak out. They don't want to be the one who lacked faith. The silence protects the healers. The shame isolates the victims. The system perpetuates itself.

Faith healing is organized like any other touring industry:

- An advance team books venues
- A marketing team promotes events regionally
- A production team sets up lights, sound, and staging
- A collections team processes offerings
- An administration team manages payroll

It's a business operation with professional infrastructure, sophisticated marketing, and revenue targets. The healing crusades aren't spontaneous moves of God. They're scheduled events with budgets, profit margins, and strategic planning.

One former staff member of a healing ministry told me: "We had spreadsheets tracking average offering per city. Some cities gave more, we'd schedule there more frequently. Cities that gave less got fewer visits." We also tracked demographics. Elderly crowds gave more. Poor communities gave at higher percentages of income.

We targeted accordingly." This is market research. Customer segmentation. Revenue optimization. It's business strategy dressed in religious language.

According to former insiders, children are the most heartbreaking victims of faith healing theology. They don't choose the beliefs. They trust their parents. They want to be healed. They pray desperately. When healing doesn't come, they believe they failed.

I've read accounts from adults who grew up with chronic illness in faith-healing environments: **"I was sick from age eight to age seventeen. Every service, I'd go forward for healing. Every time, nothing happened. I thought I was the problem."**

I thought God was rejecting me personally." My parents spent thousands on healing conferences while I deteriorated. They refused medical care because healers told them that would show lack of faith. I almost died before a family friend called CPS." I prayed every night asking God why I wasn't good enough to be healed.

I was twelve years old believing my illness proved I was spiritually defective." These aren't isolated experiences. This is the psychological cost of faith healing theology on vulnerable children who believe the lies their parents were sold.

What if faith healers said: "I can pray for you, but please see a doctor. God can work through medicine. Faith and medical care aren't incompatible." Revenue would drop. Because the business model requires desperate people choosing between faith and medicine. What if healers said: "If healing doesn't happen, it's not your fault. Theology isn't medicine. Belief doesn't override biology." The system would collapse.

Because unfalsifiable promises are the product. What if healers offered refunds when healing didn't occur? They'd go bankrupt — healing almost never occurs. The system can only exist by making promises it never has to keep, selling hope it never delivers, and blaming victims when the exploitation fails.

GOD DOESN'T NEED THE THEATER

God — if God exists and heals — doesn't need stage lights, dramatic music, manipulated wheelchair users, or suggested donation amounts. Doesn't require seed offerings to activate healing. Doesn't need tour buses with airbrushed faces. Doesn't benefit from people dying while faith healers get rich.

Every dollar collected for healing crusades is a dollar that could've paid for actual medical care. Every person convinced to refuse treatment in favor of faith healing is a person whose life could've been saved. Every child who died believing they lacked enough faith is a child killed by theology masquerading as medicine.

The miracle marketplace isn't selling God's power. It's selling false hope to desperate people and charging them everything they have. And when they die still accepting the false promise, the faith healers move to the next city and do it again.

Faith healing as an industry generates hundreds of millions in revenue. According to medical research and multiple peer-reviewed studies, faith healing as a medical intervention has a success rate statistically indistinguishable from placebo. Faith healing as a theological framework kills people who would survive with basic medical care.

The math is simple: Revenue in. Results zero. Bodies out. That's not ministry. That's a marketplace built on corpses and financed by desperate hope. God doesn't need your money to heal. But faith healers absolutely need your belief that God does. And they're willing to let you die to keep you believing.

Worship as Drug Delivery
The Neuroscience of Manufactured Religious Experience

She couldn't worship at home anymore. Only in church.

Sarah had been attending a large, non-denominational church for three years. Every Sunday and Wednesday, she arrived early to get a seat near the front. The worship set lasted forty-five minutes. By minute thirty, she was crying.

Hands raised. Eyes closed. Completely absorbed.

"It's where I feel closest to God," she told me.

Then she moved cities for work. She tried several churches. The worship was good — well-produced, professional musicians — but she couldn't feel anything.

She started driving two hours every Sunday to return to the church she'd left.

Then Wednesday nights too. Four hours of driving for 45 minutes of worship. Her friends questioned the commitment. She said she was seeking God. But what she was actually seeking was the feeling. That specific high she got from that specific environment.

Worship services trigger specific neurochemical responses. This isn't spiritual. It's biology.

Dopamine: Released during anticipation and reward. Worship builds anticipation (the bridge is coming, the crescendo is building) and delivers reward (the drop, the key change, the peak).

Oxytocin: Released during communal bonding activities. Singing together, raising hands together, and moving together create chemical bonding — the same hormone released during childbirth and breastfeeding.

Serotonin: Released during feelings of significance and belonging. Worship environments create both — you're part of something bigger, you matter, you're connected to the divine.

Endorphins: Released during prolonged physical activity and emotional intensity. Extended worship with movement (swaying, raising hands, dancing) triggers endorphin release — the same chemicals released during a runner's high.

Adrenaline: Released during heightened emotional states. Loud music, intense atmosphere, and crowd energy trigger fight-or-flight hormones that create alertness and intensity.

This cocktail of neurochemicals creates a powerful high. Euphoria. Connection. Transcendence. Meaning.

People call it experiencing God's presence. Neuroscientists call it a predictable chemical response to specific stimuli. And worship leaders know exactly how to trigger it.

Worship sets aren't spontaneous moves of the Spirit. They're carefully engineered experiences designed to produce predictable emotional and chemical responses.

Phase 1: The Build (Minutes 0-15)

Start medium energy. Familiar songs. Get people singing. Build community feeling. Release oxytocin through group participation. Lyrics focus on God's goodness, faithfulness, love. Positive emotional framing. Build trust and safety. Tempo moderate. Let people settle in. Establish baseline emotional state.

Phase 2: The Descent (Minutes 15-25)

Slow it down. Drop to intimate, vulnerable songs. Lower lights. Softer instrumentation. Lyrics shift to personal: "I need you," I'm broken," I surrender." Make it emotional. This is where dopamine starts releasing. You're anticipating something coming. The build is obvious. Your brain knows the pattern even if consciously you don't.

Phase 3: The Peak (Minutes 25-40)

Build intensity. Gradually increase tempo, volume, instrumentation. Add drums. Layer vocals. Raise lights. Repetitive lyrics: "Holy, holy, holy" repeated 20 times." I surrender all "repeated 15 times. The repetition is intentional — it bypasses cognitive processing and creates trance-like states.

This is where the full cocktail hits. Dopamine floods as anticipation meets reward. Oxytocin surges from communal experience. Endorphins release from sustained emotional intensity. Serotonin flows from feeling significant and connected. People cry. Raise hands. Some collapse. Some speak in tongues. Some have what they interpret as divine encounters.

What's actually happening: neurochemical overload producing altered states of consciousness that feel transcendent.

Phase 4: The Landing (Minutes 40-45)

Gentle descent. Softer songs. Bring people down gradually. Don't drop them abruptly-you'll lose the emotional carryover into the sermon. End with a song about commitment or surrender. Plant the seed for the altar call later. This formula isn't accidental. It's refined through trial and error, studied through observation, and passed between worship leaders as best practices.

Worship leaders use specific techniques to maximize emotional response:

The Key Change

Musicians know key changes trigger emotional elevation. Move from G to A during a chorus and watch the room respond. It's not God moving-it's musical psychology. Worship leaders strategically place key changes for maximum impact. Usually right before the final chorus. Right when you want people maximally emotional for the transition to the sermon.

The Bridge Loop

The bridge is where worship sets peak. It's the most emotionally intense section. Worship leaders will loop it-repeat it 4, 5, 6 times. Each repetition builds intensity. Your brain releases more dopamine each loop as anticipation heightens. By loop six, you're flooded with neurochemicals and completely absorbed.

This isn't spontaneous worship. It's calculated emotional manipulation.

The Strategic Pause

Watch a skilled worship leader. They'll stop singing, let the instruments fade, create a moment of silence. Then drop back in with the chorus. That pause triggers anticipation and attention. The drop back in triggers reward.

Dopamine spikes. Churches call it creating space for the Holy Spirit. Neuroscience calls it manipulating neurochemical timing.

The Emotional Anchor

Lyrics are written to create maximum emotional resonance." You're a good, good Father." Reckless love." No longer slaves to fear." These phrases trigger emotional associations-childhood, safety, freedom, love. The music becomes anchored to deep emotional needs. You're not responding to God. You're responding to language engineered to trigger specific emotional states.

The Crowd Psychology

Seeing others emotionally engaged triggers mirror neurons. When the person next to you raises their hands and cries, your brain unconsciously mimics the response. This is why worship works better in crowds. It's not that God shows up more powerfully in groups; it's that emotional contagion amplifies individual response.

Worship leaders know this. They plant people in the crowd who respond demonstratively — hands raised first, dancing first, crying first. Others follow.

The Sensory Overload

Lights, sound, visuals, movement, singing-multiple sensory inputs simultaneously. This overloads cognitive processing and makes rational evaluation difficult. When you can't think clearly, you feel more intensely. That intensity gets interpreted as spiritual significance. It's not. It's just sensory manipulation creating altered consciousness.

Here's what makes worship dangerous: it creates legitimate addiction patterns.

Pattern Recognition: Your brain learns the formula. Anticipates the build. Craves the peak.

Tolerance Development: Over time, you need more intensity to achieve the same high. Louder music. Longer sets. More extreme expressions.

Withdrawal Symptoms: When you miss worship, you feel off. Disconnected. Anxious. Spiritually empty.

Behavioral Compulsion: You prioritize worship over other activities. Rearrange schedule around services. Feel guilty missing worship.

Relationship Damage: Neglect relationships, responsibilities, self-care because worship comes first. This isn't relationship with God. This is addiction to neurochemical release that you've been trained to call God.

I've spoken with dozens of people who left church and experienced genuine withdrawal: "I'd have panic attacks on Sunday mornings. I felt like I was dying." I couldn't pray at home. I needed the environment, the music, the crowd.

Without it, God felt absent." I tried other churches but it wasn't the same. I'd leave feeling empty. I thought I'd lost my relationship with God." What they lost wasn't God. It was their drug supply.

Different churches have different "product"-different musical styles, different emotional intensities, different formulas. You get hooked on your specific dealer's specific product. When you try another church, it's like switching from cocaine to Adderall. Similar but not the same high.

So you drive hours back to your original church or stop going altogether.

Worship leaders are the most powerful people in church. More influential than pastors in some contexts. Because they control the supply. They decide the emotional journey. They employ psychological influence techniques on the chemical response. They create the experience that people attribute to God. Many worship leaders are aware of this power.

Some use it consciously. Others intuit it without understanding the neuroscience. A former worship leader told me: "I knew exactly how to move a room. When to build, when to pull back, when to trigger tears.

I told myself I was 'following the Spirit,' but I was following patterns I'd learned worked." I could predict when people would start crying, when hands would go up, when someone would fall out. Not because God was moving on schedule.

Because I'd engineered the emotional response." He quit because he felt like a manipulator, not a minister. Most don't quit. They enjoy the power. The affirmation. The feeling of being used by God. But they're not being used by God.

They're using people's neurochemistry to create experiences that benefit the church.

Here's what worship addiction takes away: the ability to encounter God outside manufactured environments. People lose capacity for:

Silent Reflection: Can't sit quietly without becoming anxious. Need constant emotional stimulation.

Personal Prayer: Can't feel God's presence without music, lights, crowd. Prayer at home feels empty.

Daily Spirituality: Compartmentalize God to worship experiences. Struggle to see the sacred in ordinary moments.

Critical Thinking: Can't evaluate teaching objectively when emotionally elevated. Become vulnerable to manipulation.

Independent Faith: Can't maintain belief without regular worship highs. Faith becomes dependent on institutional supply. This dependency is intentional. Churches want you hooked on the experience because hooked people return, give, serve, and recruit. If you could encounter God just as powerfully in your living room, you wouldn't need church. You wouldn't give. The church loses power.

So worship environments are engineered to be irreplaceable. The experience can't be reproduced alone. You need the church to access God. That's not spirituality. That's manufacturing dependence.

Megachurches have perfected worship as drug delivery:

Professional Musicians: Hired talent who know exactly how to perform.

State-of-the-Art Sound: Engineered to hit you physically. Bass frequencies you feel in your chest. High frequencies that create emotional clarity.

Lighting Design: Programmed to match emotional beats. Darkness for intimacy. Brightness for elevation. Strobes for intensity.

Visual Effects: Lyrics timed with imagery. Videos playing during songs. Multiple screens creating immersive experience.

Smoke Machines: Literally. They use atmospheric effects to create visual drama and sensory overwhelm.

Crowd Volume: Often amplified. Microphones in the audience mixed back through speakers so you hear yourself and others louder, creating illusion of bigger community response. This is concert production technology applied to religious service. It's not worship.

It's performance designed to overwhelm senses and trigger maximum chemical response. Small churches can't compete. They don't have the budget. So megachurches attract people addicted to the intensity. People who've developed tolerance and need more powerful doses.

What happens when the service ends? The chemicals fade. Dopamine drops. Oxytocin decreases. You return to baseline — which now feels empty by comparison. This is why churches schedule multiple services weekly. Keep you coming back before the high fully wears off. This is why people feel so different Monday morning.

Not because God's presence left. Because the neurochemicals depleted. This is why church hurt is so profound. You're not just leaving a community. You're losing your drug supply. The withdrawal is physical: anxiety, depression, restlessness, emptiness.

The psychological pain is real: feeling abandoned by God, questioning everything, profound sense of loss. But it's not losing God. It's detoxing from the addiction the church created.

What if churches said: "Worship is valuable, but it's not the only way to connect with God. Silence, nature, service, daily life-these are equally valid spiritual practices." People would attend less frequently. Give less consistently. The church would lose control. What if worship leaders said:

"We're using musical and psychological techniques to create emotional experiences. These feelings are beautiful but they're not the sum total of God's presence." The magic would break. People would recognize manipulation. The power would evaporate.

What if churches acknowledged: "You're experiencing neurochemical responses to specific stimuli. Enjoy them, but don't mistake manufactured intensity for spiritual depth." The addiction would end. Attendance would drop. Revenue would decline.

So instead, churches frame the chemical high as divine encounter, create dependency on the experience, and extract value from people who can't worship without them.

The deepest damage isn't physical or psychological. It's spiritual. Worship addiction trains people to:

Equate Feeling with Truth: If it feels powerful, it must be God. This makes them vulnerable to any system that generates intensity.

Confuse Emotion with Spirituality: Deep faith becomes about peak experiences rather than sustained character, ethics, service, transformation.

Depend on Institutions for God: Can't access the divine without church production. Lose autonomy and spiritual agency.

Prioritize Experience Over Justice: Care more about worship excellence than actually helping people. Invest in production while ignoring suffering.

Become Theologically Vulnerable: When emotional manipulation drives belief, any skilled manipulator can control you. This is why worship culture produces people who are emotionally elevated but ethically inert. Who cry during songs but ignore systemic injustice. Who pursue the high but not the holy. Because the high is addictive. Holiness is demanding. And churches prefer addicts to activists.

Worship has become an industry unto itself:

Worship Conferences: Thousands of worship leaders paying to learn manipulation techniques. (Though they call it "excellence in worship" or "leading people into God's presence.")

Worship Albums: Hillsong, Bethel, Elevation-these are commercial enterprises generating millions. The music is product. The labels are businesses.

Worship Training: Certification programs, online courses, coaching — all monetizing the knowledge of how to manipulate emotions through music.

Worship Consultants: Churches hire specialists to improve their worship experience. Translation: make it more addictive. None of this exists to help people connect with God. It exists because worship is profitable. The better you are at manufacturing intensity, the more people attend, the more they give, the bigger the church grows.

GOD DOESN'T NEED THE HIGH

God — if God exists and cares about worship — doesn't require:

- Professional production
- Specific musical formulas

- Neurochemical manipulation
- Manufactured intensity
- Crowd psychology
- Sensory overload

God doesn't benefit from your addiction to worship experiences. Doesn't need churches to engineer emotional responses and call them divine encounters. Doesn't demand that you mistake dopamine for the Holy Spirit. But churches need you to believe all of this. Because the addiction keeps you coming back, keeps you giving, keeps you serving, keeps you dependent. You're not a worshiper. You're a customer. The product is the high. The cost is your autonomy.

And the church is your dealer.

You can keep chasing the high. Keep needing bigger doses. Keep believing the intensity equals intimacy with God. Or you can recognize that what you're experiencing is beautiful, powerful, meaningful — and manufactured. You can acknowledge that neurochemistry doesn't negate spiritual value, but it does explain the mechanism.

You can learn to encounter God — or meaning, or transcendence, or whatever you're actually seeking-outside institutional environments that profit from your dependence. Real spirituality doesn't require a dealer. Real connection doesn't need professional production. Real worship doesn't have to be a drug.

But churches built on worship addiction need you to keep believing otherwise. Because once you realize you can connect with the divine on your own terms, in your own way, without their formula and without their control- You don't need them anymore. And they can't profit from you. That's the real threat to the church.

Not that you'll stop worshiping God. That you'll stop needing them to manufacture the experience.

"I volunteered 12,000 hours over ten years. At my hourly rate, that's $360,000 worth of labor. They called it 'serving.' I call it wage extraction with spiritual justification." — James, 52, Houston

The system has identified its targets. Now we examine how it keeps them. The mechanisms of control in exploitative churches aren't physical — they're psychological, social, and spiritual. Understanding them is the first step to breaking free.

PART 3: THE CONTROL

Chapter 9: The Pastor's Wife Prison – The Woman Who Can't Leave, Can't Speak, Can't Fail

◆◆◆

Jennifer wore makeup to cover the bruise. Sunday morning. Front row. Smiling like always. Her husband had shoved her the night before during an argument about church finances. She'd questioned where the building fund money was going. He reminded her-loudly, physically-that questioning him was questioning God's anointed.

On stage that morning, he preached about biblical marriage. How wives should submit. How God had designed men to lead. How a good Christian wife supports her husband's ministry above all else. Jennifer smiled and nodded. The congregation saw a supportive pastor's wife. She saw her prison guard getting praised for the lock on her cell.

After service, women hugged her. Told her how blessed she was. How lucky to be married to such a godly man. How inspired they were by her devotion. She wanted to scream. Instead, she thanked them and excused herself to teach children's church. Unpaid, obviously. She'd been running it for eight years.

That night, alone in the kitchen after everyone had gone to bed, she googled "how to leave your pastor husband." The search results were all articles about how to pray for restoration, how to submit better, how to be the wife a pastor needs. Nothing about how to escape. Because pastor's wives don't leave. They endure.

Or they break.

The pastor's wife occupies the most exploited position in the American church. She must be:

Visible but not authoritative. Present enough to legitimize her husband's leadership, invisible enough not to threaten the male hierarchy.

Attractive but not sexual. Pretty enough to reflect well on her husband, modest enough not to attract attention from other men or jealousy from women.

Involved but not independent. Active in ministry to prove she supports her husband, never so involved she develops independent power or following.

Spiritual but not theological. Lead women's Bible studies, but never challenge doctrine or correct her husband's teaching.

Employed but unpaid. Work 20-40 hours weekly for the church-administrative tasks, counseling, hospitality, children's ministry-receive no salary because "ministry is a calling, not a job." Perfect but relatable. Maintain impossible standards while appearing normal. Never struggle too much, never succeed too much.

One former pastor's wife told me: **"I had to be a Proverbs 31 woman, Pinterest mom, magazine model, professional counselor, event planner, and human shield — all while pretending it was effortless and acting grateful for the privilege."**

She left after fifteen years. Lost her community, most of her friends, her identity.

Gained her sanity. Most don't leave. They can't afford to.

Pastor's wives rarely have money in their own names.

The pastor receives the salary. The housing allowance. The book royalties. The speaking fees. His name is on the bank accounts. The mortgage. The car titles. The credit cards. Her contributions-years of unpaid labor, ministry work, supporting his career-give her no legal claim to assets. If she leaves, she often leaves with nothing. No savings.

No income history. No job experience churches value in secular settings. No credit in her name. She's economically dependent by design. I spoke with a woman who tried to leave her pastor husband after twenty years. She had no bank account of her own. No car in her name. He controlled everything.

When she told him she wanted to leave, he reminded her: "You have nothing. No money. No way to support yourself. Where would you even go?" He was right. She stayed five more years until her parents died and left her enough money to escape. That's not marriage. That's financial captivity dressed in religious language.

What does a pastor's wife do? Whatever the church needs, unpaid.

Children's Ministry: Often entirely her responsibility. Curriculum planning, volunteer coordination, Sunday morning execution. 10-15 hours weekly. No compensation.

Women's Ministry: Expected to lead or heavily participate. Bible studies, events, counseling, mentoring. 5-10 hours weekly. No pay.

Hospitality: Host church leaders, visiting speakers, small groups, new members. Cooking, cleaning, entertaining. Countless hours. No reimbursement for food costs.

Counseling: Women in the congregation bring marriage problems, parenting questions, spiritual crises. Often to her home or over coffee she pays for. No professional training. No pay.

Administrative: Help with bulletins, emails, social media, event planning. Whatever the church needs that they don't want to pay someone to do. No compensation.

Crisis Response: Member hospitalized? She visits. Someone dies? She coordinates meals. Natural disaster? She organizes relief. consistently on call. rarely paid. One pastor's wife calculated that she worked approximately 35 hours weekly for her husband's church. Over fifteen years at minimum wage, the church owed her $273,000.

She received nothing. Because she was "serving alongside her husband" and his salary covered both of them. Except his salary was for his role as pastor. Her labor was simply extracted free because she married him. That's not partnership. That's unpaid employment justified by marriage.

A pastor's wife carries responsibility for her husband's reputation — and the consequences when he fails-without any actual authority. She's expected to:

Cover his mistakes. When he's inappropriate, she explains he's under stress. When he's cruel, she says he's dealing with a lot. When he fails publicly, she stands by him visibly to minimize damage.

Perform happiness. Even when the marriage is broken, she must appear fulfilled. Even when he's abusive, she must seem content. Because his leadership depends on the appearance of a successful marriage.

According to denominational data, manage other women. Keep them at appropriate distance from her husband. Be vigilant without appearing jealous or controlling. If he has an affair, she often gets blamed for not being vigilant enough or not meeting his needs.

Absorb criticism. When congregants are unhappy with the pastor, they often complain to his wife. She's expected to listen, sympathize, and relay concerns gently — or shield him entirely by absorbing the complaints herself.

Protect the brand. Her behavior reflects on his ministry. If she struggles, questions, fails, or leaves-his leadership is compromised. She must maintain the image regardless of personal cost. I've spoken with women who stayed in abusive marriages for years because leaving would "harm his ministry." Not "harm him"-harm the ministry. The church mattered more than her safety.

That's not faith — it's coercion through institutional pressure.

Pastor's wives can't speak freely. About anything.

Can't criticize the church. It would undermine her husband's leadership. Make him look bad. Cause division.

Can't disclose financial information. Even when it's problematic. Even when it's illegal. She's expected to keep institutional secrets.

Can't discuss marriage problems. Because that would damage his reputation and credibility. She must suffer privately while performing publicly.

Can't express doubts. About doctrine, practices, leadership decisions. Her role is support, not challenge.

Can't establish boundaries. Saying no to ministry requests is selfish. Having personal needs is unsupportive. Wanting anything for herself is unspiritual. One woman told me: "I spent eighteen years being told that my feelings were attacks from the enemy, that my needs were selfish, that my desire for rest was lack of faith.

I wasn't a person. I was a ministry asset." That kind of systematic silencing causes profound psychological damage. Many pastor's wives develop anxiety, depression, chronic stress conditions. Some break entirely. But they can't talk about it. Because admitting struggle would harm the ministry.

Pastor's wives face unique sexual pressures. Purity culture teaches that wives should be sexually available to prevent husbands from temptation. For pastor's wives, this becomes even more intense-his sexual satisfaction is her spiritual responsibility.

If he struggles with lust, fails morally, or has an affair, she often gets blamed." She wasn't meeting his needs." She let herself go." She wasn't fulfilling her biblical duty." Meanwhile, she's exhausted from unpaid labor, emotionally drained from impossible standards, financially dependent and legally trapped, silenced and exploited.

But she's still expected to be sexually enthusiastic and available. I spoke with a woman whose pastor husband demanded sex multiple times weekly regardless of her exhaustion or health. When she refused, he'd preach about wives' biblical submission. Use scripture to coerce compliance. She felt raped by theology. Violated with Bible verses. She couldn't say no without being accused of disobeying God. That's not marriage. That's spiritual abuse weaponizing sexual coercion.

Pastor's wives often sacrifice healthcare because the church comes first. Salary barely covers family needs. Health insurance is often inadequate or absent. When resources are limited, she goes without. I've documented cases of pastor's wives who:

Delayed cancer screenings because they couldn't afford copays and their husbands prioritized church expenses.

Suffered chronic pain untreated because medical care would strain the budget and the church "needed" the money more.

Developed serious mental health conditions without treatment because therapy costs money and admitting psychological struggle would damage her husband's ministry.

According to former church staff, postponed necessary surgeries because taking time to recover would leave ministry needs unmet and create inconvenience for the church. One woman developed a treatable heart condition. She needed medication and monitoring. The church's insurance had high deductibles.

Her husband told her to "trust God" and wait until they could afford it. She had a heart attack at age forty-three. Survived, but with permanent damage. The church held a special offering — not for her medical bills, but for a new sound system. Because the church's needs consistently come first. Even over her life.

Pastor's kids are used as leverage against their mothers. If a pastor's wife considers leaving, she faces:

Losing primary custody. Courts often favor stability. He has the house, the income, the community support. She has nothing. Leaving means potentially losing her children.

Children being turned against her. The church will frame her departure as abandoning God, being deceived, choosing the world over faith. Her kids will hear this constantly.

Children losing their community. Their friends, their youth group, their identity — all tied to the church. Leaving destroys their social world, and they'll blame her.

Children suffering financially. If she leaves with nothing, she can't provide the same lifestyle. The kids suffer materially because she sought safety. So she stays. For the children. While the children watch their mother being exploited, abused, silenced, and destroyed. She's teaching them that this is normal.

That this is what faithful Christian marriage looks like. That this is what women endure for God. Her sons learn to expect this from wives. Her daughters learn to accept this as normal. The cycle perpetuates. Justified by scripture. Protected by community. Celebrated as sacrifice.

What happens when pastor's wives finally leave-through divorce or when the ministry ends? They're abandoned by the church they served for years.

Social exile. The community that praised her service ghosts her immediately. She's no longer useful to the church.

Financial abandonment. No pension. No retirement. No acknowledgment of decades of unpaid labor.

Reputation destruction. If she leaves because of abuse, the church often defends the pastor. She's labeled angry, bitter, deceived. Her testimony is dismissed.

Identity erasure. She was "Pastor So-and-So's wife "for decades. Now she's nothing in that world. Has to rebuild identity from scratch. I know women who served churches faithfully for 20+ years, then were completely cut off when the pastorate ended. No calls. No support. No acknowledgment. They'd given their youth, labor, health, and autonomy.

The church gave them nothing in return except trauma.

Let's describe the role without religious language:

Position: Support staff for organizational leader

Compensation: None

Hours: 20-40+ weekly

Benefits: None independent of spouse

Advancement opportunity: None

Authority: None

Security: Entirely dependent on marriage

Exit options: Financially catastrophic

Responsibilities:

Unpaid administrative work

Unpaid counseling services

Unpaid event planning

Unpaid childcare coordination

Unpaid hospitality

Maintain perfect public image

Absorb all criticism

Never complain

Sexual availability on demand

Sacrifice personal needs, health, autonomy

Consequences for leaving:

Loss of community

Loss of identity

Financial devastation

Potential loss of children

Social exile

Reputation destruction

Is that a calling? Or is that indentured servitude dressed in biblical language?

Most pastor's wives don't leave. Despite everything, they stay. Why?

Sunk cost. They've given so much. Leaving means admitting it was wasted.

Fear. Where would they go? How would they survive? Who would they be?

Belief. They genuinely believe this is God's will. That suffering is sanctified. That endurance proves faithfulness.

Hope. Things will get better. He'll change. The church will appreciate them. The sacrifice will be worth it.

Identity. They don't know how to be anyone except a pastor's wife. That role has consumed them.

Obligation. To God. To their husband. To the church. To their children. To everyone except themselves. So they stay. And they break. Slowly, quietly, invisibly. Some develop chronic illness-their bodies breaking under stress they can't acknowledge. Some become numb-functional but dead inside, going through motions without feeling.

Some fragment-dissociation as survival mechanism, leaving their body during the worst moments. Some become enforcers-embracing the system that oppresses them, policing other women to justify their own suffering. The church calls this faithfulness. Psychology calls it trauma response.

What if churches said to pastor's wives: "Your labor has value. You will be compensated fairly for the work you do." The church budget would reveal how much they're exploiting free labor. What if churches said: "You are a person with needs, boundaries, and autonomy.

Your wellbeing matters as much as your husband's ministry." The exploitation would become visible. The system would have to change. What if churches said: "You can speak honestly about your marriage, your struggles, your doubts.

You don't have to perform happiness to protect institutional image." The facade would crumble. The truth would emerge. The abuse would be exposed. What if churches said: "You can leave without losing everything.

We'll ensure you have financial security, community support, and practical resources." Women would leave abusive marriages. Churches would lose their free labor. Pastors would face consequences. None of these things happen. Because the system needs pastor's wives trapped, silent, exploited, and performing.

Their suffering is the cost of maintaining the church.

GOD DOESN'T NEED THE SACRIFICE

God-if God exists and cares about justice-doesn't need women to:

Endure abuse in silence

Work without compensation

Sacrifice health for ministry

Stay in exploitation for others' benefit

Perform happiness while dying inside

God doesn't require pastor's wives to be unpaid labor, trapped by marriage, silenced by theology, and destroyed by ministry demands. God doesn't benefit from their suffering. But the church absolutely does. The church gets free labor. The pastor gets unpaid support staff.

The system gets a visible endorsement of its ideology about marriage and women's roles. All it costs is the pastor's wife's health, autonomy, sanity, and sometimes life. That's not sacrifice. That's exploitation. And calling it ministry doesn't make it holy.

The most exploited person in the American church isn't the volunteer working for free. It's not the congregant giving beyond their means. It's not even the pastor burning out for low wages. It's the pastor's wife. She works more hours unpaid than anyone. She has less Open Ledger Press than anyone.

She faces more pressure than anyone. She has fewer exit options than anyone. She suffers more consequences for honesty than anyone. She receives less support when she breaks than anyone. And she's told this is God's design. That suffering proves faithfulness. That endurance demonstrates love. That her exploitation is her calling.

It's not. It's a system that needs free labor and found the perfect victim: a woman trapped by marriage, theology, economics, and community expectations. A woman who can't leave without losing everything. A woman who can't speak without threatening the system.

A woman who can't fail without disqualifying her husband. The pastor's wife isn't in ministry. She's in prison. And the church is holding the key.

Chapter 10: When Faith Becomes Fatal

◆ ◆ ◆

Faith Healing, Exorcisms, and Lethal Theologies

They don't all die the same way. But they all die for the same reason: someone told them God required it.

Alex, 17: Hanged himself after three years of conversion therapy convinced him that being gay was demonic and that death was better than temptation.

Maria, 8: Died during an exorcism when adults held her down so long she suffocated. They believed they were casting out demons. They were killing a child with epilepsy.

David, 52: Diabetic. Stopped taking insulin after a faith healer told him that using medicine showed a lack of faith. Dead within three weeks from diabetic ketoacidosis.

Rachel, 19: Developed anorexia after years of purity-culture teaching that her body was dangerous and shameful. She weighed seventy-eight pounds when her heart gave out.

Marcus, 15: Beaten to death by his parents during "discipline" their church taught was a biblical requirement for rebellious children.

They don't use knives.

But they kill efficiently — through theology that makes death seem holier than life.

This chapter is about the body count.

FAITH HEALING DEATHS

Documented practices show the pattern is consistent: treatable condition, rejected medical care, religious assurance that faith alone will heal, death that could have been prevented with basic medicine.

The Children

In 2008, **Ava Worthington**, fifteen months old, died in Oregon from pneumonia and a blood infection. Medical experts testified she would have survived with antibiotics. Her parents chose prayer instead. They were later convicted of criminally negligent homicide.

In the same religious community, **Neil Beagley**, sixteen, died after suffering from a congenital urinary tract blockage that led to kidney failure. Doctors testified that routine surgery would have saved his life. His parents relied on faith healing. He died after weeks of untreated pain.

In another Oregon case, a prematurely born infant to **Dale and Shannon Hickman** died after the parents refused neonatal medical care in favor of prayer. The baby lived less than a day. The parents were later convicted.

These deaths did not occur in the nineteenth century.
They occurred in the 2000s.
In the United States.
In churches that still exist.

The Adults:

Adults die this way too — quietly, and often without headlines.

Some stop taking insulin after being told that medicine demonstrates unbelief. Some delay or refuse surgery and chemotherapy because leaders frame treatment as fear or spiritual compromise. Others escalate giving — thousands of dollars in "seed offerings," special prayers, healing services — while their condition worsens. When they decline, the explanation is rarely that the promises were false. It's that the person didn't believe hard enough.

Court records, investigative journalism, and medical literature document numerous adult deaths in the United States linked to faith-based refusals of medical care. Conditions that modern medicine routinely treats — diabetes, infections, cancers, surgical emergencies — become fatal when theology reframes treatment as disobedience.

When death comes, silence follows. Families are often too ashamed to admit the loss was preventable. They don't want to be remembered as the ones who "lacked faith." Churches rarely document failures. They celebrate testimonies and bury outcomes. Healers move on to the next city. The system remains intact.

For every documented case, there are likely many more that never reach courtrooms or newsrooms — protected by shame, spiritual pressure, and institutions that face little accountability.

The Justifications:

When these deaths happen, churches don't admit error.

They say: "She lacked faith." "God had a higher plan." "He's healed in heaven now." "Sometimes God says no." "She gave up too soon." But never: "Our theology killed them." Never: "We were wrong." Never: "We should be held accountable." The theology is unfalsifiable.

When healing works, God is credited. When it fails, the believer is blamed. The perfect system for avoiding responsibility while continuing to collect offerings for healing services that heal nothing.

EXORCISM DEATHS

Churches teach that evil spirits cause illness, behavioral problems, mental disorders, and developmental disabilities. In some communities, the solution taught is exorcism — casting out demons through prayer, fasting, physical restraint, and sometimes extreme force. This theology has had **fatal consequences**.

There are documented cases in the United States and around the world in which individuals — including children — were harmed or killed during exorcism rituals. In one well-reported case, pastors were convicted for the death of a disabled child who died after being physically beaten during a deliverance ritual. Globally, investigative reporting and court records show that forceful restraint, prolonged fasting, and physical harm during supposed "demon casting" have led to preventable deaths in multiple countries.

The pattern is clear:

1. A behavioral, medical, or developmental difference is interpreted as demonic influence.
2. Church members or leaders perform an exorcism ritual.
3. Physical force or restraint is applied.

4. The person is injured or dies.
5. Community narratives frame the outcome as spiritual warfare or insufficient faith.
6. Leaders rarely face significant legal consequences.

Autism isn't demonic. Epilepsy isn't possession. Mental illness isn't spiritual oppression. Developmental disabilities aren't curses. But theologies that teach otherwise have led to real harm — including death — in documented cases.

The Theology:

Exorcism theology creates several lethal problems:

Delays real treatment: While performing exorcisms, families avoid medical care. Treatable conditions worsen. Sometimes fatally.

Justifies violence: If the body is possessed, hurting the body to expel demons becomes righteous. Restraint, beating, starvation — all justified as spiritual warfare.

Prevents intervention: Families hide what's happening because they believe they're doing God's work. By the time authorities discover abuse, it's often too late.

Eliminates accountability: If demons are real and exorcism is biblical, then injuries or death are collateral damage in spiritual warfare, not criminal negligence.

CONVERSION THERAPY SUICIDES

Churches teach that homosexuality is demonic, curable through prayer and therapy, and that living gay is worse than death. Teenagers believe them. And die.

The Methods:

Conversion therapy varies but commonly includes:

Shaming sessions where teens describe same-sex attractions and are told they're disgusting

Isolation from supportive peers and family

Forced viewing of heterosexual pornography

Electric shocks or induced nausea paired with same-sex images

Exorcisms to cast out "spirits of homosexuality" Extended prayer and fasting to "break strongholds" Complete identity deconstruction and reconstruction

None of it works. Sexual orientation doesn't change through therapy or prayer. What does change: mental health deteriorates catastrophically.

The Body Count

Exact numbers are impossible to track. Families often hide the role conversion therapy played in a suicide, reframing it as "mental health struggles" or "spiritual warfare." But the research is unequivocal.

According to studies published by **The Trevor Project**, the **American Psychological Association**, and peer-reviewed journals including **JAMA Pediatrics**, LGBTQ youth who undergo conversion therapy report **dramatically higher rates of suicide attempts**, depression, anxiety, PTSD, substance abuse, and self-harm than those who do not. Many survivors describe conversion therapy as the most traumatic experience of their lives — more damaging than bullying, discrimination, or even family rejection.

The Survivors Who Didn't Survive

Leelah Alcorn, 17: A transgender teenager who died by suicide after being subjected to conversion therapy. In her final message, she wrote, *"Fix society. Please."*

Blake Brockington, 18: A transgender student pressured by church teachings to change his identity. He died by suicide during his senior year of high school.

Bobby Griffith, 20: A gay young man whose evangelical mother sent him to conversion programs. He later walked into highway traffic, leaving behind writings that blamed religious teaching for his despair. His mother would later become a vocal opponent of conversion therapy.

These are not abstract "struggles with same-sex attraction," as churches often frame them. These are deaths linked to a theology that teaches young people they are broken, dangerous, or sinful for existing as they are — and that being dead is preferable to being themselves.

The Continuing Harm

Many U.S. states have banned conversion therapy for minors. Churches continue offering it anyway, rebranding it as "pastoral counseling," "discipleship," or "prayer support" to evade regulation. Teenagers are still being sent into church-run programs that inflict psychological harm in God's name.

And in some communities, the message remains unmistakable:
being gay is worse than being dead.

PURITY CULTURE CASUALTIES

Purity culture doesn't look lethal. Until it kills you. The theology is simple: Your body is dangerous. Sexual desire is shameful. Virginity determines worth. Women's bodies cause men to sin. Purity equals value. Impurity equals worthlessness. This teaching produces:

Eating Disorders:

Purity culture and eating disorders are statistically correlated. Both stem from control, shame, and body hatred disguised as virtue. When girls are taught their bodies are dangerous and shameful, they learn to punish their bodies.

When sexuality causes significant harm and bodies cause sin, eliminating the body through starvation becomes righteous. Churches rarely connect the dots. But therapists who work with eating disorder patients from religious backgrounds see the pattern constantly.

Girls dying slowly from anorexia while churches praise their "self-control" and "discipline." Sexual Dysfunction:

Decades of sexual shame don't disappear at the wedding altar. Purity culture teaches that sex is dangerous, dirty, sinful-then expects a mental switch to flip on the wedding night. It doesn't. Women can't become aroused. Men struggle with performance. Both feel profound guilt.

Some become completely unable to have sex, even in marriage — outcomes documented by therapists and in published research on purity culture effects. Churches tell them to pray more, submit better, try harder. Never: "We damaged you with harmful teaching." Some couples divorce over sexual incompatibility created by purity theology.

Some live sexless marriages in quiet desperation. Some develop such profound shame-based sexual dysfunction that they require years of therapy. The wedding night fantasy becomes a trauma trigger. The promised "gift" becomes a punishment.

All because churches taught them to hate their bodies and sexuality for decades, then expected instant reversal.

Suicides:

Some purity culture adherents die by suicide after sexual "failure":

- Women who were raped feel "impure" and worthless
- Teens who had premarital sex believe they're damaged goods
- Young adults who masturbate feel irredeemably sinful
- Assault victims who "didn't fight back enough "blame themselves

The theology makes death preferable to impurity. So they choose death. Churches call it "tragic" but never examine the theology that taught people their worth was tied to their virginity.

DISCIPLINE DEATHS

"Spare the rod, spoil the child" has a body count.

Some churches teach corporal punishment as a biblical requirement. Others go further — teaching that **severe physical punishment** is godly discipline. When obedience is framed as righteousness and pain as love, harm becomes not only permissible but virtuous.

One of the most influential texts promoting this approach is *To Train Up a Child* by **Michael and Debi Pearl**, a book that has been widely criticized by child welfare experts, pediatricians, and psychologists. The Pearls teach that physical punishment should be **early, frequent, and decisive**, framing resistance as rebellion that must be broken.

Their teachings include:

- Using pain to establish authority and compliance
- Interpreting a child's resistance as sinful defiance

- Equating obedience with moral worth
- Treating physical punishment as an expression of love

Advocacy groups and investigative journalists have linked these teachings to **multiple child abuse prosecutions**, in which caregivers cited the book's methods to justify extreme discipline. Courts and child protection agencies have repeatedly warned that such practices **increase the risk of severe injury and death**, particularly for infants and young children.

This isn't about discipline versus permissiveness.
It's about what happens when **theology sanctifies violence** and removes moral brakes by calling harm obedience.

When pain is holy, stopping becomes disobedience.
When obedience is everything, escalation is inevitable.

Children don't die because parents hate them.
They die because parents are told hurting them is love — and that God requires it.

Begin hitting children as young as 6 months

Use plumbing supply line (flexible plastic tubing)

Hit until child is completely broken

Never stop until child is submissive

Physical pain is the primary tool for godly child-rearing

This theology has killed.

Lydia Schatz, 7: Beaten to death in 2010 by parents who followed the discipline methods promoted in *To Train Up a Child*, including striking with plumbing tubing. Her parents were convicted of murder.

Hana Williams, 13: Adopted from Ethiopia and subjected to prolonged physical punishment, starvation, and exposure to freezing temperatures. She died from hypothermia and malnutrition. In court proceedings and investigative reporting, the parents' discipline practices were linked to teachings popularized by the Pearls' work.

Sean Paddock, 4: Beaten to death by caregivers who used a quarter-inch plumbing line and attended a church that promoted Pearl-influenced discipline principles. His death resulted in criminal convictions.

To Train Up a Child has sold **over one million copies** and has been **repeatedly cited in child abuse prosecutions**, where caregivers referenced its teachings to justify extreme corporal punishment. Child welfare experts and courts have warned that these methods **significantly increase the risk of severe injury and death**.

The Pearls have never retracted the book or publicly acknowledged the deaths linked to its teachings. Churches continue recommending it. Parents continue buying it. And children continue paying the price.

The Justification:

When children die from "discipline," churches defend the theology: "They took it too far, but the principle is biblical." Spanking itself isn't the problem-abuse is different." We need to discipline children; the Bible is clear." But the line from "biblical discipline" to fatal abuse is direct.

When you teach parents that beating children is God's command, when you say physical pain is godly correction, when you claim children need to be broken-you create conditions for fatal violence.

COVER-UP MURDERS

Sometimes churches don't kill directly. They just protect the people who do.

The Pattern:

Member commits abuse (physical, sexual, financial) 2. Victim reports to church leadership 3. Leadership protects abuser, silences victim 4. Abuse escalates 5. Victim dies 6. Church claims they didn't know, couldn't have prevented it

Documented Patterns

These are not rare failures. They are documented patterns.

Youth pastors who sexually abused children were reported to senior leadership, then quietly moved to different churches — where they continued abusing.

Husbands who beat their wives sought counsel from pastors, were told to "work on the marriage" and submit more fully, and later escalated the

violence — sometimes to murder.
Children showing clear signs of severe abuse were seen by church staff and volunteers. Nothing was reported. Intervention came only after the child was dead.

In case after case, churches prioritized institutional reputation over human safety.
Better to hide abuse than risk scandal.
Better to protect the abuser than support the victim.

Until someone dies.

Then come the statements.
Thoughts and prayers.
We had no idea.
If only they'd said something.

They did say something.
They said it to the church.
The church chose silence.

Investigative reporting and court records document multiple domestic-violence cases in which victims reported abuse to pastors and church leaders and were instructed to submit, pray more, and avoid divorce. In several cases, those victims were later killed by their husbands. A theology that frames submission as godly and divorce as sin creates conditions where women die trying to be faithful.

This is not accidental. It is the predictable outcome of a system that treats obedience as virtue, endurance as holiness, and institutional protection as righteousness.

Why do churches keep killing without consequences?

Religious Freedom Protections:

Courts defer to religious organizations on theological matters. If a church teaches faith healing, courts hesitate to intervene. If a church practices exorcism, it's protected as religious ritual. If a church mandates corporal punishment, it's often legal under parental rights.

Mandatory Reporter Exemptions:

Many states exempt clergy from mandatory reporting of abuse if disclosed in "pastoral counseling." Priests, pastors, and church leaders can learn of abuse and legally choose not to report. Children die because churches value confessional privilege over child safety.

Institutional Protections:

Churches have money for lawyers. Victims often don't. Churches have public support. Victims are isolated. Churches have institutional backing. Victims have trauma and stigma. The power imbalance means churches can drag out legal proceedings, bankrupt victims with legal fees, and ultimately escape meaningful consequences.

The Calculation:

THE THEOLOGY OF DEATH

Why do churches develop lethal theologies?

Martyrdom glorification: Christianity has martyrdom in its DNA. Suffering proves faithfulness. Death for belief is the ultimate witness. This makes death preferable to compromise. Better to die faithful than live unfaithfully. Better your child dies pure than lives gay. Better to refuse medicine and die trusting God than accept treatment and live doubting. Death becomes holier than life.

Body hatred: Theology that teaches bodies are sinful, flesh is corrupt, earth is temporary, and heaven is home creates death-seeking rather than life-affirming faith. If this life doesn't matter, if only eternity matters, then death isn't tragedy-it's promotion. A child dying from preventable illness just gets to heaven faster.

Authority without accountability: When religious leaders claim to speak for God, their instructions become divine command. Questioning them is questioning God. Disobeying them is disobeying God. This creates conditions where leaders can demand lethal obedience and frame resistance as sin.

Othering: Theology that demonizes difference-gay people, mentally ill people, disabled people, non-believers-makes their deaths feel less important. They're not fully human; they're possessed, broken, sinful. Their deaths are spiritual victories, not human tragedies.

THE SURVIVORS

For every death, there are survivors carrying trauma:

Parents who lost children because they believed what churches taught. They live with guilt, grief, and often continued belief that faith healing or exorcism was right — they just failed somehow.

Siblings who watched their brother or sister die preventable deaths while adults prayed instead of calling ambulances. They carry trauma, anger, often their own damaged faith.

Survivors of conversion therapy who didn't die but carry scars. PTSD, depression, anxiety, sexual dysfunction, shattered family relationships.

Former cult members who escaped before theology killed them but lost years to damaging teaching and practice. The body count is only part of the cost. The walking wounded multiply it.

THE CHURCHES THAT ACKNOWLEDGE IT

Almost none. Churches that teach faith healing don't acknowledge the deaths. They reframe them as lack of faith or God's mysterious will. Churches that practice exorcism don't admit they're killing disabled children. They claim demons fought back or the person wasn't delivered.

Churches that promote conversion therapy don't connect suicides to their teaching. They blame "the lifestyle" or "mental illness." Churches that teach severe corporal punishment don't take responsibility for murdered children.

They distinguish "discipline" from "abuse" and claim the parents went too far, not that the theology was wrong. Acknowledgment would require change. Change would require admitting error. Admission would require accountability. Better to maintain the theology and keep killing than admit centuries of teaching were wrong.

Theology that prioritizes faith over medicine

Practices that confuse disability with demons

Teaching that makes death preferable to being LGBTQ

Purity culture that produces eating disorders and suicide

Discipline methods that escalate to murder

Cover-ups that protect predators

The body count is real. The deaths are documented. The theology is traceable. Churches kill. Not accidentally. Not rarely. Systematically. Theologically. Intentionally. Because some versions of Christianity value belief over life, purity over safety, obedience over survival.

GOD DOESN'T REQUIRE THE DEATHS

God — if God exists and values human life — doesn't need:

- Children dying from treatable illnesses to prove faith
- Disabled children suffocating during exorcisms
- LGBTQ teenagers hanging themselves
- Girls starving from purity-induced body hatred
- Babies beaten to death in the name of godly discipline
- Women murdered while churches protect abusers

God doesn't benefit from theological frameworks that kill people. But institutions built on those frameworks benefit from maintaining them-even at the cost of human life. Because changing theology admits error. Admission threatens authority. And authority is what they're actually protecting. Not God. Not truth. Not life. Authority.

How many have died because churches taught them death was better than compromise, medicine was faithlessness, demons needed violent expulsion, gayness was worse than suicide, bodies needed punishment, and institutions mattered more than individuals? Thousands. Conservatively. And the deaths continue. Because the theology continues. Protected by religious freedom, defended by institutions, ignored by society. Churches kill. Not metaphorically. Not spiritually. Actually.

Verifiably. Repeatedly. And they call it faithfulness.

Chapter 11: The Tithing Deception – How 10% Became Non-Negotiable

◆◆◆

The sermon started with a threat disguised as a promise." Will a man rob God? Yet you rob me. But you ask, 'How are we extracting resources from you?' In tithes and offerings." The pastor let that sit. Malachi 3:8.

The go-to verse for financial manipulation in many churches that prioritizes money over integrity." When you don't tithe," he continued," you're not just failing to give to the church. You're robbing God Almighty. And God will not be robbed." He paused for effect.

The congregation shifted uncomfortably." But here's the good news. Malachi 3:10 says, 'Bring the whole tithe into the storehouse, that there may be food in my house.

Test me in this, says the LORD Almighty, and see if I will not throw open the floodgates of heaven and pour out so much blessing that there will not be room enough to store it.'" Translation: Give us 10% of your gross income or God will withhold blessings. Give it and God will make you wealthy.

It's a transaction. A divine vending machine. Insert money, receive blessings.

This is the Tithing Deception. And it's financing million-dollar empires while bankrupting faithful believers.

Multiple former members describe malachi 3:8-10 is the most misused passage in modern church financial teaching. Let's examine what it actually says — and what it doesn't.

The Context Nobody Mentions:

Malachi was written to Israelites under the Old Covenant. The tithe was a temple tax-literally a tax for funding the Levitical priesthood and temple operations. It wasn't voluntary giving. It was required taxation. The "storehouse" wasn't a local church. It was the temple in Jerusalem. There was one temple. One storehouse.

Specific. Defined. The tithe wasn't money. It was agricultural products-grain, wine, oil, livestock. Ten percent of your crops and herds. If you lived in the city and earned wages, you didn't tithe. The system didn't apply to you.

What Changed:

Jesus never taught tithing. Not once. He criticized the Pharisees for tithing meticulously while ignoring justice and mercy. But he never commanded his followers to tithe. Paul never taught tithing. He taught generous, voluntary giving according to what people had decided in their hearts.

2 Corinthians 9:7: "Each of you should give what you have decided in your heart to give, not reluctantly or under compulsion." Not under compulsion. Meaning no mandatory percentage. No required amount. No threats for not giving. The early church didn't practice tithing. They gave as they were able.

They sold possessions to help the needy. They supported traveling teachers and local leaders. But there was no 10% requirement.

When It Changed:

The institutional church reintroduced tithing in the Middle Ages as a revenue mechanism. Not because it was biblical. Because it was profitable. Protestant reformers initially rejected it. Then they realized they needed consistent funding. Tithing came back. By the 20th century, American evangelicalism had made tithing non-negotiable.

The Old Testament tax became New Testament command. And Malachi 3:8 became the weapon: "You're robbing God." Modern tithing teaching isn't satisfied with 10% of your income. It demands 10% of your gross income-before taxes, before healthcare, before anything. The reasoning: "Give God his portion first.

The firstfruits." But here's the problem. Your gross income isn't actually your income. It's your employer reports before mandatory deductions. You never see most of it. If you make $50,000 annually, your gross is $50,000.

But after federal tax, state tax, Social Security, Medicare, and healthcare premiums, your actual take-home might be $35,000. Churches teaching gross tithing are demanding $5,000 annually-while you're living on $35,000. That's

14.3% of what you receive. For a family barely making ends meet, that extra $417 monthly devastating.

That's groceries. Utilities. Car payment. Medical copays.

But churches frame it as faithfulness." Trust God to provide." You can't out-give God." When you honor God with your firstfruits, he'll multiply what's left." The Math They Don't Do:

A church of 500 families, average income $50,000, all tithing on gross: $2.5 million annually. That same church, if people tithed on net: $1.75 million annually. The difference: $750,000. That's three senior staff salaries, or a building expansion, or a new campus. Churches push gross tithing because their budgets depend on it. Not because God requires it.

Churches that demand tithes rarely disclose how they spend them. But leaked budgets, financial investigations, and former staff testimonies reveal consistent patterns.

Average Megachurch Budget Breakdown:

50-60%: Staff Salaries and Benefits

The senior pastor typically makes $150,000- $400,000+. Executive pastors make $80,000- $150,000. The worship pastor, youth pastor, admin staff— all paid from tithes. For a church collecting $5 million annually, $2.5-3 million goes to payroll. The people collecting the money pay themselves first.

20-30%: Facilities

Mortgage or lease payments. Utilities. Maintenance. Insurance. Technology. Often another $1-1.5 million annually. That building with the $8 million mortgage and the $200,000 annual utility bill? Funded by people who can't afford their own mortgages or utility bills.

10-15%: Programming and Marketing

Sunday services require significant production costs. Lighting, sound, video, graphics, printed materials, website, advertising. Churches spend $500,000-$750,000 making Sunday morning look professional. Because if it doesn't look polished, people won't come. And if people don't come, giving drops.

5-10%: Missions and Benevolence

The actual helping people category. Often the smallest line item. Sometimes as low as 2-3% of total budget. A church collecting $5 million might give $100,000- $250,000 to actual missions and helping people in need. The rest is institutional self-perpetuation.

The Revelation:

When people discover that 90%+ of their tithe funds the church while less than 10% helps anyone, they feel betrayed." I thought I was funding the gospel. I was funding your salary and mortgage." Churches avoid this revelation by keeping budgets private. No transparency. No accountability. Just trust us with your money.

The Faith Offering:

"God is calling someone to give $1,000 today. Not $500. Not $1,200. Exactly $1,000. If you feel that prompting, it's God speaking." This isn't God. It's the pastor needing to hit budget targets. Framing it as divine direction makes people override financial common sense. I've watched people write checks they couldn't afford because they believed God told the pastor they were supposed to give that specific amount.

The Building Fund Separate from Tithes:

"Your tithe goes to general operations. But we need a separate offering for this building expansion. God has big plans. We need to step out in faith." Translation: Your 10% isn't enough. We need 15-20%. But we can't say that directly, so we'll frame the building fund as separate and additional.

The Prophetic Offering:

"The Lord showed me that breakthrough is coming to this house. But we need to sow seed for it. I'm not talking about your regular giving. I'm talking about a sacrificial, above-and-beyond offering." Sacrifice means give what you can't afford. Above-and-beyond means give more than your tithe. It's asking people to give money they don't have for blessings that won't come.

The Emergency Appeal:

"We're $50,000 short on budget this month. If everyone here gave just $100, we'd make it. Who's willing to step up?" This creates artificial urgency and social pressure. The shortfall is often manufactured or exaggerated. But people give out of guilt and fear of what might happen if the church closes.

The Compound Expectation:

- Regular tithe (10%)
- Building fund
- Missions offering
- Special prophetic offerings
- Emergency appeals
- Plus expectations to buy pastor's books, attend conferences, support special projects

People end up giving 15-25% of income because every ask is framed as separate and necessary. One woman calculated she'd given 22% of her gross income the previous year when all offerings were totaled. She was in debt and struggled to feed her kids. But the church praised her sacrificial giving.

The promise is clear: tithe faithfully and God will bless you financially. Open the floodgates. Pour out blessing. No room to contain it. Reality: most faithful tithers never experience financial breakthrough.

The Theological Escape Clause:

When blessings don't come, churches blame the tither:

"Are you giving cheerfully or reluctantly?" Have you been consistent?" Are you tithing on gross or net?"(gross is required)

"Do you have unconfessed sin blocking your blessing?" God's timing isn't our timing. Keep tithing in faith." Never: "The theology is wrong. Tithing doesn't actually cause financial prosperity." The Survivors Bias:

Many churches elevate the rare stories of people who tithed and then got a raise, bonus, or unexpected money. These testimonies are repeated endlessly. What's rarely mentioned: the hundreds of faithful tithers who gave for decades and stayed financially struggling. They're invisible. Their stories don't get told.

This creates the illusion that tithing works. But it's selection bias. Churches show the winners, hide the losers, and claim the system is proven.

The Real Correlation:

People who can afford to tithe 10% of gross income tend to be financially stable. They're not stable because they tithe. They tithe because they're stable. People who can't afford it but tithe anyway often get poorer. They're giving money they need for necessities. Of course their financial situation worsens. The causation is backwards. Churches sell it as: tithing causes prosperity. Reality: prosperity enables tithing.

Some churches take it further: they teach you must tithe to your local church specifically. Not to any ministry or need. To the storehouse — which they define as their church.

The Teaching:

"You can give offerings anywhere. But your tithe belongs to the house where you're fed spiritually. If you attend here, your tithe must come here." This prevents people from:

- Giving directly to people in need
- Supporting other ministries
- Helping family members
- Choosing how their money is used

It centralizes all giving to the church. Maximum control. Maximum revenue.

The Enforcement:

Many churches track tithing. Many use giving software that shows exactly who gives what. In some churches, tithing is required for:

- Church membership
- Serving in leadership
- Participating in certain ministries
- Receiving pastoral care or counseling

Not tithing can get you removed from leadership, excluded from decision-making, or even disciplined publicly — practices documented in church policy manuals and member testimonies. One man told me his church refused to marry him and his fiancee because his giving records showed inconsistent tithing. They had to prove faithful tithing for six months before the church would perform the ceremony. Strip away the label of community: financial coercion remains.

Tithing theology and prosperity gospel are inseparable. Both teach transactional relationship with God. Both promise financial return on spiritual investment.

The Seed Faith Doctrine:

Your tithe is a seed. Plant it in faith, you'll reap a harvest. The bigger the seed, the bigger the harvest. This is farming metaphor applied to finances. It sounds biblical. It's actually manipulation. Because unlike actual farming, the promised harvest rarely comes. But unlike actual farming, you can't sue for crop failure. It's religion. The promises are unfalsifiable.

The Anointing Attraction:

Prosperity preachers claim that giving to anointed ministers multiplies the blessing. Their anointing covers your seed. Your return is greater if you give to them specifically. This is narcissistic theology." God favors me specially, so your money is blessed more if given to me than to others." It's also lucrative. People give to celebrity pastors believing they're investing in extra-anointed ministry. The pastor gets rich.

The giver gets nothing but the belief that someday blessing will come.

Youth pastors say," If you can't tithe $20 from your $200 paycheck, how will you tithe when you're older?" This programs children before they can think critically about it. By the time they're adults, tithing feels mandatory. They can't imagine not doing it without feeling guilty.

I've met adults who tithe even though they don't attend church, don't believe anymore, haven't darkened a church door in years. They still write a check to someone because "God's 10%" is so deeply ingrained they can't stop.

That's not faith — it's childhood indoctrination creating lifelong obligation.

What does tithing cost families who can't afford it?

Medical Care Delayed:

Families who tithe before addressing medical needs. Dental work goes undone. Prescriptions go unfilled. Necessary surgeries get postponed. One family tithed faithfully while their daughter needed braces. They couldn't afford both. They chose tithing. She went through adolescence with severe dental issues that caused pain and social anxiety. The church praised their faithfulness. Their daughter paid the price.

Debt Accumulation:

Families who tithe while carrying credit card debt. They're paying 18-24% interest on balances they could eliminate if they stopped giving 10% to the church. Basic financial advice: pay off high-interest debt before giving money away. But churches teach the opposite: tithe first, trust God with the rest. Result: families stay in debt while churches build empires.

Children's Needs Unmet

School supplies, extracurricular activities, and college savings are sacrificed because the tithe comes first.

One family couldn't afford to send their son to college. They had tithed faithfully for twenty years — **over $100,000** to their church. They never saved for education because they were told, *"God will provide."*

He didn't.

The church did nothing.

Their son went into debt for college while his parents' tithe money helped fund a new worship center.

Housing Instability:

Families who tithe while behind on rent or mortgage. Prioritizing church over shelter because that's what they've been taught is faithful. I know a family that lost their home to foreclosure. They'd given $15,000 to their church that year-money that could have caught up their mortgage payments. The church let them be homeless. But kept their money.

What if churches taught generous giving without mandatory percentages?

What Scripture Actually Says:

“Each of you should give what you have decided in your heart to give, not reluctantly or under compulsion, for God loves a cheerful giver."(2 Corinthians 9:7) Not 10%. Not required. Not under threat.

According to what you've decided.” Give to everyone who asks you, and if anyone takes what belongs to you, do not demand it back."(Luke 6:30) Give directly to those who need.

Not channeled through institutional structures that take 90% for operations.” If anyone has material possessions and sees a brother or sister in need but has no pity on them, how can the love of God be in that person?"(1 John 3:17) Help people directly. Meet actual needs. Not write checks to churches that spend it on themselves.

What Healthy Giving Looks Like:

Give what you can afford without creating financial strain. Give directly to people in need when possible. Give to organizations that transparently show how money is used. Give to causes that actually help people, not just fund institutional operations. Save for your family's future-that's also stewardship.

Pay off debt before giving away money you don't have. Take care of your own household first-that's biblical too. But churches don't teach this. Because this model doesn't generate $5 million annual budgets.

Churches accuse non-tithers of robbing God. But who's really being robbed?

Families robbed of financial stability by teaching that demands 10% of gross income regardless of need.

Children robbed of opportunities because their parents gave money to churches instead of saving for their future.

Believers robbed of autonomy by teaching that makes a specific percentage mandatory and framing anything less as sin.

Communities robbed of resources because money that could help people directly gets filtered through churches that keep 90% for themselves.

God's reputation robbed by teaching that reduces divine relationship to transactional formula and makes God look like a greedy accountant demanding payment.

The real robbery isn't people not tithing. It's churches teaching that God requires it, threatening people with curses if they don't comply, promising financial blessings that never come, taking money from people who can't afford it, spending it on themselves, and calling it holy.

GOD DOESN'T NEED YOUR 10%

God-if God exists and cares about resources-doesn't need your money routed through a church that spends 90% on self-perpetuation. God doesn't require a mandatory percentage calculated on gross income. God doesn't withhold blessings from people who can't afford to give.

God doesn't bless people financially for tithing — that's not how economics work. Doesn't curse people for failing to give to institutions. Doesn't need the tithe. The church needs the tithe. And they've convinced you that not giving to them is robbing God. That's not theology.

That's financial manipulation. And it's been robbing families for generations while enriching the institutions claiming to speak for God.

If churches were honest, they'd say: "We need your money to pay salaries, maintain buildings, and fund operations. Giving is voluntary. Give what you can afford. We'll adjust our budget to match what people willingly give." But that's not what they say. They say: "God requires 10% of your gross income.

Anything less is robbing God. Give sacrificially even if you can't afford it. Trust that God will bless you." Why the difference? Because honesty doesn't generate the same revenue as manipulation.

Because "we need money to survive" doesn't motivate like "God will curse you if you don't pay." Voluntary giving based on ability produces less than mandatory percentages enforced by guilt. The Tithing Deception isn't accidental. It's strategic. It's profitable.

And it's been devastating families while building empires. God doesn't need your tithe. But the pastor's salary, the building mortgage, and the institutional survival absolutely do. And as long as you believe tithing as practiced today is biblically mandated — rather than an evolved institutional practice whose modern application is theologically contested — they'll keep collecting.

Chapter 12: The Anatomy of the Con – How Churches Run Effective Extraction Systems

◆ ◆ ◆

The best cons don't announce themselves. They don't appear to be extraction. They look like opportunity. They don't feel like manipulation. They feel like community. They don't sound like false promises. They sound like truth you've been searching for your whole life. That's what makes them perfect.

Churches in America are running the longest, most sophisticated con in human history. And if you're reading this thinking "not MY church," that's how you know the exploitation is working. Because the first rule of a successful con: the mark never believes they're the mark. Let me show you the playbook.

What Makes a Con

A successful long con requires specific elements. Not some of them. All of them.

Element 1: Identify vulnerable targets.

People in transition. People in crisis. People searching for meaning, community, or answers. People who need something desperately enough to suspend critical thinking. Many churches call this "reaching the lost." Manipulators call it "finding marks."

Element 2: Promise something irresistible.

Something the target wants so badly they'll overlook red flags. Something that addresses their deepest need. Something too good to be true — but packaged as absolutely true. Churches promise: eternal life, divine love, purpose, community, healing, prosperity, answers to life's biggest questions. manipulators promise: wealth, love, security, belonging, transformation.

Same promises. Different vocabulary.

Element 3: Establish trust through authority and social proof.

Element 4: Create urgency and scarcity.

Start small. Build slowly. Each commitment makes the next easier. By the time the target realizes the scale, they're already deep. Churches: attend once, join small group, start volunteering, begin tithing, take leadership role, recruit others. Each step feels natural. The total commitment is massive.

Element 6: Make the product unfalsifiable.

Promise something that can't be proven or disproven. When it doesn't materialize, blame the victim, not the system.

Churches promise: blessings (undefined), God's presence (unfelt but claimed), spiritual growth (unmeasurable), eternal reward (after death, unprovable). If you don't receive what's promised: you lacked faith, had hidden sin, didn't wait long enough, misunderstood what was promised. The system can never fail. Only you can fail the system.

Element 7: Create exit costs.

Make leaving more painful than staying. Threaten loss of investment, community, identity, or future benefit. Make the mark believe leaving means losing everything. Churches: leaving means losing your community, risking your salvation, abandoning God's plan, disappointing everyone, proving you were rarely real.

Element 8: Prevent exposure.

Control information. Discredit critics. Make questioning taboo. Isolate marks from outside perspectives. Create loaded language that stops critical thinking. Churches: don't read critics (they're deceived), don't question leadership (rebellion), don't discuss doubts openly (division), stay away from "worldly wisdom"(outside information).

These eight elements define a long con.

This isn't metaphor. This isn't exaggeration. This is literal structural analysis. If it looks like a con, operates like a con, and produces outcomes like a con-it's a con.

You walked in because you needed something. Maybe you just moved to a new city and needed community. Maybe you were going through a divorce and needed support. Maybe someone you loved died and you needed answers about what happens after. Maybe you were just lonely and needed belonging. Whatever brought you, you were vulnerable. And vulnerability is the entry point.

The church didn't cause your vulnerability. But they identified it immediately.

New in town?" We'd love to help you get connected." Going through crisis?" God brought you here for a reason." Searching for meaning?" You'll find your purpose here." Lonely?" We're a family." They diagnosed your need within minutes and positioned themselves as the solution.

This is targeting. Sophisticated, effective targeting.

You thought you chose the church. The church chose you the moment you walked in the door. You fit the profile: vulnerable, searching, available.

Then came the love-bombing.

Everyone so friendly. People remembering your name by the second visit. Invitations to coffee, to small groups, to serve. Texts checking on you. Genuine seeming care. It felt like you'd found your people. Finally, a place where you belonged. What you didn't know: this is strategy.

New members get intentional attention. It's coordinated. Small group leaders are told to integrate new people quickly. Volunteers are assigned to make newcomers feel special. Everything is designed to create attachment before you think critically about what you're attaching to.

By week four, you felt like you'd been there for years.

By week eight, you couldn't imagine not being there. By week twelve, you were recommending it to your friends. The hook was set. You didn't feel it. That's how you know it worked.

Commitment increased gradually. So gradually you didn't notice the total weight until you were already carrying it.

Month 1: Just attending services. One hour Sunday morning. Easy.

Month 2: Joined a small group. Now it's Sunday service plus Wednesday night. Still manageable.

Month 3: Started volunteering. Sunday morning setup crew. Adds two hours weekly. You're serving God. Feels good.

Month 4: Began tithing. 10% of gross income. You're trusting God with finances. It's faith.

Month 6: Took a leadership role. Training meetings, coordination calls, plus your volunteer hours. Now giving 8-10 hours weekly.

Month 9: Recruiting others. Inviting friends. Bringing coworkers. You're invested in the church growing.

Month 12: Your entire social life is church. Your free time is church activities. Your money goes to church. Your identity is wrapped up in your role at church.

You didn't decide on day one to give 10-15 hours weekly, 10% of income, and your entire social world to this church. It happened incrementally. Each step felt small. The total commitment is massive. This is the boiling frog method. Increase temperature slowly, the frog doesn't jump out. Increase commitment slowly, the mark doesn't leave.

By month twelve, you're fully captured.

And now the sunk cost fallacy kicks in. You've invested so much-time, money, relationships, identity. Walking away means admitting it was wasted. So you stay. And invest more. Which makes leaving harder. Which makes you invest more. The trap closes gradually. But it closes completely.

What does the church get from you?

Financial:

According to former insiders, 10% of your gross income, every paycheck, for life. If you earn $40,000 annually, that's $4,000 per year. Over 40 years of working life: $160,000. If invested instead at 7% return: approximately $850,000 by retirement. You're not giving pocket change. You're giving your retirement security. Your kids' college fund. Your emergency savings.

Your financial future.

Labor:

Volunteering 10-20 hours weekly. That's 500-1,000 hours annually. At minimum wage, that's $7,500- $15,000 in value per year. Over a decade: $75,000- $150,000 in unpaid labor. You're not "serving." You're working a part-time job with no compensation, no benefits, no retirement, no workers comp, and no ability to negotiate conditions.

Recruiting:

Bringing in new members. Each person you recruit enters the same cycle. Gives money. Gives labor. Recruits others. You're building the church's workforce and donor base. For free. While paying them to let you do it.

What do you get in return?

Sermons: delivered to hundreds simultaneously, cost the church nearly nothing per person. Community: which you largely create through your volunteer labor and recruiting. Programs: run by volunteers (you), funded by tithes (yours).

The math doesn't remotely add up.

You give $4,000 annually plus 500 hours of labor. The church gives you maybe $200 worth of actual goods and services — and that's generous. The return on investment is catastrophically negative. For you. For the church? The ROI is extraordinary.

They extract hundreds of thousands per committed member over a lifetime, spend a fraction delivering services, and keep the difference.

That's not ministry — it's profit margin.

What were you promised?" Tithe and God will bless you financially." Serve and you'll find purpose." Commit and you'll experience God's presence." Stay faithful and you'll see breakthrough." What actually happened?

Financial blessing: Most faithful tithers rarely experience the promised prosperity. Many get poorer because they're giving away 10% they can't afford. When blessing doesn't come, you're told you lacked faith or had hidden sin. The promise is unfalsifiable.

Purpose through serving: You found exhaustion. Burnout. Resentment that you tried to suppress because feeling resentful about serving God means something's wrong with you, not the system asking too much.

God's presence: You felt it sometimes during worship-neurochemical response to engineered music, not divine encounter. The rest of the time, you wondered why God felt distant and assumed you were the problem.

Breakthrough: Still waiting. Always one more offering, one more conference, one more commitment away. It never comes. But you keep believing it will.

The promises sustain hope. Hope sustains investment. Investment sustains the church.

The promise is the product. The product doesn't have to be delivered. The hope of the product is enough.

Long cons protect themselves from exposure. Churches are expert at this.

Spiritual Language:

Questioning the system is framed as doubting God. Leaving the church is framed as abandoning your faith. Asking for financial transparency is framed as lacking trust. The conflation is intentional. If questioning the church equals questioning God, most people won't question.

Information Control:

"Don't read books by critics — they're deceived." Don't listen to people who left — they're bitter." Don't trust secular wisdom-it's worldly." If you're doubting, stop consuming content that feeds doubt." This isolates you from outside perspectives that might help you see clearly. All information is filtered through the church.

Anything contradicting the church is dismissed before you encounter it.

Loaded Language:

"Covering." Anointed." Submitted." Faithful." Rebellious." Backslidden." Worldly." These terms stop critical thinking. They're thought-terminating cliches. When someone's described as "rebellious" for questioning leadership, you stop listening to their concerns. When leaving is called "backsliding," it's pre-framed as spiritual failure.

Social Pressure:

most people around you believes. If you doubt, you're the problem. If everyone you trust is committed, your doubts feel like personal deficiency rather than reasonable assessment. This is why cults work. Isolation + group conformity = individual compliance even when individual judgment says something's wrong.

Exit Costs:

Leaving means losing your community, your identity, your sense of purpose, possibly your salvation (according to the teaching). The cost is so high that staying-even in dysfunction-feels safer than leaving. This is captivity. Not physical. Psychological and social. But captivity nonetheless.

Let's put it in a simple chart. Long con elements vs. church operations.

Identify vulnerable targets:

Long con: Find people in crisis or transition Church: "Reaching the lost," targeting seekers and people in need

Promise something irresistible:

Long con: Wealth, love, security, transformation Church: Salvation, purpose, community, blessing, eternal life

Establish trust and authority:

Long con: Credentials, testimonials, associations Church: Pastoral calling, changed lives, denominational authority

Create urgency:

Long con: "Limited time offer," Don't miss out" Church: "Today is the day of salvation," altar call pressure

Increase investment gradually:

Long con: Small asks leading to large commitments Church: Attend '?' join '?' serve '?' tithe '?' lead '?' recruit

Unfalsifiable promises:

Long con: "Results vary," blame victim when it fails Church: "God's timing," You lacked faith," unfalsifiable blessings

Create exit costs:

Long con: Threaten loss of investment, opportunity Church: Lose community, identity, salvation, divine blessing

Prevent exposure:

Long con: Discredit critics, control information Church: Critics are "deceived," outside info is "worldly" Every single element matches.

This isn't similarity. This is identical structure. If any other organization operated this way, we'd call it a scam immediately. Because it is one.

Most pastors aren't consciously scamming people. They were recruited young. They went through the same system. They genuinely believe. They've structured their entire life around this being true. Asking them to see it as a con requires admitting they've been conned. And that they're now conning others.

That's psychologically unbearable.

So they rationalize." I'm not getting rich-I make a modest salary."(While living better than most congregants and having expenses covered they don't.)" The church provides real value-community, teaching, support."(Value created mostly by unpaid volunteers and funded by people who can't afford it.)" People give willingly-no one's forcing them."

(Coercion through guilt, social pressure, and spiritual threats isn't force, but it's not voluntary either.)" God really does bless faithful givers."(Survivorship bias — they remember the few who prospered, ignore the many who didn't.

But belief doesn't change structure.

A con that the conman believes is still a con. Sincerity doesn't make extraction legitimate. Good intentions don't override harmful outcomes. The system is the scam. The people running it are often victims of it too. That doesn't make it less of a scam. It makes it more insidious.

This isn't small-time operation. This is the largest ongoing con in American history.

The numbers:

300,000+ churches in the United States

40+ million evangelical Christians actively participating

According to Giving USA Foundation's annual reports and the National Council of Churches, religious organizations receive an estimated $50+ billion annually in tithes and offerings

Millions of hours of unpaid labor weekly

Generational wealth transfer from families to institutions

For comparison:

Bernie Madoff's Ponzi scheme: $65 billion over 17 years before collapse. Church wealth extraction: Trillions over centuries, still running, legally protected, culturally celebrated.

This is exploitation through con artistry, scaled to billions.

And it's legal. Tax-exempt. Constitutionally protected. Socially encouraged. You can't prosecute it because it's "religion." You can't regulate it because "religious freedom." You can't expose it effectively because believers defend it and critics are dismissed. It's the perfect crime. No accountability. No oversight. No consequences.

Just continuous wealth transfer from the many to the few, justified by theology and protected by law.

How do you know it's a con? Look at outcomes.

If tithing brought blessing:

Faithful tithers would be noticeably wealthier than non-tithers. They're not. Many are poorer because they're giving money they need.

If the church helped the poor:

Most church budgets would go to poverty relief. They don't. 70-90% goes to salaries and buildings. 3-5% actually helps people in need.

If leadership was servant-hearted:

Pastors would live modestly. They don't. Celebrity pastors have multi-million dollar homes, luxury cars, private jets.

If it was about community:

Leaving wouldn't destroy your social network. It does. The community is conditional on continued participation and compliance.

If it was about truth:

Questioning would be encouraged. It's not. Doubts are suppressed. Critics are silenced. Outside information is discouraged.

If it was healthy:

Financial transparency would be standard. It's not. Most churches refuse to disclose detailed budgets to their own members.

When promises rarely materialize, investment keeps increasing, leadership gets wealthy while members struggle, questioning is punished, and leaving is made traumatic-it's a con. The outcomes prove the structure. The structure proves the intent. The intent doesn't require consciousness-systems reveal themselves through results.

When confronted with this analysis, churches and believers use predictable defenses:

"You're bitter/hurt/angry." Ad hominem. Attacks the critic's emotional state rather than addressing the argument. Whether I'm bitter is irrelevant to whether the structure is exploitative.

"Not many churches are like this." True. And not all used car salesmen are dishonest. But the ones using high-pressure tactics, hiding

information, and extracting maximum profit are scamming. Same with churches.

"You're attacking faith/God/Christianity." Conflation. Critiquing institutions isn't attacking God. If God exists, God doesn't need defending from structural analysis of organizations claiming to represent God.

"People give voluntarily." Coercion through guilt, social pressure, spiritual threats, and information control isn't voluntary. Voluntary requires informed consent and freedom from pressure. Churches provide neither.

"The church does good work." Some do. Most of the "good work" is done by volunteers using their own time and money. The church extracts resources, takes credit, and spends most of the budget on itself.

"You just don't understand spiritual things." Thought-terminating cliche. Claiming special knowledge that exempts the system from normal analysis is exactly what cons do." You have to be in it to understand it "is cult logic.

None of these defenses address the structural argument.

They deflect, dismiss, and distract. Because addressing the argument honestly requires admitting the structure is exploitative.

How do people finally see it? Usually not through argument. Through experience.

Something breaks the spell:

The church asks you to give more when you're already struggling financially, and you realize they don't actually care about your wellbeing. Your pastor gets exposed for financial impropriety or moral failure, and the church protects him instead of the victims. You try to leave and experience the shunning, the guilt, the loss — and realize it was never actually about love.

You see behind the curtain-the budget, the strategy meetings, the manipulation techniques — and can't unsee it.

Every sermon becomes a sales pitch. Every testimony becomes marketing. Every offering becomes extraction. Every call to serve becomes free labor recruitment. The spell breaks. And you realize: this was always a con. You just couldn't see it while you were in it.

That's not your fault.

The con is sophisticated. It's been refined over centuries. It uses your best qualities-faith, hope, generosity, desire for community-against you. Smart people fall for cons. Good people fall for cons. The shame is the final hook. Don't take it.

Churches won't admit this because the entire model depends on you not seeing it clearly.

If they said:

"We need your money to pay our salaries and maintain our buildings. We'll spend 70-90% on ourselves. We'll use guilt and social pressure to extract it. The promises we make are unfalsifiable. If you leave, you'll lose everything you've built here." No one would join.

So they say: "God loves you. This is a family. Give and you'll be blessed. Serve and you'll find purpose. Stay faithful and breakthrough is coming." The theology is the marketing. The marketing is the exploitation.

And it works because people are desperate for meaning, community, and answers to life's hardest questions. Churches aren't providing those things. They're selling the promise of those things while extracting resources and providing minimal actual value.

The product is hope. Hope is renewable. Hope doesn't require delivery. Hope sustains investment indefinitely.

GOD DOESN'T NEED THE CON

God — if God exists — doesn't need a system that extracts through guilt, exploits labor under the guise of service, or enforces compliance through spiritual threats. Doesn't need churches that operate like cons to accomplish divine purposes.

If the system requires conning people, it's not God's system.

It's a human system that benefits from using God's name. And once you see that distinction-between God and the institutions claiming to represent God-everything changes. You're free to reject the exploitation without rejecting faith. You're free to leave the church without leaving God. You're free to protect yourself without sinning.

Because God requires no con. But the church absolutely does.

And recognizing that difference is how the exploitation finally ends.

Now you know the playbook. You can't unknow it. You can't unsee it. The pattern is too clear. The structure is too obvious.

Your choice:

Stay and participate, knowing it's a con. Some people do this. Eyes open, accepting the cost, getting what

Research on church finances indicates they can from it. That's your right. Leave and rebuild. Hard, painful, necessary for many. You'll lose community, identity, certainty. You'll gain freedom, autonomy, clarity. Try to reform from inside. Usually doesn't work. Systems protect themselves. But some try anyway. That's also your right.

What you can't do anymore is pretend you don't see it.

The con is exposed. The structure is clear. The outcomes are documented. Churches in America are running a long con. Sophisticated, effective, protected by law and culture, sustained for centuries.

And now you know exactly how it works.

What you do with that knowledge is up to you. But you can't say you weren't warned.

Chapter 13: Touch Not My Anointed – How One Misquoted Verse Creates Untouchable Leaders

◆ ◆ ◆

"Touch not my anointed ones; do my prophets no harm." — Psalm 105:15 Five seconds after you question anything a pastor does, you'll hear this verse.

Ask why the pastor needs a second home?" Touch not God's anointed." Wonder why financial records aren't available?" Do my prophets no harm." Question a decision that seems self-serving?" You're touching the Lord's anointed." This single verse-ripped from context, weaponized beyond recognition, and deployed as a nuclear option-has created a class of religious leaders who operate above accountability, immune from criticism, protected from consequences.

It's not theology. It's a Get Out of Jail Free card for spiritual tyrants. And it's built on a fundamental misrepresentation.

What the Verse Actually Says

Let's look at the actual passage. Psalm 105:8-15, written about God's protection of the Israelite patriarchs: "He remembers his covenant forever, the promise he made, for a thousand generations, the covenant he made with Abraham, the oath he swore to Isaac.

He confirmed it to Jacob as a decree, to Israel as an everlasting covenant: 'To you I will give the land of Canaan as the portion you will inherit.' When they were but few in number, few indeed, and strangers in it, they wandered from nation to nation, from one kingdom to another.

He allowed no one to oppress them; for their sake he rebuked kings: 'Do not touch my anointed ones; do my prophets no harm.'" Context: God protecting Abraham, Isaac, and Jacob-the patriarchs-as they wandered through foreign lands. These men had no institutional power. No buildings. No budgets. No staff. No security teams.

They were vulnerable wanderers in hostile territory.

God was warning foreign kings: don't harm these powerless refugees under my protection.

Modern application by pastors: "Don't criticize me, the powerful religious leader with a platform, money, and institutional backing." It's the exact opposite meaning.

Who were the "anointed ones" in this passage? Not religious professionals. Not institutional leaders. Not people with power and wealth.

The anointed ones were:

Abraham: A nomad with flocks and family, no nation or institution

Isaac: A shepherd, living in tents, vulnerable to neighboring tribes

Jacob: A wanderer who literally wrestled with God and walked with a limp

They were called "anointed" because God chose them for a purpose, not because they held religious office. And they were vulnerable. Powerless. At the mercy of foreign kings who could have destroyed them. God's warning to those kings: "These are mine. Don't harm them." Modern megachurch pastor invoking this verse:

- Has institutional power
- Controls millions in budget
- Commands staff and security
- Owns property and assets
- Has legal protections
- Wields social influence
- Can destroy critics financially and socially
- He's the king in this analogy, not the wandering patriarch.

When a powerful religious leader uses "touch not my anointing" to silence critics, he's positioning himself as the vulnerable one needing God's protection from oppression. He's not. He's the oppressor using God's name to avoid accountability.

How It Became a Weapon

The transformation from protective promise to silencing tactic happened gradually.

Phase 1: Elevate pastoral authority

Teach that pastors are God's specially chosen representatives. They hear from God directly. They're anointed for leadership. Their authority comes from divine appointment, not human consensus. This creates hierarchy. Pastor above congregation. Pastor as mediator between people and God.

Phase 2: Equate criticism with spiritual rebellion

Once the pastor is positioned as God's anointed, questioning him becomes questioning God. Disagreeing with him becomes disagreeing with God's will. Challenging him becomes rebellion against divine authority. The equation is: Pastor = God's Anointed = God's Voice = God's Authority Therefore: Criticizing Pastor = Attacking God

Phase 3: Deploy the verse as defense

When anyone questions, raise concerns, or demands accountability, quote Psalm 105:15.

"You're touching God's anointed. You're doing harm to His prophet. God will judge you for this." The verse becomes threat, warning, and silencing mechanism all at once.

Phase 4: Demonstrate consequences

Make examples of people who "touch the anointing." Publicly shame them. Remove them from positions. Excommunicate them. Spread rumors about their spiritual condition. This teaches everyone else: questioning leadership has severe consequences. Stay silent. Submit. Don't touch.

In churches that weaponize this verse, **"anointing"** becomes magic.

The *anointed* pastor is believed to have special:

- Access to God

- Spiritual authority
- Prophetic insight
- Divine protection
- Supernatural power

Everyone else is cast as:

- Needing the anointed one's mediation
- Dependent on his spiritual gift
- Subject to his authority

This creates two-tier system. The anointed and the un-anointed. The special and the common. The untouchable and the expendable.

It's spiritual aristocracy.

And like all aristocracies, it serves those at the top while exploiting those beneath.

The pastor's anointing means:

He can't be questioned (anointed authority)

He can't be corrected (anointed knowledge)

He can't be removed (anointed position)

He can't be held accountable (anointed protection)

Your lack of anointing means:

You must submit without question

You must trust without verification

You must obey without understanding

You must stay silent when you see wrong

This isn't Christianity. This is dictatorship with Jesus branding.

What Actually Makes Someone Anointed

In biblical context," anointed "meant chosen for specific purpose.

Old Testament anointing:

Kings were anointed for governance

Priests were anointed for temple service

Prophets were sometimes anointed for their calling

The anointing was:

Temporary (ended with death or removal)

Purpose-specific (for a task, not permanent status)

Accountable (anointed kings were judged harshly for failure)

No protection from consequences (many anointed leaders were removed, judged, even killed for corruption)

King Saul was anointed. God removed him.

Anointed priests in the Old Testament were held to HIGHER standards, not exempted from accountability.

Anointed kings who abused power faced God's judgment directly.

Being anointed never meant being above accountability. It meant being under greater scrutiny.

Modern pastors have inverted this completely.

They claim anointing exempts them from accountability rather than subjecting them to it.

"Touch not my anointing" functions as spiritual protection racket.

The pastor tells you:

"I'm anointed by God. Criticizing me invites God's judgment on you. If you challenge me, you're fighting God. You'll lose." This creates:

Fear of questioning (spiritual consequences)

Isolation of critics (they're painted as rebellious)

Self-censorship (people monitor their own doubts)

Protection of leadership (no accountability possible)

It's the perfect defense against accountability.

You can't expose financial corruption if exposing it means touching God's anointed. You can't report abuse if reporting means doing harm to God's prophet. You can't demand transparency if demanding means rebelling against God's authority.

The verse becomes shield against all oversight.

And pastors who abuse this verse know exactly what they're doing. They've seen it work. They've deployed it successfully. They teach other pastors to use it. It's strategic. Calculated. Effective.

What happens when pastors become untouchable?

Financial abuse goes unchecked:

Pastor uses church funds for personal expenses. When questioned, he invokes anointing. Board members who push for audit are removed for "touching God's anointed." Result: pastor extracts resources for years, builds personal wealth, faces no consequences.

Sexual abuse continues:

Pastor has affair with staff member or congregant. When exposed, he claims spiritual warfare and attacks on anointing. Victim is labeled Jezebel, troublemaker, spiritually deceived. Result: pastor remains in position, continues abusing, victims are silenced and blamed.

Doctrinal error compounds:

Pastor teaches questionable theology. When challenged by members with legitimate concerns, he dismisses them as rebellious and touching anointing. Result: congregation follows false teaching because questioning was equated with spiritual rebellion.

Families destroyed:

Pastor counsels couple to divorce (benefits him somehow-maybe the wife is useful to his ministry). When family members object, they're told not to touch God's anointed. Result: family separated because no one could challenge pastoral authority.

These aren't hypothetical. These are documented patterns.

"Touch not my anointing" has covered up financial exploitation, abuse, heresy, and destruction of families. The body count is real.

Here's what's darkly funny: the Bible is full of people questioning, challenging, and even rebuking anointed leaders.

Nathan confronted King David (anointed king) about his adultery and murder. God sent Nathan specifically to rebuke the anointed king. (2 Samuel 12)

Paul publicly rebuked Peter (anointed apostle) for hypocrisy. Publicly. In front of everyone. (Galatians 2:11-14)

Moses faced constant challenges from the Israelites. God didn't strike them all dead for "touching His anointed." Some He judged. Others He let Moses address.

Jesus called out religious leaders constantly. The Pharisees, Sadducees, teachers of the law — all anointed religious authorities. Jesus called them whitewashed tombs, blind guides, snakes, vipers. (Matthew 23)

If "touch not my anointing" meant what modern pastors claim, these biblical examples are all sin.

Nathan sinned by confronting David. Paul sinned by rebuking Peter. Jesus sinned by calling out Pharisees. Obviously not.

The verse never meant "leaders can't be questioned." It meant "God protects His vulnerable servants from oppressive power." Modern pastors are the oppressive power. Not the vulnerable servants.

WHO'S REALLY UNTOUCHABLE

In churches that weaponize this verse, notice who actually can't be touched.

The senior pastor can:

- Control all finances without disclosure
- Make unilateral decisions without input
- Remove anyone who questions him
- Live luxuriously while congregants struggle
- Teach whatever he wants without correction
- Abuse power without consequence

But you can't:

- Ask where your tithe money goes
- Question theological teaching
- Raise concerns about leadership decisions
- Demand accountability
- Leave without being labeled *backslidden*

The anointing doesn't protect the faithful.
It protects the powerful — from the powerless.

It should be the reverse. If God protects anyone's anointing, it's the vulnerable congregant who can be crushed by institutional power. But churches don't quote Psalm 105:15 to protect members from pastoral abuse. They quote it to protect pastors from accountability.

What does the Bible actually say about church leaders?

Timothy 5:19-20:

"Do not entertain an accusation against an elder unless it is brought by two or three witnesses. But those elders who are sinning you are to reprove before everyone, so that the others may take warning." Leaders can be accused. With proper witnesses, they should be rebuked publicly.

Peter 5:2-3:

"Be shepherds of God's flock that is under your care, watching over them — not because you must, but because you are willing, as God wants you to be; not pursuing dishonest gain, but eager to serve; not lording it over those entrusted to you, but being examples to the flock." Leaders shouldn't lord authority over people. Shouldn't pursue dishonest gain. Should serve, not rule.

Matthew 20:25-28:

Jesus called them together and said," You know that the rulers of the Gentiles lord it over them, and their high officials exercise authority over them. Not so with you. Instead, whoever wants to become great among you must be your servant, and whoever wants to be first must be your slave-just as the Son of Man did not come to be served, but to serve." Leadership is servanthood. Authority is service. Greatness is humility.

Modern "anointed" pastors often do the opposite of this.

They **lord authority**, pursue personal gain, rule rather than serve, silence accusers, reject rebuke — and when confronted, hide behind *"touch not my anointed."*

So let's be clear about what **biblical anointing** actually looks like.

Jesus was anointed. His anointing meant:

- Healing the sick *(not building mansions)*
- Feeding the hungry *(not buying luxury cars)*
- Serving the least *(not demanding service)*
- Confronting religious corruption *(not participating in it)*
- Dying for others *(not enriching himself)*

The apostles were anointed. Their anointing meant:

- Suffering for the gospel *(not prosperity)*
- Living simply *(not accumulating wealth)*
- Serving sacrificially *(not being served)*
- Facing persecution *(not demanding protection from criticism)*
- Accountability to one another *(not exemption from oversight)*

If modern pastors who claim anointing lived like the biblically anointed, they would:

- Give away their wealth
- Live among the poor
- Refuse luxury
- Welcome accountability
- Serve rather than demand service
- Accept criticism with humility
- Submit to oversight

Why this works

- Parallel structure makes hypocrisy unmistakable
- Parentheticals sharpen contrast without editorializing
- Ends with a moral mirror instead of an insult

They don't.

They accumulate wealth, demand service, reject accountability, silence critics, and hide behind anointing when questioned.

That's not biblical anointing. That's counterfeit authority.

If pastors want to quote Old Testament verses about anointed leaders, here's one they should actually fear:

Ezekiel 34:2-4, 8:

"Son of man, prophesy against the shepherds of Israel; prophesy and say to them: 'This is what the Sovereign LORD says: Woe to you shepherds of Israel who only take care of yourselves! Should not shepherds take care of the flock?

You eat the curds, clothe yourselves with the wool and slaughter the choice animals, but you do not take care of the flock. You have not strengthened the weak or healed the sick or bound up the injured. You have not brought back the strays or searched for the lost. You have ruled them harshly and brutally.

Therefore, you shepherds, hear the word of the LORD: As surely as I live, declares the Sovereign LORD, because my flock lacks a shepherd and so has been plundered and has become food for all the wild animals, and because my shepherds did not search for my flock but cared for themselves rather than for my flock.

I am against the shepherds and will hold them accountable for my flock." God is against shepherds who:

Take care of themselves instead of the flock

Eat the best while the flock starves

Rule harshly

Don't care for the weak, sick, injured

Plunder the flock

That describes modern megachurch pastors exactly.

Living in luxury while congregants struggle. Ruling through control and manipulation. Extracting resources while providing minimal care. Focusing on their comfort while ignoring actual needs.

If they're anointed, God is against them.

Breaking the Spell

How do you respond when someone quotes "touch not my anointing" to silence you?

Option 1: Context

"That verse is about protecting powerless refugees from oppressive kings. You're a powerful leader with institutional backing. You're the king in this scenario, not the refugee." Option 2: Accountability

"If you're truly anointed like biblical leaders, you should welcome accountability. Anointed leaders in scripture were held to higher standards, not exempted from them." Option 3: Jesus Standard

"Jesus, the most anointed person in history, accepted challenges, answered questions, and welcomed scrutiny. If He could handle accountability, so can you." Option 4: Direct

"Using that verse to avoid accountability is spiritual abuse. If you're doing nothing wrong, transparency shouldn't threaten you." Option 5: Walk

"Any leader who hides behind that verse when questioned is admitting they can't defend their actions on merit. I'm done participating in this system." The spell breaks when you refuse to be intimidated.

Anointing isn't magic immunity. It's not a force field against accountability. It's not permission to abuse power. And pastors who claim it is are revealing exactly why they need accountability.

Here's what Psalm 105:15 actually protects:

Vulnerable people from powerful institutions.

Powerless individuals from oppressive authorities.

Those who cannot defend themselves from those who can harm them.

If anyone in churches needs that protection, it's: The congregant who can be expelled for questioning. The volunteer whose years of labor can be dismissed instantly. The member whose reputation can be destroyed by leadership. The victim whose abuse can be covered up by institutional power. The family who can lose their entire community for leaving.

These are the vulnerable ones. These are God's "anointed" who need protection from harm.

And the harm they need protection from? Often comes from the very pastors quoting this verse to protect themselves.

GOD DOESN'T NEED UNTOUCHABLE LEADERS

God doesn't need leaders who hide from accountability behind claims of divine authority positioned as too anointed to be challenged.

If leadership requires immunity from accountability to function, it's not godly leadership.

It's tyranny with a Bible verse attached. Real spiritual authority doesn't need protection from questions. It welcomes them. Answers them. Grows through them.

Counterfeit authority demands silence and calls it submission.

True authority invites dialogue and calls it growth.

Pastors who weaponize "touch not my anointing" know exactly what they're doing. They're not protecting God's purposes. They're protecting their position. They're not defending divine authority. They're defending institutional power. They're not preventing harm to God's work. They're preventing accountability for their actions.

And they use God's name to do it.

That's not just manipulation. It's blasphemy. Taking God's protective promise to vulnerable people and twisting it into a weapon to protect powerful leaders from consequences? That's using the Lord's name in vain. That's exactly what God warned against.

"Touch not my anointing" isn't theology. It's tyranny. It's a single verse, ripped from context, weaponized to create a class of religious dictators who operate above law, ethics, and accountability.

And it only works if you let it.

The moment you recognize it as manipulation rather than scripture, its power evaporates. The moment you choose accountability over intimidation, the spell breaks. The moment you walk away from leaders who hide behind this verse, you're free.

God doesn't need untouchable leaders.

But corrupt leaders absolutely need untouchable status. And "touch not my anointing" is the verse they hide behind. Don't let them. Touch the anointing. Question the authority. Demand accountability. Because if they're really anointed by God, they should be able to withstand scrutiny. And if they can't? They were never anointed in the first place.

Chapter 14: The Altar Call Machine – How Emotional Peaks Create False Commitments

◆◆◆

The lights dimmed. The worship band played softly. The pastor's voice dropped to a whisper." Every head bowed. Every eye closed. This is between you and God." But it wasn't. It was between you and 500 people watching, even if they weren't supposed to be.

"If you've never accepted Jesus, or if you've walked away and need to come back, or if you're here and you know something's not right with God-I want you to come forward. Right now. Don't wait. Don't think about it.

Just come." The music swelled." Just As I Am "playing for the fourth time. People shifting in seats. The tension unbearable." I'm going to wait. I sense God's not done. Someone needs to come forward. Don't let this moment pass." More music. More waiting. More pressure building.

Finally, someone walks forward. Then another. Then five more. The floodgates open. People crying. Hugging. Praying. Celebrating. Lives changed. Souls saved. Victory. Except most of those people will be gone within six months. Many within six weeks. Because what just happened wasn't a spiritual encounter.

It was a manufactured emotional crisis resolved through public commitment under psychological duress. It's not the Holy Spirit. It's the formula. And it works every single time.

Altar calls follow a predictable pattern. Because they're engineered, not spontaneous.

Step 1: Create emotional elevation (30-45 minutes)

Start with high-energy worship. Get people singing, moving, emotionally activated. Release dopamine, oxytocin, endorphins through music and communal experience. Then shift to slower, more intimate songs. Bring emotion to vulnerability. Get people feeling, not thinking. By the end of worship, you're emotionally elevated, defenses lowered, rational thinking suspended.

Step 2: Deliver message that creates internal crisis (20-30 minutes)

The sermon isn't teaching. It's problem agitation. Establish that something wrong with you. You're broken, lost, wandering, incomplete, in danger. The problem is framed as urgent and severe. If you're not saved: you're going to hell, could die tonight, eternity in torment awaits. If you are saved but not "all in": you're lukewarm, God will spit you out, you're living in compromise, missing God's best. Either way, there's a crisis. And it must be resolved immediately.

Step 3: Present the solution (only one)

The solution to your crisis is typically the same: come forward. Make a public commitment. Right now. Not "think about it." Not "pray about it privately." Not "talk to someone later." Come forward. Now. Publicly.

Step 4: Apply maximum pressure at peak emotion

This is where the manipulation intensifies." Every head bowed, every eye closed" — Creates illusion of privacy while maintaining public accountability. You think no one's watching, but everyone is." Don't let this moment pass" — Creates urgency. Now or never. Miss this and you miss everything.

"I sense God's not done" — Extends the pressure. Makes people who are resisting feel like they're fighting God." Just come" — Bypasses rational thought. Don't think. Just act. The music plays. And plays. And plays. The emotional tension becomes unbearable. The only release is to walk forward.

Step 5: Celebrate the decision publicly

When people come forward, everyone applauds. Celebrates. Validates the decision. This creates:

Social reward (you did the right thing)

Emotional release (the tension breaks)

Public commitment (harder to reverse)

Witnesses (accountability to the decision)

The person feels relief, acceptance, significance. The crisis is resolved. But the crisis was manufactured. And the resolution won't last.

Altar calls are psychologically effective for producing immediate responses. Here's why:

Emotional decision-making:

Under intense emotion, the prefrontal cortex (rational thinking) is suppressed. The limbic system (emotional response) dominates. You make decisions based on feeling, not analysis. When you calm down later, rational thinking returns. And you realize: I don't actually believe what I committed to.

Social pressure:

According to former church staff, the combination of public setting, peer observation, and authority figure creates enormous pressure to comply. Saying no means:

Resisting in front of everyone

Disappointing the pastor

Appearing hard-hearted

Standing out as the one who didn't respond

It's easier to walk forward than to resist publicly.

Manufactured crisis:

The sermon created a problem that didn't exist before you walked in. Now you have a crisis that demands immediate resolution. But after you leave, the crisis dissipates. Because it was never real. It was induced.

False correlation:

You feel emotional during worship and the altar call. You correlate that emotion with divine presence. But the emotion is neurochemical response to music, social bonding, and psychological manipulation. Not God. When the emotion fades (and it will), you assume God's presence left. You wonder what you did wrong. Nothing. The feeling was never God in the first place.

Churches count "decisions" but rarely track actual conversion.

What research shows:

80-90% of altar call "decisions" don't result in lasting change. Most people who walk forward during evangelistic altar calls:

- Never return to that church
- Don't integrate into faith community
- Revert to previous life within weeks
- Often don't remember making the decision

Re-dedication altar calls are even less effective:

- People re-dedicate multiple times
- Same person, different crisis, same response
- No lasting transformation
- Provides temporary emotional relief, not actual change
- But churches keep doing it. Why?

Because it looks like results. High numbers. Visible response. Something is happening. And it funds growth. "50 people came forward tonight" becomes "God is moving" becomes "join us next week" becomes new attendance becomes new giving. The altar call serves the church's growth metrics even when it doesn't serve actual spiritual formation.

"Every head bowed, every eye closed. This is between you and God." No, it's not.

This phrase creates false privacy while maintaining public pressure.

People believe no one is watching, so they feel free to respond. But everyone is actually watching peripherally. They see who goes forward. And once you're forward, you're fully visible. Everyone sees. Everyone knows. You can't take it back. This is manipulation.

If it were truly private, it would be "go home and pray about this." If it were truly about conviction, it wouldn't require public demonstration. The public element serves the church, not the individual. It creates social accountability, witnesses to the commitment, and visible "success" for the service.

Different churches use slightly different scripts, but the elements remain consistent:

Evangelical version:

"If you died tonight, do you know where you'd go? If there's any doubt, come forward now. Tomorrow isn't promised." Charismatic version:

"God is moving in this place. I sense breakthrough for someone. Don't resist the Holy Spirit. Come now." Seeker-sensitive version:

Documented practices show: "Maybe you've never made this decision. Or maybe you made it once but you've drifted. Wherever you are, you

can come home today. Just come forward." Prosperity version:

"Are you ready for breakthrough? Ready for God to open doors? Then come forward and make this commitment. Your breakthrough is waiting." Different words. Same formula. Same manipulation.

Notice when altar calls happen: Typically after emotional worship. Rarely before. Usually during specific songs." Just As I Am," I Surrender All," Come Just As You Are." Consistently with music playing throughout. Rarely in silence.

Why?

Music maintains emotional elevation. Prevents rational thinking. Creates urgency through building intensity. The repetition-playing the same chorus 6, 8, 10 times-creates trance-like state. Your mind stops analyzing and starts feeling. Skilled worship leaders know exactly how to time the music to the pastor's prompts.

Build intensity when he's calling people forward. Pull back when he pauses. Crescendo when people start walking. It's choreographed. Rehearsed. Calculated. And it works because music bypasses cognitive processing and directly triggers emotional response.

The most manipulative version: altar calls for children. Kids as young as 4 or 5 are asked to make "decisions for Jesus" during Vacation Bible School, children's church, or youth camp.

The problem:

Children that young don't have capacity for informed spiritual decisions. They're responding to:

- Wanting to please adults
- Peer pressure (other kids are going)
- Fear of hell (if they understood the message)
- Desire for acceptance and approval

A five-year-old walking forward isn't making a theological commitment. They're complying with adult authority in an environment designed to produce compliance.

But churches count these as conversions.

And worse, they use these childhood "decisions" as leverage later: "You made this decision when you were six. Don't walk away from that now." The child didn't make an informed decision. The child was manipulated by adults who should have known better.

Many Christians "re-dedicate" their lives multiple times. Same person. Different services. Repeated altar calls.

Why does this happen?

Because the altar call produces temporary emotional relief, not actual transformation. You feel distant from God. You walk forward. You experience emotional catharsis. You feel close to God. Three weeks later, you feel distant again. Because the feeling was neurochemical, not spiritual. It fades like any emotional high. So you walk forward again. And again. And again.

Churches present this as spiritual warfare or personal failure.

"The enemy is attacking." You need to fight for your commitment." Your problem is lack of discipline." The actual problem: the altar call created an emotional response that was never sustainable. You're chasing a feeling that was artificially induced and can't be maintained.

After you walk forward, you fill out a card. Name. Phone. Email. Address. Information about your decision.

This serves multiple purposes:

Data collection: You're now in the database. They can contact you. Track you. Count you.

Commitment device: Writing it down makes it feel more real and binding.

Legal protection: If you later claim you were manipulated, they have your signature saying you made the decision freely.

Metrics: Decision cards become statistics. "400 decisions this year" looks good in reports to donors and denominational bodies. But most decision cards represent people who will never return. The church knows this. They keep doing it anyway because the metrics matter more than the actual outcomes.

Altar calls use escalating pressure tactics:

Phase 1: General invitation

"If anyone needs to come forward."

Phase 2: Specificity

"God is speaking to someone specifically about [issue]. That's you. Come forward."

Phase 3: Urgency

"Don't wait. Don't let this moment pass. Come now."

Phase 4: Threat

"This might be your last chance. You might not make it home tonight. Come now."

Phase 5: Emotional manipulation

"I sense someone resisting. You're fighting God right now. Just surrender."

Phase 6: Extended time

"I'm going to wait. I'm going to have the band play one more time. Someone needs to come." Each phase increases pressure. Makes resistance harder. Eventually, people break and walk forward just to end the tension.

That's not conviction. That's coercion.

What Happens After

Most people who walk forward experience one of three outcomes:

Outcome 1: They disappear

Never return to that church. The decision didn't stick because it was made under pressure, not genuine conviction. They feel embarrassed or guilty for "failing" but can't sustain what they committed to.

Outcome 2: They cycle

Keep coming back, keep re-dedicating, keep walking forward. Chasing the emotional high they felt the first time. Never experiencing lasting change because change doesn't come from emotional manipulation.

Outcome 3: They stay and conform

Become part of the system. Participate in the same altar calls. Eventually staff them, facilitate them, perpetuate them. They made it work through sheer willpower and now believe everyone else should too. None of these outcomes represent genuine spiritual transformation. They represent compliance with a system that uses psychological manipulation to generate visible results.

What would genuine spiritual decision-making look like?

Private reflection: "Take time this week to think and pray about what you heard. There's no rush." Informed consent: "Here's what this commitment entails. Here are the expectations. Here's what's required. Consider carefully." No pressure: "This decision is between you and God.

Make it in your own time, when you're certain." Follow-up that isn't tracking: "If you want to talk more about this, here are resources. We're available. No pressure." But this doesn't generate the visible, immediate results churches need for growth metrics and emotional momentum.

So they keep using altar calls. Keep manipulating emotions. Keep creating false commitments. Because the church's needs matter more than genuine spiritual formation.

Jesus didn't use altar calls. The apostles didn't use altar calls. The early church didn't use altar calls. According to church historians including Nathan Hatch

(The Democratization of American Christianity) and scholars of American revivalism, the modern altar call was popularized in the 1820s-1830s by evangelist Charles Finney as a revivalist technique. They're roughly 200 years old, not 2,000. For most of Christian history, the faith spread without this form of public pressure.

People made genuine decisions through teaching, reflection, and personal conviction. Altar calls work for generating immediate visible response. They don't work for producing lasting transformation. But churches prioritize the immediate visible response because that's what funds growth.

If you made a decision at an altar call, consider:

Were you in emotional peak state? High from worship, vulnerable, defenses down?

Was there social pressure? Public setting, people watching, pastor waiting?

Did they create urgency?" Now or never," don't wait," this is your moment"?

Did the emotion fade? Did you feel different days or weeks later?

Have you re-dedicated multiple times? Same commitment, repeated attempts? If yes to any of these, your decision wasn't made freely. It was produced through manipulation. That doesn't mean your faith isn't real. But it means the altar call wasn't the genuine encounter you thought it was. You can have real faith.

Real commitment. Real transformation. But it won't come from walking forward during emotional manipulation. It comes from genuine conviction, informed decision-making, and sustained commitment made when you're thinking clearly — not when you're emotionally compromised.

GOD DOESN'T NEED THE MANIPULATION

God doesn't need manufactured emotional crisis to reach people. Doesn't need psychological pressure to produce genuine faith. Doesn't need public displays to validate private conviction. Doesn't need music manipulation and social pressure to draw people.

If the altar call is the only way people can encounter God, then God is weak. But churches use altar calls because they're effective at producing measurable results that fund growth. Not because they're effective at producing genuine spiritual transformation. The altar call serves the church. Not God. And certainly not you.

Here's a different kind of invitation: If you've made altar call decisions that didn't stick, you're not a spiritual failure. You were manipulated. If you've re-dedicated multiple times, you're not weak. The system is designed to keep you cycling. If you walked forward out of pressure rather than conviction, that's not your fault. The environment was designed to break your resistance.

You're free to:

Make spiritual decisions in your own time, without pressure, when you're thinking clearly. Trust your own discernment about what you believe and when.

Reject emotional manipulation as a requirement for valid faith. Walk away from systems that require public performance to validate private conviction.

Walking an aisle under emotional duress isn't a divine requirement. Churches need these tactics to generate visible results. And once you see the difference, you can finally make genuine choices — free from manipulation.

You've seen the system. You've seen who it targets. You've seen how it maintains control. Now let's look at the specific scripts — the exact words and techniques used to separate you from your money. These aren't theories. They're documented practices you may have experienced yourself without recognizing the pattern.

PART 4: THE EXTRACTION TACTICS

Chapter 15: The Urgency Trap – Manufactured Crisis and the 90-Second Shakedown

◆ ◆ ◆

"God just spoke to me. Someone here needs to sow a seed of exactly one thousand dollars." The pastor paused. Scanned the room." Not nine hundred. Not eleven hundred. Exactly one thousand.

And when you sow that seed, God's going to release a harvest in your life like you've rarely seen." I watched a woman in the third row reach for her checkbook. She was behind on rent. I knew because she'd come to the church for financial help earlier that week.

Now the church was extracting a thousand dollars from her under the guise of "sowing a seed." The harvest never came. But the church got its money. This isn't fundraising. This follows patterns associated with confidence schemes in non-religious contexts.

With specific scripts, tested formulas, and psychological manipulation refined over decades. Let me show you exactly how they do it.

SCRIPT 1: "GOD TOLD ME A SPECIFIC NUMBER" The Full Script:

"Before service, God spoke to me. He said someone here needs to give [specific amount]. I don't know who you are, but you know. This is your moment. When you obey, God's going to do something supernatural in your life. Don't let doubt stop you. Step out in faith." Why This Works:

"God told me" can't be questioned without questioning God Himself. The specific number creates the illusion of genuine prophecy. " $1,000" sounds more divinely inspired than "give what you can." I don't know who you are "makes multiple people think it's them." Supernatural "is vague enough that anyone can imagine anything.

The Reality:

God didn't speak. The pastor calculated what the church needs and what's realistic to extract.

The specific number is based on donor capacity, not divine revelation. Multiple people will respond because the framing is designed to make many feel targeted.

Variations:

"God showed me three people need to give $500." I sense someone needs to sow $100 weekly for the next month." God said five people will give $2,000 today." The Result:

If the pastor says "three people at $500," he's asking for $1,500 total. But the specificity makes it feel prophetic, so often 5-7 people respond. Total haul: $2,500- $3,500. Not prophecy. Strategy.

SCRIPT 2: "SOW YOUR SEED, REAP YOUR HARVEST" The Full Script:

"Your offering isn't just giving-it's sowing. When a farmer sows seed, he expects a harvest. The Bible says you reap what you sow. Sow finances, reap finances. Sow generously, reap generously. This is how the kingdom works. So I'm asking: what do you need to reap? Sow a seed equal to that need." Why This Works:

Agricultural metaphor feels natural, biblical, unstoppable. The promise is embedded in the metaphor: plant seed, get harvest. Guaranteed. Proportional thinking: bigger seed = bigger harvest. Creates pressure to give more." Kingdom principle "frames it as divine law, not manipulation.

The Reality:

Farmers plant seeds in their own fields and reap their own harvests. They don't give seeds to someone else and expect return. Economics: giving money away makes you poorer, not richer. That's math. The Bible verses about sowing and reaping are about moral consequences, not financial transactions.

The Harvest That rarely Comes:

Track 100 people who "sow financial seeds" for a year. Maybe 5-10 experience financial improvement (probably unrelated to giving). The other 90 stay the same or worse (because they gave money they needed). Churches celebrate the 5-10. Ignore the 90. Claim the system works.

When It Fails:

"Keep sowing." The harvest is coming." God's timing." Maybe you didn't sow in faith." The system is unfalsifiable. Success proves it works. Failure is your fault.

SCRIPT 3: "FIRST FRUITS OFFERING" The Full Script:

Multiple former members describe "God requires the first fruits. Not the leftovers. Not what's left after bills. The first and the best. When you honor God with your first fruits, He protects the rest. But when you give God leftovers, you're saying He's not your priority. And God won't bless what He's not priority in." Why This Works:

Creates guilt: if you pay bills first, you're dishonoring God. Creates fear: if you don't give first, God won't protect your finances. Creates hierarchy: God must come before practical needs or you're failing spiritually.

The Reality:

"First fruits" in the Bible was agricultural-first of the harvest, not first of paycheck. Giving before ensuring basic needs (food, shelter, medicine) isn't faithfulness. It's financial irresponsibility. God doesn't need to be proven priority through payment sequence.

The Real Purpose:

Churches want access to your full paycheck before you budget for actual needs. If you pay rent and buy groceries first, less money is available for church. By demanding "first fruits," they get money before realistic budgeting happens.

The Harm:

People give rent money and then can't pay rent. Families skip medical care to give "first." Parents don't buy food for kids because they gave "first fruits." When crisis hits, church says they didn't give enough or didn't give in faith.

SCRIPT 4: "SACRIFICIAL OFFERING" The Full Script:

"I'm not asking for comfortable giving. I'm asking for sacrifice. Give until it hurts. Give what you can't afford. That's when it becomes a sacrifice that God honors. Comfortable giving doesn't require faith. But sacrificial giving? That's when God moves. That's when breakthrough happens." Why This Works:

Reframes financial prudence as lack of faith. Makes pain the metric: if it doesn't hurt, it doesn't count. Promises breakthrough for suffering.

The Reality:

Sacrificial giving means the giver suffers while the church prospers. God doesn't require financial pain to prove devotion. That's abusive logic. The only breakthrough: church's finances break through. Yours don't.

Notice:

The pastor isn't sacrificing. He has guaranteed salary, healthcare, retirement. He asks you to sacrifice while ensuring he never has to.

The Dangerous Outcome:

People give money needed for medical care, prescriptions, necessary purchases. Families go into debt to meet the church's definition of sacrifice. Meanwhile, the pastor lives comfortably on guaranteed income funded by their sacrifice.

SCRIPT 5: "PROPHETIC SPECIFIC AMOUNTS" The Full Script:

"As I was praying, God gave me specific numbers. Some of you need to give $50 today. Some $100. Some $500. I feel like there are three people who need to give $1,000. And someone-I don't know who-needs to write a check for $5,000. As I call these amounts, if you feel God speaking, respond." Why This Works:

Menu of options: most people finds a number within their capacity (or that stretches it). Specific numbers feel prophetic, not calculated. Social proof: when others respond to their number, pressure builds on you.

The Reality:

The pastor is doing math, not prophecy. Covering all ranges (low to high) ensures maximum participation and maximum haul. If 200 people attend, some can give $50, some $100, some more. Hitting all ranges captures everyone's capacity.

The Formula:

Call out 5-7 amounts from low to high. Watch who responds to each. Celebrate each response to build momentum. Keep going until enough respond.

Example Math:

people × $50 = $2,500 30 people × $100 = $3,000 15 people × $500 = $7,500 3 people × $1,000 = $3,000 1 person × $5,000 = $5,000

Total: $21,000 from one offering.

That's not divine revelation. That's donor segmentation.

SCRIPT 6: "THE TESTIMONY SETUP" The Full Script:

"Before we receive the offering, I want to share a testimony. Last month, someone sowed a $1,000 seed. This week, they got a $10,000 bonus at work. God is faithful. He honors seed sowing." [After testimony]

"Who's ready to sow your seed and watch God move?" Why This Works:

Provides "proof" the system works. Social proof: others have succeeded doing this. Hope injection: that could be you.

The Reality:

Selection bias: Church only shares successes, never the hundreds who sowed and got nothing.

Causation assumption: The bonus probably wasn't related to the seed. Job performance, company profits, scheduled raises-actual causes ignored.

Reusability: One testimony gets used for months. One person's bonus becomes justification for extracting hundreds of thousands from others.

Honest Version:

"500 people sowed $1,000 seeds this year. One got a bonus that may or may not be related. The other 499 are still waiting. That's a 0.2% success rate. Anyone want to sow?" Nobody would give. So churches curate testimonies. Winners only. Losers blamed for lack of faith.

SCRIPT 7: "BREAKTHROUGH OFFERING" The Full Script:

"Some of you have been believing for breakthrough. It's coming. But breakthrough requires a breakthrough offering. You need to sow something significant. Something that gets God's attention. Something that breaks you out of normal into supernatural." Why This Works:

Appeals to delayed promise: you've been waiting, it's almost here. Requires action: you need to do something to unlock it. Escalates amount: normal giving isn't enough.

The Reality:

"Breakthrough" is always coming but never arrives. God's attention doesn't require purchasing. Either God cares or doesn't. Money doesn't change that. The only breakthrough: church finances.

The Pattern:

Person gives breakthrough offering. Nothing changes. Next month, another breakthrough offering needed. Nothing changes. Cycle repeats indefinitely. Church collects continuous breakthrough offerings. Congregant never breaks through anything except their bank account.

SCRIPT 8: "THE EMERGENCY APPEAL" The Full Script:

"We're short on budget this month. If we don't raise $50,000 by Sunday, we'll have to cut staff, cancel programs, might not make payroll. We need everyone to give above your tithe. This is urgent. Our ministry depends on it." Why This Works:

Crisis creates urgency. Guilt: staff will suffer if you don't give. Framed as temporary: just this once to get through crisis.

The Reality:

Often the crisis is manufactured or exaggerated. If budget is consistently short, that's mismanagement, not emergency. After the crisis, no transparency about whether it was real or how money was used.

The Pattern:

"Emergency" happens 3-4 times per year. Each time, crisis rhetoric extracts extraordinary giving. Then another crisis emerges a few months later. No accountability. No transparency. Just repeated crises requiring repeated extraordinary giving.

SCRIPT 9: "OBEDIENCE TEST" The Full Script:

"God just gave me an instruction. Everyone here is to give $100 today. Not $99. Not $101. Exactly $100. This is a test of obedience. Those who obey will see God move. Those who don't will miss their season of blessing." Why This Works:

Divine command: not a request, an order from God. Precision test: exact amount proves you're listening. Binary outcome: obey and be blessed, disobey and miss out.

The Reality:

God didn't give instruction. Pastor needs money and framed it as divine order. The "test" is manipulation. God doesn't need financial obedience tests.

The Math:

people attend. 200 give exactly $100 = $20,000. That's not prophecy. That's revenue generation with religious packaging.

SCRIPT 10: "FAITH OFFERING FOR YOUR MIRACLE" The Full Script:

"What do you need from God? Healing? Financial breakthrough? Restored relationship? Whatever you need, I want you to sow a faith offering equal to the size of your need. If you need a $10,000 miracle, sow $10,000. God honors faith." Why This Works:

Proportional logic: bigger need = bigger offering. Frames it as faith investment: sowing to receive. Makes need the measure of giving: desperate people give more.

The Reality:

People in crisis are most vulnerable. This script exploits desperation. Someone needing $10,000 probably doesn't have $10,000 to give. That's why they need it. Asking desperate people to give money they don't have is predatory.

The Outcome:

People go into debt to give "faith offerings." The miracle doesn't come. They're now deeper in crisis — and blamed for insufficient faith.

These scripts aren't accidental. They're taught. Pastoral conferences. Fundraising seminars. Church growth workshops. Books and courses on increasing offerings.

Actual training topics include:

- *"How to Triple Your Offerings in 90 Days"*
- *"Prophetic Giving: Hearing God's Voice for Your Budget"*
- *"The Psychology of Generosity"*
- *"Creating Urgency Without Desperation"*
- *"Testimony Selection for Maximum Impact"*

Pastors literally share scripts that work. They test variations. They refine approaches.

Ministry training? Hardly.
This is sales training.

And it's justified using God's name — employing manipulation techniques that would face legal scrutiny in nonreligious contexts.

When specific amounts are called out:

- The room is segmented into giving tiers
- Leaders calculate what percentage can afford each amount
- Figures are pitched high enough to create pressure, but low enough to ensure response

Strategic targeting follows predictable lines:

- **New members:** asked for smaller amounts to build the habit
- **Long-term members:** pressed for larger gifts based on loyalty
- **Wealthy members:** approached privately for major contributions

This isn't spontaneous generosity.
It's engineered extraction.

The goal:

Extract maximum from each tier without losing anyone.

These scripts cause real harm.

Financial Harm:

Families in debt from "faith giving." Elderly on fixed incomes giving sacrificially while pastors live in luxury. People skipping medical care to give "first fruits." Psychological Harm:

Constant guilt about not giving enough. Shame when breakthrough doesn't come. Anxiety that God's love depends on financial performance.

Spiritual Harm:

God becomes transactional: give to get, pay for blessings. Faith becomes financial: how much you give determines God's favor. Questioning becomes rebellion: doubt the offering, doubt God.

Notice: pastors using these scripts never sow sacrificially from their own money. They ask you to sacrifice while keeping their income guaranteed. They promise breakthrough for your giving while ensuring their comfort.

If seed faith worked:

The pastor sowing most should reap most. But pastors using these scripts get rich collecting your seeds, not sowing their own.

They get wealthy from your sacrifice. You stay broke from your sowing.

And they call this "God's blessing." God requires no SCRIPTS

God doesn't need manufactured urgency, psychological manipulation, or scripted appeals exploiting vulnerability that never come.

If God's work requires manipulation to be funded, maybe it's not God's work.

Maybe it's institutional machinery that needs money to operate and uses God's name to extract it.

They call it ministry.

They call manufactured urgency "Holy Spirit leading." They call manipulation "faith building." They call exploitation "kingdom principle." It's not.

It follows patterns associated with financial exploitation. Scripted. Refined. Deployed effectively. And God's name is attached to techniques that would face legal scrutiny in non-religious contexts.

You're allowed to recognize it.

Those "prophetic words" about specific amounts? Not prophecy. Strategy. Those seed faith promises? Not biblical. Get-rich-quick schemes that only enrich the church. Those breakthrough offerings? Not spiritual requirement. Revenue targets in religious packaging.

None of it is from God.

It's from institutional need for money and willingness to use any technique-including manipulation, guilt, false prophecy-to extract it. And once you see the scripts, you can't unsee them. Every offering appeal becomes transparent. Every prophetic word about money becomes obvious manipulation. Every testimony becomes curated marketing.

That's not cynicism. That's clarity.

And clarity is the first step to freedom.

Chapter 16: The Seed Offering Exploitation – Exact Scripts They Use

◆◆◆

"I need you to grab your checkbook right now. God is speaking to me, and He says there are ten people in this room — ten people only — who are about to experience their financial breakthrough. But you need to move fast. You have ninety seconds to write a check for ten thousand dollars. Not nine thousand. Not eleven thousand.

Exactly ten thousand. If you hesitate, you'll miss it. The anointing is here right now, but it won't wait. Ninety seconds. Who's going to be obedient?" I watched a pastor say these exact words on a Sunday night in a packed sanctuary.

And I watched ten people — including a single mother, a man facing foreclosure, and a couple who'd maxed out their credit cards — run to the altar waving checks they couldn't afford to write. Within two minutes, $100,000 moved from desperate people's bank accounts into a system designed to extract maximum cash in minimum time.

This chapter documents exactly how that extraction works.

THE SETUP: "GOD JUST SPOKE TO ME" The offering has already been collected. People are settling back into their seats. The sermon is winding down. Then the pastor pauses.

"Hold on. hold on." The music swells slightly. The pastor's expression changes — eyes closed, hand raised, listening to something no one else can hear.

"God is speaking to me right now." Everything stops. This is the moment. This is why people came tonight. Not for the sermon. Not for the worship. For this. The prophetic word. The breakthrough moment. The announcement that God is about to move.

"The Holy Spirit just interrupted me." The congregation leans forward. Phones come out — not to scroll, but to record. Because what happens next needs to be captured. Documented. Shared. This is where miracles happen.

"I wasn't planning to say this, but God just told me there are people in this room who are about to step into their financial breakthrough. But you have to move NOW." Notice what just happened.

The pastor created divine authority. You can question a man, but you can't question God. The pastor suggested spontaneity — this wasn't planned, this is the Holy Spirit moving. But watch this same pastor next week. Same pause. Same setup. Same "God is speaking" moment. It's not spontaneous. It's scripted.

The pastor bypassed rational thought. When God speaks, you don't deliberate. You don't calculate. You don't check your bank balance. You obey.

And the pastor made refusal into disobedience. If you don't respond, you're not declining an offering. You're rejecting God.

This is manipulation masquerading as prophecy. And it's about to get much worse.

THE ESCALATION LADDER: BUILDING THE FRENZY

"God is saying there are one hundred people who need to sow a seed of one hundred dollars right now." Hands go up. People move toward the altar. The band plays softly — usually something repetitive, something that builds. The atmosphere is charged. This is safe. A hundred dollars. A hundred people. You're not alone.

The pastor watches. Counts. Nods.

"That's good. That's good. But God is saying something else." The music swells slightly.

"There are fifty people — fifty people who are going to sow five hundred dollars. And these are the people who are going to see their blessing multiplied. Five hundred dollar seeds. Who's going to be obedient?" More people move. The dollar amount just quintupled, but the number of people halved. Now you're in a smaller, more elite group. You're special. You're one of the fifty. The energy in the room intensifies.

People who gave $100 are now pulling out their phones, checking accounts, reconsidering.

"Wait. God is speaking again." Another pause. More intensity.

"There are ten people. Ten people only. God says you're going to sow one thousand dollars, and you're going to see a ten-thousand-dollar return. But you have to move NOW. One thousand dollars. Ten people. Who's going to step out in faith?" Now we're at serious money.

But we're also at maximum social pressure. The people who gave $100 are watching the people who gave $500. The people who gave $500 are watching to see who gives $1,000. Nobody wants to be the person who stopped too early. Nobody wants to miss their moment.

And the pastor isn't done.

"Hold on. hold on. God just said there are FIVE people — five people in this room who are being called to sow TEN THOUSAND DOLLARS. And God says if you do this in the next ninety seconds, you're going to see a HUNDRED-THOUSAND-DOLLAR return within ninety days. But you have ninety seconds. Starting. NOW." This is the climax. This is what everything was building toward. Ten thousand dollars. Ninety seconds. A hundred-thousand-dollar promise. And the countdown has begun.

Watch what happens next.

THE COUNTDOWN: WEAPONIZING TIME PRESSURE

Ninety seconds is not arbitrary. It's calculated.

Ninety seconds is too short to think. Too short to calculate. Too short to call your spouse. Too short to check your bank balance. Too short to remember that God doesn't operate on game-show timelines.

But ninety seconds is long enough to write a check. Long enough to pull out a credit card. Long enough to run to the front. Long enough to make a decision you can't unmake.

The pastor starts the timer.

"Ninety seconds. You have ninety seconds to respond to what God is saying." The band intensifies. Drums build. The atmosphere becomes electric.

"Eighty seconds. Don't miss this. God's window is closing." People are moving now. Running. Desperate. Some are crying. Some are shouting. The people who gave $1,000 are pulling out their phones, fingers shaking, trying to access mobile banking to see if they can go higher.

God doesn't need your money in 90 seconds. But pastors who've perfected this script need your decision made before rational thought kicks in.

"Sixty seconds. If you don't move now, you're going to regret this tomorrow. The anointing is HERE. The blessing is HERE. But it won't wait." A woman is writing a check at her seat, hand trembling. A man is literally running toward the stage, waving a check in the air. Another couple is arguing in whispered, urgent tones — one pulling toward the altar, the other pulling back.

"Thirty seconds. This is it. This is your moment. Don't let fear hold you back. Don't let doubt block your breakthrough." More people surge forward. The altar is crowded now. Checks are being waved. Cash is being thrown. Credit cards are being handed to ushers. Some people are writing on offering envelopes balanced on their knees, on Bibles, on the backs of other people.

"Ten seconds. MOVE NOW. The door is closing." Final sprint. People who were hesitating make their decision. Checks get written for amounts that aren't in the account. Credit card debt gets added. Retirement savings get tapped. Rent money gets redirected.

"TIME." The music crashes to a climax. The pastor raises his hands.

"Those who obeyed God, I want you to bring your seeds to the altar. Wave them in the air. This is your seed. This is your breakthrough. God is about to do something SUPERNATURAL." And people do. They wave checks like victory flags. Ten thousand dollars. Five thousand. Fifteen thousand. Some wrote checks for amounts they've never had in their account at one time. But they're waving them anyway, because in this moment, in this frenzy, it feels like faith.

It's not faith. It's financial extraction under psychological duress. And it's perfectly legal.

THE PROMISE: GUARANTEED RETURNS THAT NEVER COME

"Now let me tell you what's going to happen. Those of you who sowed ten thousand dollars, God is going to give you a hundred-thousand-dollar return. Not ninety thousand. Not a hundred and ten thousand. EXACTLY one hundred thousand dollars. And it's going to happen within ninety days." The crowd erupts. Shouting. Crying. Hands raised. This is it. This is the miracle. This is why they came.

But notice the language.

"God is going to give you." Not "I promise you." Not "The church guarantees." God. Not the pastor. The pastor is just the messenger. The promise comes from God. Which means if it doesn't happen, it's not the pastor's fault. It's yours. You lacked faith. You had sin. You didn't believe hard enough.

"Within ninety days." Not tomorrow. Not next week. Ninety days. Long enough that you'll forget exactly when the ninety days started. Long enough that when nothing happens, the pastor can say," Well, God's timing isn't our timing." Long enough that you'll come back and sow ANOTHER seed to "activate" the first one.

"Exactly one hundred thousand dollars." Specificity creates credibility. Vague promises (" God will bless you") are easy to dismiss. But exact numbers? That sounds prophetic. That sounds like God. Except it never happens exactly. Ever.

This is investment language without a contract. This is a promise without accountability. This is a guarantee that can't be enforced.

Watch what happens when the ninety days pass.

THE AFTERMATH: FINANCIAL DEVASTATION AND SPIRITUAL GASLIGHTING

Three months later, that single mother who gave $10,000 is being evicted. The money she used for rent went to the seed offering. She believed. She obeyed. She had faith.

But ninety days passed. No $100,000. No $10,000. No return at all. Just an eviction notice and a daughter asking why they have to leave their apartment.

The man facing foreclosure who gave his last $5,000? His house was sold at auction. He had one month to catch up on payments. He used that money to sow his seed instead. The pastor said God would give him $50,000 to save his house. The pastor was wrong. Or God was silent. Or the man lacked faith. Take your pick.

The couple who maxed out their credit cards to give $15,000? They're filing for bankruptcy. The promised $150,000 rarely came. But the credit card companies don't care about prophetic promises. They want their money. With interest.

And when these people come back to church — when they ask questions, when they seek answers, when they dare to suggest that maybe the promise didn't come true — watch what happens.

"You must have sin in your life blocking your blessing." You didn't believe hard enough." God is testing your faithfulness. Sow another seed." The harvest is coming. God's timing is perfect. Just wait." Maybe you weren't one of the ten God was actually talking to." This is gaslighting.

This is spiritual abuse. This is taking someone's financial devastation and making it their fault. You gave $10,000 you couldn't afford because the pastor said God demanded it. The promise didn't come. But somehow, it's your failure. Your lack of faith. Your sin. Your problem.

According to former church staff, meanwhile, the pastor who collected $100,000 in ninety seconds? He's driving a new car. Wearing a new watch. Announcing plans for a new building expansion. His wife just posted vacation photos from the Bahamas.

The money didn't disappear. It just didn't go where you were told it would.

THE LEGAL LOOPHOLE: WHY THIS ESCAPES LEGAL SCRUTINY (TECHNICALLY)

Here's why pastors can do this without going to jail:

It's called an "offering," not a purchase. You weren't buying anything. You weren't entering a contract. You were making a donation. Donations aren't refundable. Donations don't come with guarantees. You gave voluntarily.

Except it wasn't voluntary when the pastor said you had ninety seconds to obey God or miss your breakthrough. But try explaining that in court.

The promise came from "God," not the pastor. The pastor didn't promise you $100,000. God did. The pastor was just delivering the message. If God didn't come through, take it up with God. The pastor has no legal obligation to fulfill prophecies. Even specific ones. Even ones that included dollar amounts and timelines.

It's "spiritual law," not a contract." Sow and reap "is presented as a spiritual principle, not a financial guarantee. When you plant seeds in soil, sometimes they don't grow. Same with money seeds, apparently. The pastor can't be held liable if your spiritual seed didn't produce a spiritual harvest. That's between you and God.

It was a "donation," so no refunds. Churches are tax-exempt nonprofits. Donations are donations. Once the money is given, it belongs to the church. You can't demand it back when the promised result doesn't materialize. You can't sue for false advertising. You can't pursue legal action. Because technically, it wasn't a transaction. It was an offering.

If a financial advisor did this, they'd lose their license. When a pastor does it, it's called ministry.

But here's what it actually is:

It's financial exploitation obscured by religious language. It's extortion masquerading as prophecy. It's a manipulative financial scheme that would be illegal in any other context. If a financial advisor promised you a 10x return in ninety days and failed to deliver, they'd lose their license. If a salesman used a ninety-second countdown to pressure you into a purchase you couldn't afford, that's predatory lending.

But when a pastor does it? It's called ministry. It's called anointing. It's called obeying God.

And it's causing significant harm to lives.

THE EVIDENCE: THIS HAPPENS EVERYWHERE

Search YouTube for "seed faith offering." You'll find hundreds of examples. Same script. Same setup. Same countdown. Different churches, different denominations, different states, but identical tactics.

"God is speaking to me right now." There are [number] people who need to sow [amount]." You have [short timeframe] to respond." God promises [specific return]." This isn't a few rogue pastors. This is a systematic, taught, refined technique. There are books about how to "raise offerings." There are conferences where pastors learn these scripts. There are ministry schools that teach the psychology of urgency-based giving.

This is a playbook. And it works.

Documented practices show walk into a prosperity gospel church on a Sunday night — when emotions are highest, when people are most tired, when rational thinking is lowest — and watch the altar calls. Watch the countdown. Watch people run forward with money they don't have to give, chasing promises that will never come.

You'll see the single mother choosing between rent and seed faith. You'll see the elderly couple giving their medication money because the pastor said healing was in the seed. You'll see the young man putting his tuition on a credit card because breakthrough was promised in ninety seconds.

And you'll see the pastor counting the money while the worship team plays.

This isn't isolated. This isn't exaggerated. This is documented. This is real. This is happening in churches across America every single week.

WHO FALLS FOR THIS: UNDERSTANDING VULNERABILITY, NOT STUPIDITY

Let's be clear: The people who respond to these altar calls aren't stupid. They're desperate.

They're the mother whose child has cancer and insurance won't cover treatment. The pastor promised a healing seed would open heaven's resources. What mother wouldn't give everything for her child's life?

They're the father who lost his job six months ago and is about to lose his house. The pastor said ten thousand dollars sowed in faith would bring a hundred-thousand-dollar breakthrough. When you're facing homelessness, that's not stupidity. That's desperation.

They're the woman trapped in an abusive marriage with no money to leave. The pastor promised that faithfulness in giving would unlock provision. She gave her secret savings — the money she'd been hiding for years to eventually escape. Now she's trapped with nothing.

They're the student drowning in loans, the couple who can't conceive, the man with a terminal diagnosis. They're people in crisis, people in pain, people taught since childhood to trust spiritual authority.

And they're being hunted.

Because prosperity preachers don't target the wealthy. They target the desperate. The vulnerable. The afraid. The people who have nothing left to lose and everything to hope for.

They target people who were raised in church culture, where questioning the pastor is questioning God. People who were taught that doubt is sin. People who learned that obedience means giving even when it doesn't make sense.

They target people who are sleep-deprived from late-night services, emotionally exhausted from high-intensity worship, psychologically primed by testimonies of breakthrough that may or may not be true.

This isn't stupidity. This is exploitation of vulnerability. And it's calculated.

THE PSYCHOLOGICAL WARFARE: HOW THE COUNTDOWN WORKS

The ninety-second countdown isn't random. It's psychological warfare.

It eliminates rational thinking. Under time pressure, the prefrontal cortex — responsible for logical decision-making — goes offline. The amygdala — responsible for fight-or-flight responses — takes over. You're not thinking. You're reacting.

It creates artificial scarcity." Only ten people." Ninety seconds only." This anointing won't wait." Scarcity drives action. FOMO (fear of missing out) overrides caution. You don't want to be the person who was in the room when God moved but didn't respond.

It triggers social proof. When other people start moving, running, giving, you feel pressure to do the same. If everyone else is responding, maybe you're wrong to hesitate. Maybe they know something you don't. Maybe your doubt is blocking your blessing.

It weaponizes commitment. The moment you stand up and walk toward the altar, you've publicly committed. Now you can't back down without admitting you were wrong to move. So you write the check. Not because you can afford it. Because backing out would mean embarrassment.

It bypasses spousal consultation. Ninety seconds isn't enough time to turn to your spouse and have a real conversation." Honey, should we give $10,000 we don't have?" I don't know, let me think — " TIME'S UP." Decisions that should involve discussion are made unilaterally under pressure.

It creates emotional frenzy. The music builds. The pastor's voice intensifies. People are crying, shouting, running. You're caught in a wave of emotion. And emotion is the enemy of rational financial decisions.

This is manipulation. This is psychological exploitation. This is using every cognitive bias, every emotional trigger, every social pressure point to extract maximum money in minimum time.

And they know exactly what they're doing.

HOW TO RECOGNIZE THE SHAKEDOWN: RED FLAGS

If you hear these phrases, you're being manipulated:

"God just spoke to me about your finances." God doesn't need a middleman. And God doesn't time His messages to coincide with offering moments.

"You have [short timeframe] to respond." God doesn't work on countdown timers. Urgency is a sales tactic, not a spiritual principle.

"There are [specific number] people who need to give [specific amount]." This creates artificial scarcity and competition. It's marketing, not prophecy.

"If you don't move now, you'll miss your breakthrough." This is threat-based motivation. God doesn't threaten you into giving.

"Sow [amount] and receive [larger amount] in return." This is investment language. It's transactional. It's not giving — it's buying. And what you're buying is a promise that won't be kept.

The money didn't disappear. It just didn't go where you were told it would.

"Your obedience in the next [timeframe] determines your future." This makes refusal into disobedience and giving into faithfulness. It's manipulation wrapped in spiritual language.

"Don't let your mind talk you out of what your spirit knows is right." Translation: "Don't think. Don't calculate. Don't be rational. Just give." If you hear these phrases, you're not being invited to worship through generosity. You're being worked by someone who knows exactly how to extract money from vulnerable people.

What Legitimate Generosity Looks Like

Real, healthy, biblical generosity doesn't look like a shakedown. Here's what it looks like:

No time pressure." We have these needs. Pray about it. Give as you're led. There's no deadline." No promised returns." Your giving supports this ministry. It helps people. That's the return — impact, not profit." No manipulation." Here's our budget. Here's where the money goes.

Give if you want to support this. Don't give if you can't or don't want to." No prophecy tied to money." God speaks to hearts about many things. If He's telling you to give, that's between you and Him.

I'm not claiming to have a word from God about your wallet." Full transparency." Here's where every dollar goes. Here's my salary. Here are our expenses. Everything is disclosed." Respect for autonomy." This is your decision. We're not going to pressure you. We're not going to time you.

You're an adult. You decide." Just: Here's the need. Here's how you can help. The choice is yours.

But that doesn't generate $100,000 in ninety seconds. That doesn't create viral moments. That doesn't fund private jets and luxury cars.

And that's exactly why prosperity preachers don't do it that way.

THE TRUTH THEY WON'T TELL YOU

God needs nothing from you in ninety seconds. God needs no payment.at all. The God who created everything doesn't depend on your checking account. The God who owns the cattle on a thousand hills doesn't need you to go into debt to fund His work.

But pastors who've built empires on exploitation? They need your decision made before rational thought kicks in. They need the frenzy. They need the pressure. They need the countdown. They need the FOMO.

Because if you had time to think — time to check your bank balance, time to talk to your spouse, time to ask if a good God would really demand rent money from a single mother, time to remember that God doesn't operate on game-show timelines — you'd keep your money.

And they know it.

So they don't give you time to think. They give you ninety seconds to react. And they frame that reaction as obedience.

It's not obedience. It's extraction.

And the devastation it causes — the evictions, the foreclosures, the bankruptcies, the credit card debt, the broken marriages, the shattered faith — is the cost of their wealth.

The ninety-second shakedown isn't ministry. It would be considered robbery in any non-religious context. It just happens to be legal.

God doesn't speak in countdowns. God doesn't deal in timers. God doesn't weaponize urgency to empty your bank account.

But predators do.

And some of them wear suits and stand in pulpits and claim to speak for God.

The countdown isn't coming from heaven. It's coming from someone who knows exactly how long it takes to bypass your rational thinking and access your wallet.

Ninety seconds is all they need.

Don't give it to them.

Chapter 17: Celebrity Pastor Syndrome – When Shepherds Become Rockstars

◆ ◆ ◆

He walked in surrounded by four men in suits. Earpieces. Scanning the room. Moving people aside. The pastor wasn't arriving. He was making an entrance. Bentley Mulsanne out front. Custom wheels. Tinted windows. A driver standing by. The car cost more than most congregants earned in five years. Inside, he didn't sit with people.

He had a green room. His own space. His handlers kept people away unless specifically invited for private audience. When he took the stage, the crowd erupted. Not reverence. Hysteria. Screaming, crying, hands reaching toward him. Women trying to touch him as he passed. He preached for thirty-five minutes. Mentioned his new book eleven times.

Referenced his upcoming conference. Promoted his podcast. Dropped names of other celebrity pastors he'd spent time with that week. The sermon was marketing. The appearance was performance. The whole event was brand management. After service, a line of women waited. Some wanted prayer. Some wanted photos. Some wanted. more.

His handlers managed the queue. The pretty ones got longer access. The wealthy ones got private meetings scheduled. He left the same way he arrived: surrounded by security, into the Bentley, parishioners taking photos as he drove away. This wasn't a pastor.

This was a celebrity using the church as his platform and the congregation as his fanbase. And it's become the dominant model of American megachurch leadership.

How does a pastor become a celebrity? It's systematic.

Phase 1: Church Growth

Start with a charismatic personality and decent preaching. Grow the church to 1,000+. This gets you noticed.

Phase 2: The Platform

Write a book. Any book. Get it published through the church's platform or connections. It doesn't have to sell well initially — it just needs to exist so you can call yourself "bestselling author." Start a podcast. Build social media following. Get invited to speak at other churches. Expand beyond your local congregation.

Phase 3: The Conference Circuit

Get invited to speak at large conferences. This is the breakthrough moment. You're now among the celebrity pastors. You're part of the club. Other celebrity pastors cross-promote each other. You speak at their conferences, they speak at yours. The network perpetuates itself.

Phase 4: The Brand

Everything becomes branded. Your name is the product. Your church is secondary to your personal platform. Launch a media company. Start a conference series. Create merchandise. Build the empire.

Phase 5: Untouchable

Once you're a celebrity pastor, accountability becomes impossible. Your platform is too big. Your influence too wide. Your income too diversified. Your followers too loyal.

You're no longer a pastor. You're a CEO, influencer, brand, and celebrity who happens to use religious content.

Watch how celebrity pastors present themselves. It's deliberately styled after hip-hop culture.

The Fashion:

Designer sneakers: $1,200 limited edition Yeezys or Air Jordans. Fitted jeans, often distressed or designer brands: $400- $800. Luxury brand hoodies or streetwear: $500- $2,000. Expensive watches: Rolex, Audemars Piguet, $20,000- $100,000+. Multiple rings, chains, bracelets: tens of thousands in jewelry. This isn't modest clergy attire. This is hip-hop mogul aesthetic applied to religious leadership.

The Persona:

Confident, bordering on arrogant." God told me." Used constantly to assert authority while avoiding accountability. Surrounded by yes-men. No one in their inner circle challenges them. Name-dropping other celebrities. Athletes, musicians, influencers-constantly referenced to show status and access. Exclusive circles. Private jets. Green rooms. VIP access. Creating aspiration and separation from regular people.

The Language:

"My haters." Criticism framed as jealousy or spiritual attack." God blessed me." Wealth presented as divine endorsement." I'm called to this." Luxury justified as necessary for ministry reach." Touch not God's anointed." Shield against accountability. It's prosperity gospel meets hip-hop culture meets megachurch infrastructure.

Celebrity pastors don't drive cars. They drive statements.

Common Vehicles:

Bentley Continental or Mulsanne: $200,000- $350,000 Rolls-Royce Ghost or Phantom: $300,000- $500,000 Range Rover Autobiography: $150,000- $200,000 Mercedes-Benz S-Class or G-Wagon: $100,000- $150,000 Porsche or Maserati: $80,000- $150,000 Custom details:

- Personalized plates referencing ministry or scripture
- Window tinting maxed out for privacy
- Custom wheels and details
- Often wrapped in unique colors

The Justification:

"I need reliable transportation for my travel schedule." A Honda Accord is reliable. A Bentley is a flex." God wants to bless His servants." God didn't buy the car. Tithes did.

"My success attracts people to church." Your wealth attracts certain people. It repels others. And Jesus had neither car nor wealth." I paid for it with my book money, not church salary." Book money earned using church platform, church audience, church branding, and church-provided visibility. Still church money, indirectly.

The Reality:

These vehicles cost more than many congregants earn annually. The insurance, maintenance, and fuel alone exceed what some families have for groceries monthly. When a pastor drives a $300,000 car while preaching that God wants to bless faithful givers, while congregants struggle financially-that's not ministry. That's mockery.

Celebrity pastors don't travel alone. They move with teams.

The Security Detail:

Often 2-4 bodyguards. Actual security personnel with earpieces and suits. Not just deacons helping with crowd control-hired protection like celebrities and politicians have.

Why?" Safety." Wisdom." Necessary for crowds." Reality: It creates separation, elevates status, makes the pastor seem important enough to need protection. It's theatrical. Jesus walked among crowds. Touched people. Let them approach. No bodyguards. No separation.

Celebrity pastors need barriers between themselves and the very people they claim to serve.

The Staff Team:

Personal assistant managing schedule and communications. Social media manager documenting everything for content. Sound/video team to record sermons for distribution. Handler coordinating appearances and managing people requesting access. Often a personal stylist or image consultant. This isn't pastoral ministry. It's celebrity management.

The Yes-Men:

Everyone close to a celebrity pastor agrees with everything they say. Challenges don't exist. Correction is impossible. Why? Because people who disagree get removed from the inner circle. Only loyalty is rewarded. Only compliance is tolerated. This creates echo chambers where narcissism flourishes unchecked.

The uncomfortable reality: celebrity pastors have groupies. Women (and sometimes men) who pursue them like fans pursue rockstars.

The Dynamic:

Attractive congregants seek private prayer sessions, mentorship, or just face time with the celebrity pastor.

Some are genuinely seeking spiritual guidance. Others are seeking proximity to power and status. Some are seeking more. Celebrity pastors cultivate this attention. The pretty women get more access. The wealthy ones get private meetings. The young attractive volunteers get positions close to leadership.

The Scandals That Follow:

Celebrity pastor affairs are so common they're predictable. Why? Power is aphrodisiac. Celebrity creates attraction. Access creates opportunity. Lack of accountability creates conditions where boundaries dissolve.

Add to this: traveling without spouse, hotel rooms, private meetings, women who view the pastor as special and anointed-the recipe for affairs is complete.

When exposed, churches defend the pastor or blame the woman." She seduced him." She was troubled." He was going through a hard time." Never: "The celebrity system created conditions that make this inevitable." The Worship of Men:

I've watched women cry just being in the same room as certain celebrity pastors. Not because of God's presence. Because of the pastor's celebrity. I've seen women compete for attention. Dress strategically. Position themselves for notice. Volunteer for opportunities that put them near leadership. This isn't worship of God. It's worship of men who've positioned themselves as extraordinary.

How much do celebrity pastors make? Usually impossible to know.

Church Salary:

Rarely disclosed." Private personnel matter." Between leadership and him." Not appropriate to discuss publicly." When pressed, churches claim modest salaries. $100,000- $150,000." Not excessive for the responsibility." But that's incomplete reporting.

Book Royalties:

Written on church time, using church platform, marketed to church audience. But royalties go to the pastor personally. Not the church. A bestselling Christian book can earn $500,000- $2,000,000 in royalties. Some celebrity pastors have multiple books.

Speaking Fees:

Churches pay $20,000- $50,000+ for celebrity pastors to speak. An active speaker can earn $500,000- $1,000,000 annually just from appearances.

Conference Income:

Hosting conferences generates revenue. Ticket sales, vendor fees, sponsorships. Much of this flows to the celebrity pastor who is the draw.

Consulting and Coaching:

Many celebrity pastors charge other pastors for consulting, coaching, or mentorship. $5,000- $20,000 per

engagement.

Media Companies:

Some own production companies, podcasting networks, or publishing imprints. These generate income separate from church.

Total Compensation:

While claiming a $150,000 church salary, a celebrity pastor might actually earn $2-5 million annually from all sources — all built on the church platform and congregation. But because it's not all "church salary," they can claim to be modestly compensated while living like millionaires.

Celebrity pastors answer to no one. Here's why:

Board Capture:

Church boards are supposed to provide oversight. But celebrity pastors appoint their own board members. The board serves at the pastor's pleasure. If a board member questions anything, they're removed and replaced with someone compliant. The board becomes rubber stamp, not oversight.

Financial Control:

The pastor controls information flow. Board sees what the pastor wants them to see. Full financial details remain private. When everything is filtered through the celebrity pastor and his team, actual accountability is impossible.

Celebrity Shield:

The bigger the platform, the harder to challenge. Questioning a celebrity pastor means fighting his entire fanbase. His followers attack dissenters. The celebrity pastor is protected by thousands of loyal defenders who view any criticism as attack on God's anointed.

Multi-Church Structure:

Many celebrity pastors lead multi-site or multi-campus operations. Each location has local leadership, but all authority flows to the celebrity pastor at the top. This creates even more distance from accountability. The celebrity pastor is too busy, too important, too high up to be questioned by anyone.

The Network Protection:

Celebrity pastors protect each other. When one gets caught in scandal, others defend him." We all fall short." Show grace." Restoration, not judgment." Unless the scandal is too big to defend, the celebrity pastor network shields its own.

Celebrity pastors don't pastor churches. They run religious corporations.

Staff of 50-200+:

These aren't churches. They're businesses with HR departments, marketing teams, operations managers, and corporate structure. The celebrity pastor is CEO, not shepherd.

Multi-Million Dollar Budgets:

Annual budgets of $10-50 million are common for large celebrity-led churches. That's corporate scale.

Real Estate Portfolios:

Multiple campuses, rental properties, commercial spaces. The church owns assets worth tens of millions.

Business Ventures:

Coffee shops, bookstores, conference centers, media production facilities. These generate revenue separate from offerings.

Brand Management:

Everything is branded. The church name is a brand. The pastor's name is a brand. Merchandise, media, events — all brand extensions. This is business. Sophisticated, well-run, highly profitable business.

Celebrity pastors stop living in the same world as their congregants.

No Normal Interactions:

They don't grocery shop. Don't pump gas. Don't wait in lines. Don't experience what regular people experience. Assistants handle everything. Staff manages details. Life becomes curated and insulated.

Financial Disconnect:

When you earn millions, you forget what it's like to worry about rent, utilities, medical bills. You lose capacity to relate to financial stress. Preaching about trusting God for provision when you have millions becomes tone-deaf. But celebrity pastors don't see it because they're too removed.

Surrounded by Affirmation:

Everyone around them says they're anointed, gifted, blessed, special. No one tells them they're wrong, excessive, or problematic. This creates narcissistic delusion. They believe their own mythology. They think God really does favor them specially.

Access Only to Elite:

They hang out with other celebrity pastors, wealthy donors, athletes, musicians. Their world becomes exclusive and rarified. They lose touch with the struggles, needs, and reality of the average person they're supposed to serve.

What does celebrity pastor culture cost churches?

Resource Extraction:

Massive budgets funneled to maintain celebrity lifestyle and infrastructure. Less available for actual ministry and helping people.

Spiritual Damage:

When Christianity looks like celebrity worship and wealth pursuit, the gospel message gets distorted. People think faith is about prosperity, platform, and personal success.

Leadership Pipeline Broken:

According to denominational data, young pastors see celebrity culture and either try to replicate it (leading to compromise and manipulation) or burn out trying to compete with impossible standards.

Accountability Eliminated:

When the pastor can't be questioned, abuse goes unchecked. Financial impropriety continues. Harm compounds.

Congregants as Fans:

People become consumers of celebrity pastor content rather than participants in spiritual community. They attend for the show, not for transformation or connection.

Describe celebrity pastor culture without religious language:

Leader who demands exclusive access and deference

Paid enormous salary plus undisclosed additional income

Drives luxury vehicles worth more than followers earn annually

Surrounded by security and handlers keeping regular people away

Makes decisions unilaterally without input or accountability

Uses organization's resources for personal benefit

Travels extensively at organization expense

Has affairs with followers while preaching against immorality

Punishes anyone who questions or challenges them.

Lives lavishly while followers struggle financially.

That's not ministry — it's a **cult of personality**. It's the same structure seen in entertainment, politics, organized crime, and cults. Call it a church and people defend it. Call it anything else and people recognize it as exploitative.

God — if God exists and calls people to leadership — doesn't need:

- Pastors who live like rappers and rock stars
- Bentleys and Rolls-Royces to spread the gospel
- Bodyguards separating leaders from the people
- Entourages and handlers managing image
- Multi-million-dollar personal incomes
- Celebrity status and platform worship
- Churches run like corporations
- Pastors treated as untouchable royalty

When leadership requires luxury and distance, it isn't spiritual authority — it's brand management.

Jesus had no entourage. No luxury vehicle. No bodyguards. No green room. No handlers. No exclusive access. No wealth. No celebrity status. He walked with people. Ate with them. Touched them. Taught them. Served them. The contrast between Jesus and celebrity pastors is complete.

Yet churches celebrate these men as anointed leaders.

Celebrity pastor culture is antithetical to Christianity. It's narcissism baptized in religious language. It's wealth worship disguised as blessing. It's exploitation framed as excellence. It's corporate structure called church. It's celebrity culture with Jesus branding.

And it's destroying any remaining credibility Christianity had. Because when pastors live like millionaires while preaching that God loves the poor, when they drive Bentleys while congregants struggle, when they need bodyguards to separate themselves from the people Jesus died for- The message is clear: it's not about Jesus.

It's about them. And God doesn't need that. But their egos, their bank accounts, and their empires absolutely do.

The tactics are exposed. The system is documented. What remains is the hardest part: what to do about it. The final section addresses leaving, healing, and rebuilding — because escaping a system is only the beginning. The work of recovery takes longer than the exploitation itself.

PART 5: THE RECKONING

Chapter 18: Leaving Without Losing Everything – A Survival Guide for Church Exit

◆ ◆ ◆

The decision took three years. The actual leaving took three minutes. Sarah had been planning quietly. Building external friendships. Saving money. Preparing her kids. But she didn't tell anyone at church. Couldn't risk the intervention, the pressure, the manipulation she knew would come. One Sunday, she just. didn't go.

Turned off her phone. Stayed home. Made breakfast. It felt strange and terrifying and liberating all at once. By Monday, the messages started.

Dozens of texts." Where were you?" Are you okay?" Pastor wants to talk." We're concerned about you." Not: "We miss you." Not: "How can we help?" Always: "You need to come back." You're making a mistake." This is dangerous for your soul." Within a week, the tone shifted.

The loving concern became accusations." You're in rebellion." You're deceived." You'll regret this." Friends stopped calling. Her kids' friends' parents suddenly weren't available for playdates. Invitations dried up. The community she'd known for a decade evaporated.

But Sarah was prepared. She'd known this would happen. She'd built a safety net. She'd counted the cost. Three months later, she told me: "Leaving was the hardest thing I've ever done. But staying would have killed me." This chapter is for people like Sarah.

People who know they need to leave but don't know how to survive it.

BEFORE YOU LEAVE: PREPARATION

Don't leave impulsively. Plan strategically.

Financial Preparation (6-12 Months Before):

Stop tithing gradually. Don't announce it. Just reduce." Financial constraints "if asked. Save that 10% as emergency fund. Target: 3-6 months expenses saved. You'll need cushion for the transition and any unexpected costs.

Separate church and personal finances completely. If the church has access to your bank accounts for auto-debit tithing, remove authorization. Use different bank if necessary.

Cancel recurring church donations. Building fund subscriptions, missions commitments, any automatic transfers-end them. Do it quietly.

Document your giving. If you've given significantly, document it. Not for legal reasons-for psychological ones. When they tell you've abandoned God, remember how much you gave.

Social Preparation (6-12 Months Before):

Build external friendships. Join community groups, hobby clubs, neighborhood associations. Create social connections outside church. Don't tell church people you're doing this. They'll view it as spiritual drift and intervene.

Connect your kids with outside activities. Sports, arts, clubs-anything that gives them social connection beyond church. This cushions the impact when church friends disappear.

Research other communities. Not necessarily churches. Support groups, meet-ups, community organizations. Know where you can find belonging after leaving.

Identify safe people. Who in your life won't judge you for leaving? Family, old friends, coworkers. Strengthen those relationships. You'll need them.

Emotional/Spiritual Preparation:

Journal your reasons for leaving. Write down specific incidents, patterns, teachings that drove you away. When you doubt yourself later, you'll need this clarity.

Research religious trauma. Read books, articles, listen to podcasts about leaving high-control religious groups. Recognize that what you're experiencing has a name and others have survived it.

Find a therapist if possible. Ideally one who understands religious trauma. You'll need professional support navigating the aftermath.

Practice saying no. Start setting small boundaries now. Say no to volunteering requests. Skip a service. Test how the church responds to your autonomy.

When you're ready to leave, you have choices about how:

The Quiet Fade:

Just stop going. No announcement. No explanation. Let attendance records show you've left.

Pros: Minimizes drama. Avoids confrontation. Protects from pressure to stay.

Cons: People will pursue you. You'll get calls, texts, visits. Pastoral intervention likely. If you choose this: block numbers if needed. Don't respond to pressure. Don't explain yourself. You don't

owe them justification.

The Formal Exit:

Write a resignation letter to leadership. Clear, brief, final." I'm no longer attending. Please remove me from membership. Do not contact me." Pros: Creates clarity. Establishes boundaries. Makes your intention undeniable.

Cons: May trigger aggressive retention efforts. Might result in public church discipline. If you choose this: be prepared for push back. Don't negotiate. Don't explain extensively. Keep it simple and final.

The Slow Transition:

Gradually attend less. Start visiting other churches. Ease into exit over months.

Pros: Less jarring socially. Gives kids time to adjust. Allows relationship preservation with some people.

Cons: Prolongs the difficulty. Creates ambiguity. May result in more manipulation attempts.

Which to Choose:

Depends on your situation. High-control churches: quiet fade or formal exit. Moderate churches: slow transition might work. Trust your instincts.

Handling the Intervention

The Concerned Check-In:

According to former church staff, pastor or leader calls." Just checking on you. Noticed you've been gone. Everything okay?" This sounds caring. It's assessment. They're gathering information to determine intervention strategy.

How to respond: "I'm fine. Taking some time to process things. I'll reach out if I need anything." Don't elaborate. Don't explain. Don't give them material to argue with.

The Coffee Meeting Request:

"Let's grab coffee. No pressure. Just want to hear where you're at." This is pressure. It's an opportunity for them to convince you to stay, diagnose your "spiritual condition," and deploy manipulation.

How to respond: "I appreciate the offer, but I'm not ready for that conversation." You're allowed to decline. You don't owe them a meeting.

The Concerned Friend Visit:

Someone shows up at your house." We're worried about you. Can we talk?" This is coordinated. Leadership sent them. It's intervention disguised as friendship.

How to respond: Set boundaries." I'm working through things privately. I'll reach out if I want to talk." You're allowed to not invite them in. Your home is your space.

The Spiritual Diagnosis:

They attribute your leaving to sin, deception, spiritual attack, emotional wounds, or false teaching." You're listening to the enemy." Someone's deceived you." You're hurt and not thinking clearly." This invalidates your agency. Your reasons aren't real-you're just compromised somehow.

How to respond: "I've made a thoughtful decision. I'm not open to being diagnosed." Don't defend yourself. Don't argue. Don't try to make them understand. They're not trying to understand — they're trying to change your mind.

The Ultimatum:

"If you continue this path, you're in rebellion. We'll have to move forward with discipline." This is threat. Comply or face consequences.

How to respond: "I understand. I'm still moving forward." Church discipline only has power if you care what they think. Once you've genuinely left emotionally, their judgment can't harm you.

Protecting Your Children

This is often the hardest part. Your kids will lose friends, face questions, experience confusion.

Before You Leave:

Talk to them age-appropriately. Don't trash the church. Don't burden them with adult details. Frame it as: "We're making some changes. You'll make new friends.

It'll be okay." Documented practices show prepare them for friend loss." Some of your church friends might not be able to play anymore. That's not your fault. Their parents make those decisions." Establish new activities quickly. Sign them up for sports, clubs, activities where they'll make friends fast.

Don't let them sit in a social vacuum.

After You Leave:

Monitor their emotional state. Kids may feel guilty, confused, angry. Make space for them to process without judgment.

Don't force them to hate the church. They may have positive memories. That's okay. Let them have complicated feelings.

Help them make sense of it." Sometimes organizations aren't healthy even when people in them are nice. We had to leave for our family's wellbeing." Be the stable presence. Your consistency, love, and emotional stability helps them through the transition.

If They Want to Go Back:

This is complicated. Teenagers especially might want to return for social reasons.

Option 1: Allow occasional visits with someone else (not you). Monitor if the church manipulates them against you.

Option 2: Explain why you can't support their attendance. Set boundary: "This organization harmed our family. I can't participate in you being there." Option 3: Let them attend if old enough to make informed choice, but stay connected to their experience. Ask questions. Watch for manipulation.

No perfect answer. Prioritize your child's emotional health and family unity.

Rebuilding Community

Leaving creates social void. You must intentionally rebuild.

Where to Find Community:

Hobby groups: Running clubs, book clubs, maker spaces, art classes, sports leagues.

Volunteer organizations: Animal shelters, food banks, community centers, political campaigns.

Online communities: Ex-church forums, deconstruction groups, recovery communities. Start online, transition to in-person meetups if available.

Therapeutic communities: Group therapy, support groups, recovery programs.

Other churches (maybe): If you want to try church again, look for: financial transparency, democratic governance, no celebrity pastor, clear accountability structures, healthy boundaries.

What Community Rebuilding Looks Like:

It's slower than church. Church creates instant community through shared beliefs and regular gatherings. Secular community builds gradually through repeated interaction and genuine connection. Be patient. Show up consistently. Be vulnerable when appropriate. Invest in relationships. It takes time but it's real.

Managing Guilt and Doubt

You will doubt your decision. That's normal.

The Guilt Thoughts:

"What if I'm wrong?" What if I'm deceiving myself?" What if God is angry with me?" What if I'm damaging my kids spiritually?" What if I was just being selfish?" The Reality:

These thoughts are programming. They were installed by theology designed to prevent exit.

Counter them with:

"I left for good reasons. Those reasons are still valid." I've thought about this carefully. I'm not being impulsive." If God exists and is good, God doesn't want me in an abusive system." My kids will benefit from healthy modeling more than from staying in dysfunction." Taking care of myself and my family isn't selfish. It's responsible." Keep your journal of reasons handy. When doubt hits hard, read it. Remember why you left.

Many people try to go back. Especially in moments of crisis or loneliness.

High-Risk Situations:

Major life crisis (death, illness, job loss)

Holidays and significant dates

Intense loneliness

Family pressure

Kids begging to return to see friends

If You're Tempted to Return:

Pause. Don't act immediately. Give yourself 48 hours.

Review your reasons. Read your journal. Remember the harm.

Reach out to safe people. Call someone outside the church who knows your story.

Ask: "Am I actually wanting to return, or am I just wanting relief from this hard moment?" Remember: Going back won't actually solve the crisis you're facing. It will add church dysfunction back into your life.

If You Do Go Back:

No shame. Many people cycle through several times before finally leaving permanently. Each attempt teaches you something. Each return shows you more clearly why you can't stay. When you're ready to leave again, you will.

Financial Recovery

Stopping tithing can dramatically improve finances.

What to Do with the 10%:

First: Build emergency fund. 3-6 months expenses.

Second: Pay off high-interest debt.

Third: Save for kids' education/future.

Fourth: Invest for retirement.

Fifth: Give to causes you choose, in amounts you decide, when you're financially stable.

Typical Timeline:

Most people see significant financial improvement within 12-18 months of leaving. The money that was going to church gets redirected to actual family needs. Some people report feeling guilty about having more financial stability. That's also programming. Your family having enough isn't unfaithful. It's what should have been happening all along.

You might be reading this because your friend, family member, or partner is leaving and you're staying.

What Not to Do:

Don't pressure them to stay. Don't spiritually diagnose them. Don't cut them off. Don't turn their children against them. Don't tell them they're going to hell. Don't make it about you.

What to Do:

Ask if they're okay. Listen without trying to fix. Maintain the relationship if they're willing. Respect their boundaries.

Let them know you love them regardless.

If Your Spouse Is Leaving and You're Not:

This is crisis. Get marriage counseling-neutral counselor, not church-affiliated. Recognize this might end the marriage. Religious incompatibility can be insurmountable, especially in highcontrol churches. Protect your children from being weaponized by either side.

Leaving is just the beginning. Healing takes years.

What Recovery Looks Like:

Year 1: Acute grief. Anger. Disorientation. Relief mixed with guilt. Building new community. Figuring out who you are outside church.

Year 2-3: Processing trauma. Reexamining beliefs. Establishing new identity. Relationships stabilizing. Finances improving. Anger cooling.

Year 4-5: Integration. You're no longer "ex-church person"-you're just you. The church experience is part of your history but doesn't define you. Relationships healthy. Life stable.

Ongoing: Occasional triggers. Anniversaries. Seeing church people. Hearing certain music. These fade with time.

Professional Help:

Therapy specifically for religious trauma is invaluable. Look for therapists familiar with:

High-control religious groups

Spiritual abuse

Complex trauma

Faith deconstruction

Resources:

Books: "Leaving the Fold" by Marlene Winell," The Subtle Power of Spiritual Abuse "by David Johnson," Faith After Doubt "by Brian McLaren Websites: RecoveringFromReligion.org, ExvangelicalTruth.com, ReligiousTraumaInstitute.com Podcasts: "Life After"," The Deconstructionists"," Straight White American Jesus" Support groups: Check online for local ex-church, deconstruction, or religious trauma support groups.

Eventually, you'll realize: you're free. Free to question without fear. Free to think for yourself. Free to have boundaries. Free to say no. Free to prioritize your family. Free to spend your money on what you choose. Free to explore spirituality on your own terms — or not at all. Free from manipulation. Free from guilt. Free from the performance. The cost was high. The grief was real. The losses hurt.

But the freedom is worth it.

God-if God exists and is good-doesn't need you to stay in systems that harm you. God doesn't require you to sacrifice your wellbeing for institutional loyalty. God doesn't punish people for protecting themselves and their families. God doesn't condemn people for leaving destructive environments. The church needed you trapped. God doesn't. And recognizing that difference is the beginning of actual freedom.

You can leave. You can survive it. You can rebuild. Thousands have done it before you. You're not alone. You're not crazy. You're not betraying God. You're choosing life over the system that was slowly killing you. And that choice-that courageous, terrifying, necessary choice-is the beginning of everything good that comes next.

You are not alone. You were not wrong. And you are finally allowed to name what was done to you.

For everyone who left and still carries what happened.

For everyone who stayed silent because speaking cost too much.

For everyone who reported and wasn't believed.

This chapter is for everyone who knew something was wrong but was told the problem was them.

Nothing will.

And until churches are willing to answer that question honestly — What would have to change for them to stop?

The most dangerous question is this:

The most dangerous question isn't whether pastors use God to get sex and money.

Why does everyone reading this know exactly what I'm talking about?

If the patterns I've described weren't real — Why would accountability be so impossible to find?

If church systems weren't designed to protect predators — Why would this chapter feel so threatening?

If pastors weren't using God to get sex and money — THE QUESTION YOU'RE AFRAID TO ASK

Until accountability becomes cheaper than protection — until transparency becomes easier than concealment — until victims matter more than institutions — the pattern will continue.

And churches have built systems that make this not only possible but predictable.

Not all. Not most. But more than churches want to admit.

Some pastors use God to get sex and money.

These aren't bugs. They're features of a system designed to concentrate power in individuals without creating corresponding accountability.

The pastorate, as currently constructed in most churches, creates perfect conditions for predation. Concentrated authority. Spiritual leverage.

Normalized private access. Victim-discrediting mechanisms. Institutional protection incentives. Accountability voids.

The answer is structural.

Why do churches have better systems for silencing accusations than for preventing abuse?

Why is "restoration" always available for pastors but never for victims?

Why do the same patterns appear across denominations, across continents, across decades?

Why do church systems consistently protect abusers and consistently punish victims?

Bad apples exist in every profession. The question isn't whether some Some pastors engage in patterns of abuse toward their power. Of course they do.

This is not about bad apples.

Here's what I want you to understand:

The Bottom Line

Churches operate in a regulatory void — and they've filled that void with systems that protect their own.

What law requires churches to background check volunteers? What law requires financial transparency? What law prevents churches from rehiring pastors who've been "restored"? What law prohibits NDAs in misconduct settlements?

Not technically above the law. But practically? Yes.

The result is institutions that are functionally above the law.

Narrative immunity: Control the story through careful public statements and media-trained spokespeople.

Financial immunity: Use donor money to fund legal defense and settlements.

Social immunity: Create insular communities where questioning leadership means exile.

Legal immunity: Use religious freedom protections to shield internal practices from oversight.

Theological immunity: Frame everything as spiritual so secular standards don't apply.

Churches have developed sophisticated defenses against accountability:

The Institutional Immune System

Every instruction for reconciliation has been perverted into a tool for continued abuse.

Every call to grace has been twisted into a demand for silence.

Every verse designed to promote healthy community has been weaponized to protect predators.

Used to mean: If you really loved the church, you'd cover this up. Exposing sin isn't love — it's betrayal.

"Love covers a multitude of sins."(1 Peter 4:8)

Used to mean: Demanding accountability is unforgiveness. Pursuing justice is bitterness. Real Christians let it go.

"Forgive as the Lord forgave you."(Colossians 3:13)

Used to mean: You cannot go public. You cannot warn others. You must handle this privately, where they can control the narrative and pressure you to stay silent.

"If your brother sins against you, go to him privately."(Matthew 18:15)

Used to mean: Unless multiple people witnessed the abuse simultaneously, the accusation is invalid. One victim is never enough.

"Do not receive an accusation against an elder except on the basis of two or three witnesses."(1 Timothy 5:19)

Used to mean: You cannot criticize, question, or hold accountable anyone in spiritual leadership. Doing so is attacking God's chosen.

"Touch not my anointed, and do my prophets no harm."(1 Chronicles 16:22)

These are the scriptures used to silence victims:

The Theological Manipulation

Every single time.

If protecting the ministry requires sacrificing victims, that's a price churches have proven willing to pay.

What they're actually protecting is the organization. The brand. The revenue. The power structure.

Churches tell themselves they're protecting "the ministry." The mission. The kingdom.

The institution's survival matters more than individual victims.

Silencing her — however much it costs in hush money — is cheaper than the alternative.

She doesn't generate revenue. She threatens reputation. She creates legal liability. She complicates the narrative.

The accuser is a cost center.

Protecting him — however much it costs in settlements and legal fees — is cheaper than replacing him.

Losing him means losing his followers. His donors. His influence. His revenue stream.

He draws crowds. He generates donations. He builds the brand. He IS the brand.

The pastor is a profit center.

Here's why churches protect predator pastors:

THE COST-BENEFIT CALCULATION

Churches have made sure of that.

There is no accountability structure that works.

The media? Maybe. If your story is compelling enough. If you have documentation. If you're willing to have your life examined publicly. If you're prepared for the church to mobilize its members against you. If you can handle being called a liar by thousands of people who've never met you.

Civil courts? You can sue. If you have evidence. If you have money for lawyers. If you haven't signed an NDA. If you're prepared for the church's legal team to destroy your reputation in discovery. If you can survive years of litigation while the church uses congregational donations to fund its defense.

The police? For what? Unless there's criminal behavior — and even then, good luck proving it — there's no law against pastors sleeping with congregants. It's not illegal to have affairs. It's not illegal to manipulate people spiritually. It's not illegal to be a predator if your prey technically consented.

The denomination? If there even is one. Many churches are independent — no denominational authority, no oversight structure, no one to appeal to. If there is a denomination, they have their own institutional interests to protect. They don't want scandals any more than the local church does.

The church board? They're hand-picked by the pastor. They're loyal to him. They're invested in protecting the institution. They will investigate the way HR investigates complaints against the CEO.

You want to report pastoral misconduct. Where do you go?

The Accountability Void

Not by addressing it. By silencing anyone who tries to expose it.

This is how churches "handle" misconduct.

If you speak, we sue. If you name names, we litigate you into bankruptcy. If you go public, our legal team will make your life hell.

Sign this agreement. Take this money. Never speak of this again.

Churches have lawyers too. And they use them — not to pursue justice, but to purchase silence.

NDAs. Non-disparagement agreements. Confidential settlements.

Legal silencing.

The church has weaponized scripture to silence victims. Every accusation can be reframed as the accuser's spiritual failure. Every demand for accountability can be labeled division. Every pursuit of justice can be condemned as unforgiveness.

"You're just bitter. You need to check your heart." Speaking against leadership is speaking against God." We don't air dirty laundry — that's divisive." Forgiveness means not holding grudges." Who are you to judge?" Touch not God's anointed."Spiritual silencing.

Most people can't pay that cost. Churches know this. They count on it.

The cost of speaking is total social annihilation.

People who hugged you last Sunday will cross the street to avoid you. People who called you "sister" will call you a liar. People who prayed with you will pray against you.

Accuse the pastor and watch how fast those relationships evaporate.

Speaking up means losing everything. Your church community is probably your entire social network. Your friends are church friends. Your support system is church-based. Your identity is wrapped up in church participation.

Social silencing.

Here's how churches manufacture silence:

The Silence Machine

It restores nothing to the people he harmed.

Restoration restores the pastor to power.

The money extracted from congregants. The years taken from volunteers. The trust destroyed in families.

The victims' reputation. The victims' community. The victims' faith. The victims' careers.

What is NOT restored?

It means his platform is restored. His income is restored. His authority is restored. His access to vulnerable people is restored.

What does restoration mean?

He's written a book about his "journey." He's got a testimony about God's grace. He's been "restored." The pastor reappears. Different church, maybe. Different role, sometimes. But back in ministry.

Eighteen months later. Maybe two years. Long enough that people have stopped asking questions.

Step 3: The Return

The victims are protected from nothing.

The pastor is protected from his congregation, from the media, from accountability.

During this time, the church handles things internally. Pays off victims. Collects NDAs. Manages the narrative. Makes sure any public statements are carefully controlled.

The pastor goes away. Sometimes to a "restoration ministry" that specializes in rehabilitating fallen leaders. Sometimes just to another state where nobody knows his name.

Step 2: The Disappearance

Healing. Not accountability. Not justice. Not making amends. Healing. As if he's the victim. As if what he needs is care, not consequence.

Season. Not permanent consequence. A season. Temporary. Time-limited. With an implicit promise of return.

Note the language. Voluntary. Not fired. Not removed. Voluntarily stepping down — as if this is his noble choice rather than a response to being caught.

The pastor "voluntarily steps down" for a "season of healing."Step 1: The Announcement

It works like this:

It's called "restoration." When pastoral misconduct becomes undeniable, churches have developed a standard response:

The Restoration Scam

This is not consent. This is manufactured compliance.

The final crossing feels less like violation and more like inevitability.

She's been tested and her boundaries have been gradually eroded.

She's been given theological frameworks that make resistance feel like sin.

She's been told this is normal, spiritual, God-ordained.

She's been elevated to "special" status that makes her invested in the relationship.

She's been isolated from people who might raise concerns.

By the time physical crossing happens, the victim has been psychologically prepared.

The grooming process manufactures compliance.

This is not consent. This is coercion with scripture references.

The victim is trapped in a theological framework that makes her responsible for protecting her abuser.

When secrecy is framed as "sacred trust," exposing it means you're violating something holy.

When intimacy is framed as "spiritual connection," questioning it means you're spiritually inferior.

When a relationship is framed as "God's will," refusing it means refusing God.

The spiritual framing eliminates autonomous choice.

This is not an environment where consent can be freely given.

Practical consequences: If you work for the church, you lose your job. If your family attends, you lose your family's community too.

Social consequences: You lose your community. Your friends. Your support system. Your identity.

Spiritual consequences: You're rejecting God's anointed. You're in rebellion. You're opening yourself to demonic attack.

What catastrophic consequences exist for saying no to a pastor?

Consent requires the genuine ability to say no without catastrophic consequences.

A pastor is not a peer. He is a spiritual authority who claims to speak for God. He controls access to community, to belonging, to salvation itself. He has information about your deepest secrets from counseling sessions. He has the ability to destroy your reputation with a single sermon illustration.

The power differential is absolute.

Let me explain why consent doesn't exist in these relationships.

The Consent Collapse

It means protecting children from knowing what pastors actually do.

The church talks about protecting children.

Some grew up in the shadow of megachurch empires, watching their biological fathers preach about family values while denying their existence.

Some were abandoned entirely. The pastor moved to a new church, a new state, a new story — leaving behind children who would never know why daddy disappeared.

Some of these children were paid off. Monthly support in exchange for permanent silence. Blood money for paternity.

The children who learn, eventually, that they were the inconvenient evidence of a powerful man's "moral failure" — and that their entire existence was managed as a liability.

The children whose existence is the church's most guarded secret.

The children whose mothers signed NDAs that prohibited them from ever naming the father publicly.

The children born from pastoral affairs who grow up without fathers because acknowledging them would expose the scandal.

Let me tell you about the children.

THE CHILDREN THEY DON'T TALK ABOUT

The system protects its own. And women have never been its own.

This IS the system.

This is not a failure of the system.

When a pastor exploits vulnerable women, plural, across years — when the evidence is overwhelming — the church writes him a severance check and protects his reputation.

When a pastor assaults a staff member, the staff member loses their job. The pastor gets counseling.

When a pastor has an affair with a congregant, the pastor stays. The woman leaves. Or is made to leave. Or leaves because staying is impossible.

Here's the pattern documented across hundreds of cases:

The man returns to ministry. The woman lives with the consequences.

The man gets another chance. The woman gets erased from the story.

The man gets a restoration process. The woman gets exile.

The female victim: Asked what she did to cause it. Accused of seduction. Blamed for not stopping it. Questioned about her own spiritual state. Told she should have known better. Told she should forgive quietly.

The male pastor: Described as "struggling." Battling temptation. A good man who made mistakes. Human. Fallen. In need of grace and restoration.

Watch what happens when misconduct surfaces:

The Gender Equation

And churches have built systems that concentrate power in individuals while eliminating accountability for how that power is used.

It was always about power.

Because it was never about sex. It was never about money.

The same pastors who manipulate people sexually manipulate people financially. The same systems that enable sexual predation enable financial extraction. The same silencing mechanisms that protect sexual abusers protect financial abusers.

Hush money to victims. Legal fees for NDAs. Payoffs to families. Consulting fees to "restoration" ministries. Book deals about the "journey back." There's always money involved.

Watch what happens when pastoral sexual misconduct surfaces:

Both are expressions of power without accountability. Both require silencing victims. Both depend on institutional protection. Both extract value from people who've been conditioned to give.

They are the same problem expressed differently.

Sexual misconduct and financial exploitation are not separate problems.

Here's what you need to understand:

The Money Connection

He's "restored." She's erased.

If she speaks anyway, she's the one who gets destroyed.

She's warned that no one would believe her anyway.

She's reminded that speaking would destroy his family, his church, his calling.

She's told to keep silent for the good of the ministry.

When the pastor tires of the relationship, or when risk increases, the victim becomes a liability.

Stage 5: Extract and Discard

The victim is now complicit. She can't report without implicating herself in what she's been told is a sacred secret.

Now the inappropriate relationship has a theological framework. It's not sin — it's spiritual. It's not abuse — it's anointing. It's not wrong — it's misunderstood by lesser believers.

"This is between us and God. No one else needs to know." "King David had many wives." "The Spirit moves in mysterious ways." "God sometimes gives leaders special relationships that others wouldn't understand." "What we have is different. It's spiritual intimacy."

If she doesn't pull back, he escalates.

If she pulls back, he adjusts." I'm sorry, that was just the Spirit moving." The pastor tests reactions. Pushes slightly. Watches for resistance.

"Has anyone ever told you how beautiful you are? That's God's design." I feel such a spiritual connection with you." Come here, let me pray over you."(Hands on shoulders. Then neck. Then lower.)

"You can tell me anything. It's between us and God."

Each step isolates the target further from people who might notice something wrong.

Each step seems natural. Pastoral. Caring.

The relationship moves from public to private. From group settings to one-on-one. From office hours to off-hours. From professional to personal.

"I don't share this level of insight with just anyone." "Let's meet privately so we can really dig into what God is doing in your life." "You need more spiritual covering than what you're getting in the general congregation." "I'd like to mentor you personally."

Once a woman believes God is speaking through this man, questioning him becomes questioning God.

These aren't compliments. They're positioning statements. They establish the pastor as God's mouthpiece and frame the relationship as divinely ordained.

"I believe God has connected us for a reason." "God is going to use you for something significant." "I see something in you that no one else sees." "God told me you're special."

This is how a pastor uses God to get sex:

THE PLAYBOOK: HOW SPIRITUAL GROOMING WORKS

What other profession has developed institutional silencing into an art form?

So churches develop expertise — not in preventing abuse, but in managing it. Containing it. Silencing it. Paying it off. Making it disappear.

Every scandal damages the brand. Every accusation threatens donations. Every lawsuit costs money. Every public failure empowers critics.

Protecting the institution.

Not protecting victims. Not protecting truth. Not protecting justice.

The church has one overriding interest: protecting itself.

Institutional protection.

What other profession allows serial predators to simply relocate and restart?

Three years later, he's back on stage. Platform restored. New congregation. No criminal record. No professional license revoked. No public registry of offenses.

He writes a book about his "journey" and his "healing." He goes to a different state. A different church. A different denomination.

The pastor "steps down" for a "season of restoration." When pastoral misconduct surfaces, what actually happens?

Consequences that can be managed.

What other profession offers this level of built-in victim-discrediting?

The accuser has shame, isolation, and a community that would rather believe she's lying than believe their pastor is a predator.

Meanwhile, the pastor has a congregation full of character witnesses. Years of "faithful service." A wife standing beside him. A reputation that must be protected.

She's asked what she was wearing. Whether she led him on. Whether she misunderstood his "pastoral concern" for something inappropriate. Whether she's bitter, unstable, attention-seeking.

If a woman accuses a pastor, what happens?

Victims who won't be believed.

What other profession normalizes private emotional intimacy with congregants as part of the job description?

A man in any other profession spending that much private time with female subordinates would raise flags. In ministry, it's called "shepherding." The pastoral role requires private access to people — including women, including the vulnerable, including people in crisis.

Counseling sessions. Private prayer meetings. Discipleship relationships. Hospital visits. Office hours.

Normalized private access.

What other profession lets the accused define whether the accusation is valid?

Questioning him isn't questioning a man. It's questioning God.

He's also the one who interprets God's will. Who decides what's sin and what's sanctified. Who determines whether your discomfort is legitimate concern or spiritual rebellion.

When a pastor crosses a line, he's the authority you'd report to.

When a therapist crosses a line, the client can report them. When a doctor crosses a line, there's a board to complain to. When a boss crosses a line, HR exists.

Unquestionable authority.

What other profession offers this level of access to desperate people who have been pre-conditioned to trust you absolutely?

A pastor doesn't need to seek out vulnerability. It comes to him. It sits in his office. It confesses its deepest secrets. It trusts him with information it hasn't told anyone else. It believes he represents God.

And predators go where the vulnerable congregate.

Many churches collect people in crisis. Divorce. Grief. Addiction. Depression. Financial ruin. Spiritual searching. These are the people who walk through church doors looking for help.

Access to vulnerable people.

Let me explain why pastoral ministry attracts predators the way a watering hole attracts lions.

The Perfect Hunting Ground

The question is why it keeps happening here.

When the same patterns repeat — across denominations, across cities, across decades, across continents — the question is no longer whether it can happen.

But outrage is not an argument. And silence is not innocence.

The outrage comes fast." How dare you." That's slander." You're attacking the church."Are pastors using God to get sex and money?

That question is this:

Because answering it honestly would collapse the entire system.

Not because it's crude.

Chapter 19: Sacred Predators – How Spiritual Authority Becomes Sexual Currency

◆ ◆ ◆

The call came at 2 a.m.

A woman I'll call Sarah had found my contact information through a mutual friend. She'd been trying to tell her story for three years. Every time she started, something stopped her — shame, fear, disbelief that it had really happened, terror of not being believed.

She'd been twenty-four when it started. New to the church. Struggling with anxiety and a recent breakup. The pastor noticed her. Told her God had shown him she was "special." Started mentoring her privately.

Within six months, she was in his office after hours, convinced that what was happening was somehow spiritual. "He told me this was how God worked through him," she said. "That I was receiving something sacred. That my confusion was just the enemy trying to block my blessing." She was thirty-one when she called me.

Still untangling what had happened. Still wondering if it was her fault.

Sarah's story is not unusual. It is, in fact, a pattern so predictable that anyone who works with survivors can identify the stages before they're described.

This chapter names that pattern. Not to sensationalize. Not to attack all pastors. But because predators thrive in silence, and the church has been silent for far too long. — ## THE ANATOMY OF SPIRITUAL SEXUAL ABUSE

Sexual abuse by clergy follows a remarkably consistent pattern. Understanding this pattern is the first step in recognizing it, preventing it, and believing survivors when they come forward.

Stage 1: Selection

Predators don't choose victims randomly. They select strategically.

Who gets targeted:

- People in crisis: recent divorce, job loss, grief, illness, depression
- People new to the church: haven't yet learned the social dynamics, eager to belong
- People with trauma history: often have damaged boundaries, may not recognize red flags
- People who are isolated: fewer people watching, fewer people to tell
- People who deeply admire the pastor: admiration can be leveraged into compliance
- Young adults, especially those from strict religious backgrounds: often sexually naive, trained to obey authority How selection happens:

The pastor notices vulnerability. Maybe she cried during worship. Maybe he shared a prayer request about his struggling marriage. Maybe she came forward for prayer about her anxiety. Maybe he mentioned financial stress.

The pastor files this information away. Begins paying special attention. Makes the person feel seen, valued, chosen." God told me to invest in you." I sense something special about your calling." You have a gift that needs to be developed. I want to mentor you personally." This isn't pastoral care. It's reconnaissance.

Stage 2: Grooming

Grooming is the process of preparing a victim for abuse while simultaneously ensuring they won't report it. In church contexts, grooming is devastatingly effective because it exploits existing religious frameworks.

Isolation:

The relationship becomes increasingly private. Meetings move from public spaces to private offices. Communication shifts to personal channels — texts, calls, messages that bypass church systems." This mentoring is just between us. Others wouldn't understand our connection." Don't tell anyone about our sessions. They might get jealous or misinterpret." The victim is slowly separated from community accountability.

Anyone who might notice something wrong is pushed to the periphery.

Special status:

The victim is made to feel uniquely chosen. Not just one of the congregation — someone the pastor has specifically selected for deeper spiritual work." God has shown me you're different from the others." Most people couldn't handle what I'm teaching you." You have a calling that requires special preparation." This creates investment. The victim doesn't want to lose their special status. They become compliant to maintain it.

Boundary erosion:

Boundaries are crossed incrementally. Each violation is small enough to rationalize but moves the relationship further from appropriate.

- Extended eye contact becomes normal
- Hugs become longer, more intimate
- Conversations become more personal, more emotionally vulnerable
- Meetings happen later, in more private settings
- Touch becomes more frequent, lingers longer

By the time anything overtly sexual happens, dozens of boundaries have already been crossed. The victim has been conditioned to accept escalation.

Spiritual framing:

This is where church-based abuse becomes uniquely damaging. The grooming process is wrapped in religious language." God is doing a deep work in you through our connection." The intimacy you feel is spiritual. Don't let your carnal mind confuse it." This is how prophets poured into their disciples. It's biblical." The victim can't separate the abuse from their faith. Rejecting the pastor feels like rejecting God.

Questioning the relationship feels like questioning their spiritual discernment.

Stage 3: Abuse

By the time physical abuse occurs, the victim has been so thoroughly groomed that they often don't recognize it as abuse.

How it's framed:

-" This is a spiritual impartation. Receive it."-" Your body is reacting to the anointing."-" God is healing your sexuality through this."-" This is covenant intimacy. It's sacred."Why victims comply:

They've been trained to trust this person absolutely. They've been isolated from anyone who might offer perspective. They believe rejecting the pastor means rejecting God. They fear losing their spiritual covering, their community, their identity. They're confused — this doesn't feel right, but the pastor says it's from God, and who are they to question God's anointed?

The abuse itself:

This chapter won't describe specific acts. What matters is understanding that the abuse is rarely violent. It doesn't have to be. The grooming has already accomplished compliance. The victim participates not because they want to, but because they've been manipulated into believing they should.

And afterward, the spiritual framing continues: "Don't let the enemy take what God did today." "If you feel shame, that's not from God. That's the accuser." "This is between us and God. No one else would understand."

Abuse is rarely a single incident. Predators need ongoing access. This requires maintaining control over the victim.

Continued spiritual manipulation:

- "God showed me we need to continue this work."
- "Your breakthrough depends on our continued connection."
- "If you pull away, you'll lose everything God is doing in your life."

Implied and explicit threats:

- "No one would believe you. I'm the pastor."
- "If this comes out, it will destroy the church. Do you want that on your conscience?"

- "Your reputation would be ruined. People would say you seduced me."
- "I'll tell everyone about your struggles. Everything you shared in confidence."

Trauma bonding:

Victims often develop complex emotional attachments to their abusers. This isn't Stockholm syndrome — it's the natural result of intimacy, even coerced intimacy, combined with the isolation that prevents perspective.

The victim may genuinely believe they love the pastor. May feel responsible for protecting him. May fear that ending the relationship will cause him harm.

This is by design. Trauma bonding keeps victims silent. — ## WHY THE CHURCH IS UNIQUELY VULNERABLE

Sexual predators exist everywhere. But churches create conditions that make abuse easier to perpetrate and harder to expose.

Unquestioned authority:

Pastors are granted spiritual authority that few other professions enjoy." Touch not God's anointed "becomes a shield against all accountability. Questioning the pastor is framed as questioning God.

This means victims can't trust their own perception. If the pastor says it's spiritual, maybe it is. Who are they to disagree with God's chosen vessel?

Access to vulnerability:

Pastoral care involves intimate knowledge of people's deepest struggles. Confession, counseling, prayer — all create asymmetric vulnerability. The pastor knows everything about you. You know nothing about the pastor's inner life.

This information asymmetry is a predator's dream.

Institutional investment in silence:

When abuse surfaces, churches face devastating consequences: scandal, legal liability, loss of members and donations, destruction of the pastor's family, potential criminal charges.

The institution has enormous incentive to suppress allegations. And churches have power to suppress:

- Control over who speaks and what's said
- Ability to frame accusers as bitter, deceived, or immoral
- Threat of church discipline against those who "cause division"-

Community pressure to protect the church's reputation Victims face the entire institution when they come forward. Most don't.

Theology that enables abuse:

Certain doctrines create fertile ground for predators:

Purity culture: Teaches that victims are damaged goods, that sexual sin (even when coerced) brings shame, that women are responsible for men's behavior. Victims blame themselves. Predators blame victims.

Male headship: Positions men as spiritual authorities over women. Normalizes female submission. Creates power dynamics that predators exploit.

Forgiveness theology: Pressures victims to forgive quickly, reconcile with abusers, and avoid "bitterness." Silences legitimate anger. Protects perpetrators from consequences.

Touch not the anointed: Makes accountability impossible. Protects leaders from scrutiny.

Isolation from secular resources:

Many church members are taught to distrust secular institutions — including law enforcement, therapists, and journalists." Handle it within the church." Don't bring the world into this." We don't air dirty laundry." This keeps abuse hidden from anyone with power to address it. — ## HOW CHURCHES RESPOND (BADLY)

When abuse allegations surface, churches typically follow a predictable, damaging pattern.

Disbelief and minimization: "That doesn't sound like Pastor. Are you sure you understood what happened?" He's been in ministry for thirty years. This must be a misunderstanding." Maybe you're remembering it differently than it actually was."Victim investigation:

Instead of investigating the allegation, the church investigates the victim." What were you wearing?" Why did you keep meeting with him if it made you uncomfortable?" Have you struggled with sexual sin before?" Were you attracted to him?" The victim's character, history, and credibility are scrutinized. The pastor's are protected.

Spiritual reframing: "This is a spiritual attack on the church. The enemy is trying to destroy Pastor's ministry." You need to examine your own heart. Is there unforgiveness? Bitterness?" Have you considered that you might be deceived?" The accusation itself becomes evidence of the victim's spiritual deficiency.

Pressure to stay silent: "Think about Pastor's family. His wife. His children." The church can't survive this kind of scandal." If you go public, you'll hurt so many people." Can't we handle this internally, like a family?" Victims are made responsible for protecting everyone except themselves.

Quick, quiet "resolution":

If the church can't suppress the allegation entirely, they move to contain it:

- Private "reconciliation" meeting where the victim is pressured to forgive
- Pastor takes a brief sabbatical for "restoration"
- Non-disclosure agreement in exchange for financial settlement
- Pastor quietly moves to another church, credentials intact

The victim gets no justice. The predator faces no real consequences. And in a new church, with new victims who know nothing, it starts again. — ## WHY VICTIMS DON'T REPORT

Outsiders often ask: "Why didn't she say something sooner? Why didn't she go to the police?" The question reveals ignorance of how abuse actually works.

They don't recognize it as abuse:

The grooming process convinces victims that what's happening is normal, spiritual, or their own fault. Many don't have language for what happened until years later.

They fear not being believed:

Pastors have credibility. Victims — especially those who've been framed as troubled, emotional, or spiritually unstable — don't.

They'll lose everything:

Community. Friends. Church family. Spiritual identity. Sense of God. In high-control churches, leaving means losing your entire social world.

They've been threatened:

Not always explicitly. But victims understand the consequences of speaking. They've seen how churches treat accusers.

They blame themselves: "I should have recognized the red flags." I kept going back." I didn't fight hard enough." Maybe I led him on." Predators cultivate this self-blame deliberately.

The process is retraumatizing:

Reporting means telling the story repeatedly. To people who may not believe you. Facing the person who abused you. Watching the institution protect him. The process itself causes harm.

Most victims calculate — consciously or unconsciously — that reporting will cost more than staying silent. They're usually right. — THE PREDATOR PROFILE

Not every pastor who crosses boundaries is a calculated predator. Some are genuinely struggling with their own issues and make terrible decisions. This doesn't excuse harm, but it's a different category.

Predatory clergy, however, share recognizable characteristics:

Pattern of behavior:

It's never just one victim. Predators have histories. If you're aware of one allegation, there are almost certainly others.

Grooming sophistication:

Image management:

Public persona is carefully constructed. Often charismatic, beloved, seen as particularly godly. The gap between public image and private behavior is enormous.

DARVO response:

When accused, predators follow a predictable pattern: Deny, Attack, Reverse Victim and Offender. They deny the abuse, attack the accuser's credibility, and position themselves as the real victim." She's lying." She's unstable." She seduced me." I'm being persecuted for my faith."Enabler network:

Predators surround themselves with people who protect them. Loyal staff. Devoted congregants. Board members who owe their position to the pastor. When allegations surface, this network activates to suppress them. — WHAT PROTECTION LOOKS LIKE

Prevention isn't complicated. But it requires churches to prioritize safety over image.

Structural accountability:

- No private meetings between pastors and congregants of the opposite sex
- All counseling in observable spaces
- Mandatory background checks for all staff and volunteers
- Clear reporting procedures that bypass the pastor
- External board oversight, not just internal

Cultural accountability:

- Teach congregations that questioning leaders is healthy, not rebellious
- Remove "touch not the anointed" from your vocabulary
- Train everyone — staff, volunteers, members — on grooming patterns and red flags
- Create multiple reporting channels that don't require going through

The pastor Believe survivors:

When someone comes forward, believe them first. Investigate second. Don't reverse that order.

The overwhelming majority of abuse allegations are true. The overwhelming majority of false allegations are easily identified through investigation. Leading with belief protects victims while investigation establishes facts.

Remove predators:

Not restoration. Not reconciliation. Removal.

Predatory behavior disqualifies someone from ministry permanently. There is no rehabilitation that makes a predator safe to lead vulnerable people again.

Report to law enforcement. Cooperate with investigations. Don't handle it "internally." — A WORD TO SURVIVORS

If this chapter described your experience, I want you to know:

It wasn't your fault. Grooming works. Manipulation works. You were targeted because of your vulnerability, not your weakness. The shame belongs to the person who exploited you, not to you.

You're not alone. The isolation you felt was manufactured. There are others. There are communities of survivors who understand. You don't have to carry this alone.

Your perception is valid. If it felt wrong, it was wrong. You don't need anyone else to validate that. Trust yourself.

Healing is possible. It takes time. It often requires professional help from therapists who understand religious trauma. But people do heal. You can too.

You don't owe forgiveness. Whatever you've been told, you are not required to forgive your abuser. You're not required to reconcile. You're not spiritually deficient for being angry. Your anger is appropriate. It's protective. Don't let anyone take it from you before you're ready.

It's never too late to tell. Whether it happened last month or thirty years ago, your story matters. You don't have to report publicly. But if you choose to, there are people who will believe you. — ## GOD WASN'T IN THAT ROOM

The most insidious aspect of spiritual sexual abuse is the theological damage.

When abuse is framed as sacred, victims can't separate the trauma from their faith. God becomes associated with violation. Church becomes unsafe. Spirituality itself becomes triggering.

God was not in that room.

Whatever your abuser told you, whatever spiritual language was used to justify what happened — it was a misrepresentation — calculated and manipulative, designed to ensure your compliance and silence.

God does not violate. God does not exploit vulnerability. God does not use spiritual authority to take what isn't freely given.

What happened to you was human evil using God's name as cover. That's blasphemy. It's the abuser's blasphemy, not yours.

You can reject what happened without rejecting God — if you want to. You can also reject God — if that's where you land. Your spiritual journey after abuse is yours to determine. No one else gets to dictate what you believe or where you find healing.

But know this: the God your abuser described — the one who sanctioned what happened — doesn't exist. That was a weapon manufactured to control you.

Whatever is actually divine, actually sacred, actually holy — it wasn't that. — ## THE SILENCE ENDS HERE

Churches have protected predators for generations. Survivors have been silenced, shamed, and driven away while their abusers continue in ministry.

This has to end.

If you're a church leader: create accountability structures. Believe survivors. Remove predators. Stop protecting your institution at the expense of vulnerable people.

If you're a church member: demand transparency. Ask how your church handles allegations. Watch for the red flags described in this chapter. Be someone safe for survivors to talk to.

If you're a survivor: your story has power. You don't have to share it publicly. But if you do, it might be the thing that protects someone else. It might be the thing that finally holds a predator accountable.

The church has been a haven for predators because it's been silent about predation.

No more.

God doesn't need your silence. The predator does. — For support and resources, see Appendix A.

Chapter 20: If This Is You – Recognizing Yourself in These Pages

If you recognized your church in this book, you're not imagining things. If you felt your stomach tighten reading certain chapters, that's not coincidence. If you've been telling yourself for years that something felt wrong but you couldn't name it-now you can. This chapter is for you.

You're reading this book secretly. Maybe on your phone where no one can see. Maybe you bought it with cash so there's no digital record. Maybe a friend sent you the PDF and you're reading it in pieces when you're alone. You're afraid someone will find out you're reading this. That says everything.

Here's what I want you to know:

Your discomfort is information. Your body is telling you something your mind hasn't been allowed to process. Trust that feeling. The fact that you're afraid to read a book is evidence that you're in a system that controls information. Healthy organizations don't fear outside perspectives. Controlling ones do.

You're not:

- Being deceived by the enemy
- Letting doubt undermine your faith
- Opening yourself to spiritual attack
- Being divisive or overly critical
- Failing to trust God

You are:

- Thinking critically
- Trusting your instincts
- Recognizing patterns
- Protecting yourself
- Starting to see clearly

You don't have to leave immediately. You don't have to make any decisions today. But start preparing. Quietly build external friendships. Start saving money. Document the things that concern you. Research other communities. When you're ready-if you're ready-you'll know. And when that time comes, you'll have done the work to make leaving survivable.

You left six months ago. Or six years ago. Or six days ago. You're reading this and crying because someone finally named what happened to you. Someone finally said: "Yes, that was real. Yes, that was harmful. Yes, you had good reasons." Here's what I want you to know:

You're not crazy. The gaslighting was real. The manipulation was real. The harm was real. You didn't leave because you were weak. You left because you were strong enough to recognize toxicity and brave enough to walk away.

The guilt you feel? Programming. It was installed to keep you compliant. It's not God. It's not truth. It's conditioning.

The fear that you made a mistake? Also programming. Designed to make you doubt yourself so thoroughly that you return.

The grief? That's real. You lost community, identity, certainty, belonging. Those losses are legitimate. Grieve them. But don't confuse grief with regret. You can mourn what you lost while knowing you made the right choice.

What to do now:

Give yourself time. Healing isn't linear. Some days will be hard. Some will be freeing. Both are okay. Find community-therapy, support groups, online forums. You need people who understand religious trauma. Be patient with yourself. You're not just leaving an organization. You're rebuilding your entire framework for understanding reality. That takes time.

You're a pastor, elder, staff member, or ministry leader. You're reading this and recognizing your church in these patterns. Maybe you've been uncomfortable for years but couldn't articulate why. Maybe you've pushed back on certain practices and been shut down. Maybe you've tried to create change and faced resistance.

Here's what I want you to know:

You have more power than congregants do. And more responsibility. If you see this clearly and stay silent, you're complicit. I know that's hard to hear. But it's true.

Your choices:

Option 1: Try to change it from inside.

Raise concerns. Demand transparency. Push for accountability. Advocate for congregants. Be prepared: you'll likely be labeled divisive, undermined, and eventually pushed out. Systems protect themselves. But maybe you create enough disruption that something shifts. Maybe you help some people see clearly. Maybe your courage gives others permission to speak up.

Option 2: Document and leave.

If you can't change it and staying means participating in harm, leave. But first, document what you've seen. Financial irregularities. Abuse cover-ups. Manipulation tactics. Whatever you have access to that proves the patterns. You don't have to go public immediately. But having documentation protects you and might help others someday.

Option 3: Stay and participate.

If you stay silent, keep taking the salary, keep playing your role-you're choosing the system over the people it harms. I understand the financial pressure. The career investment. The identity wrapped up in ministry. The hope that maybe it'll get better. But it won't get better if people with power and knowledge stay silent.

What to do now:

Make a choice. You've seen clearly now. You can't unsee it. Staying neutral is choosing the status quo.

Someone you love left church. You're hurt. You feel betrayed. You think they're deceived, rebellious, or throwing away their faith. You might have bought this book to understand their reasons. Or to find ammunition to bring them back.

Here's what I want you to know:

They didn't leave lightly. This decision cost them everything. They wouldn't have done it without compelling reasons.

What they need from you:

Not attempts to save them. Not spiritual diagnosis. Not withdrawal of love. They need you to listen without trying to fix. To maintain relationship without conditions. To love them regardless of religious agreement.

What you think is happening:

They're being deceived. Walking away from God. In danger spiritually.

What's actually happening:

They're protecting themselves from harm. Walking away from a church. In danger from people who can't let them go.

Your choice:

You can prioritize the church over the relationship. You can cut them off, pray against them, wait for them to "come back." Or you can prioritize the person. You can stay connected. You can trust that they're capable of making decisions about their own spiritual life. One choice keeps the relationship. The other destroys it.

You started questioning the church. Now you're questioning God. Doctrine. The Bible. Everything. This is terrifying. Your entire framework for understanding reality is collapsing. You don't know what you believe anymore.

Here's what I want you to know:

This is normal. This is the deconstruction process. It's painful but necessary. You can't rebuild a healthy faith on a damaged foundation. Sometimes you have to demolish everything and decide what's worth rebuilding.

This doesn't mean:

- You've lost your faith permanently
- You're going to hell
- You were never really saved
- God has abandoned you

This means:

- You're thinking critically
- You're distinguishing between institutional religion and actual faith
- You're reevaluating what you believe — and why
- You're becoming autonomous

Where this goes:

Some people rebuild faith in a healthier form. Some leave religion entirely. Some stay in the questions indefinitely. All three are okay. There's no timeline. No required destination.

What to do now:

Give yourself permission to not know. To question. To doubt. To explore. Read widely. Different perspectives. Different traditions. Different worldviews. See what resonates. Find community in the questions. Online groups for people deconstructing. People who won't try to give you easy answers. Trust yourself. You've been told not to trust yourself for so long. Learn to trust yourself again.

Your friend, sibling, parent-someone you care about is still in a church that concerns you. You see the manipulation. The control. The harm. They don't. Or they do but aren't ready to leave.

Here's what I want you to know:

You can't force them out. You can't argue them out. You can't rescue them.

What you can do:

Be available. Let them know you're safe to talk to. That you won't judge. That you'll listen.

Plant seeds. Share articles, books, podcasts that might resonate. Don't force. Just offer.

Model healthy life. Show them what life outside the system looks like. Happy. Stable. Free.

Be patient. People leave when they're ready. Not before. Your timeline doesn't matter.

Maintain relationship. Stay connected even while they're still in. So when they're ready to leave, you're still there.

What not to do:

Don't attack their church. It'll make them defensive and push them deeper in. Don't issue ultimatums." Leave or else "doesn't work. Don't cut them off out of frustration. That leaves them more isolated.

Remember:

Most people who leave had someone who stayed connected during their time inside. Someone who represented an alternative. Someone safe. Be that person. That's the most powerful thing you can do.

IF YOU'RE A THERAPIST, COUNSELOR, OR HELPING PROFESSIONAL

You have clients processing religious trauma. Maybe you picked up this book to understand what they're experiencing.

Here's what I want you to know:

Religious trauma is complex trauma. It involves:

- Betrayal by trusted authorities
- Disruption of belief systems
- Loss of community and identity
- Spiritual abuse and manipulation
- Often financial exploitation
- Sometimes physical or sexual abuse

Your clients need:

Validation. Their experiences were real and harmful. They're not overreacting.

Permission. To question. To doubt. To deconstruct. To leave.

Tools. For managing guilt, fear, grief, and anger. For rebuilding identity. For creating new meaning.

Time. This isn't quick. Years often. Don't rush them.

Understanding. Of high-control group dynamics. Of spiritual abuse tactics. Of how religious systems create psychological captivity.

Resources for You:

Marlene Winell's work on Religious Trauma Syndrome

Dr. Steven Hassan's BITE model for cult analysis

Dr. Janja Lalich's research on bounded choice

The Religious Trauma Institute

What to avoid:

Don't minimize." Many churches have problems "isn't helpful.

Don't spiritualize their recovery. They might not be interested in "finding a healthier church." Don't push forgiveness prematurely. Forgiveness might come. But first comes safety, processing, and healing.

You're investigating religious institutions, documenting abuse, exposing systems.

Here's what I want you to know:

This work matters. The patterns documented in this book aren't isolated. They're systematic. And they need exposure.

What to investigate:

Financial opacity in megachurches. Where does the money go? Why no transparency? Leadership accountability structures. Who has power? Who can check that power? What happens when abuse occurs? Labor practices. How many unpaid hours do volunteers work? What's the value extraction? Real estate holdings. What does the church own? How did they acquire it? Who profits? Educational institutions. What gets taught? How is dissent handled? What happens to people who leave?

What victims need:

Protection. Many can't speak publicly without retaliation. Validation. Their stories being believed and documented. Platform. Not most people can write books or give interviews. Help tell their stories. Change. Not just exposure-actual policy changes, legislative action, cultural shift.

Wherever you are in this process-inside and questioning, recently left, years into recovery, trying to help someone else-you're not alone. Thousands of people have walked this path. Thousands more are walking it now. You have community waiting. Resources available. People who understand.

The work ahead:

This isn't just personal healing. It's cultural change. Churches won't reform themselves. They benefit too much from current structures. Change requires people speaking up. Sharing stories. Demanding accountability. Supporting each other. That's how systems eventually fall. Not through external attack. Through internal exodus and refusal to participate.

Your role:

Whatever you're ready for. If that's just saving yourself and your family, that's enough. If it's speaking publicly, advocating loudly, demanding change-that's valuable. Both matter. Personal survival and systemic change are both necessary.

You have permission to:

Trust yourself. Your instincts. Your observations. Your conclusions.

Set boundaries. With church. With family. With anyone who won't respect your autonomy.

Change your mind. About beliefs. About participation. About what you're willing to tolerate.

Grieve. What you lost. What was taken. What never was.

Be angry. At systems. At leaders. At the harm. Anger is information.

Protect yourself. Physically. Financially. Emotionally. Spiritually.

Leave. If that's what you need. Without guilt. Without shame. Without explanation.

Stay. If you choose to, for your own reasons. With open eyes and boundaries.

Heal. On your timeline. In your way. With the support you need. You have permission to be autonomous, complex, questioning, human. You consistently had that permission. But you've been told otherwise for so long. So here it is again: you have permission.

God doesn't need your participation in systems that harm you. God doesn't require your submission to human authorities who abuse power. God doesn't condemn you for protecting yourself. God doesn't need the church to survive. If you're in and need to leave, you can.

If you're out and carrying guilt, you shouldn't. If you're questioning everything, that's okay. If you're helping someone else through this, thank you. If you're reading this in secret, afraid of being found out-I'm sorry. You deserve better. And it's waiting for you when you're ready.

This Is You

If any of this resonated. If any of this felt true. If any of this named something you've been feeling but couldn't articulate. This is you. And you're going to be okay.

Chapter 21: God Never Threatened You – The Church Did

She was afraid to stop tithing. Not because she couldn't afford groceries because she was terrified God would curse her finances. She was afraid to miss a service. Not because she'd miss community-because she believed God was keeping track and disappointment meant judgment. She was afraid to question the pastor.

Not because she lacked conviction-because she'd been taught that questioning leadership was questioning God. She was afraid to leave. Not because she'd miss the church-because she genuinely believed leaving meant losing her salvation, inviting demonic attack, and risking eternal damnation. Every fear. Every threat.

Every consequence she'd been warned about. None of it came from God. It all came from the church using God's name. And there's a massive difference.

Let's catalog the threats churches make in God's name:

Financial:

"If you don't tithe, God will curse your finances." You're robbing God and He won't bless you." Windows of heaven will close if you're not faithful with your giving." Spiritual:

"If you leave this church, you'll backslide." You're opening yourself to demonic attack by questioning leadership." God will remove His hand of protection if you rebel."

Eternal:

"If you're not really saved, you'll go to hell." Lukewarm Christians will be spit out." There's no salvation outside the church."

Relational:

"If you don't submit to your husband, you're out of God's will." Honoring your parents means obeying your pastor." Leaving this church means abandoning God's family."

Behavioral:

"God sees everything you do. He's keeping a record." That sin will find you out and God will judge you." You can't hide from God." Every single one is a threat.

And every single one is designed to produce compliance through fear.

None of these threats appear in scripture the way churches present them.

"Robbing God"(Malachi 3:8):

Context: God speaking to corrupt priests who were extracting resources from offerings meant for widows and orphans. Not about church members failing to tithe. Church use: Weaponized against congregants to extract 10% of income.

"Touch not my anointed"(Psalm 105:15):

Context: God protecting powerless wandering patriarchs from hostile foreign kings. Church use: Powerful pastors protecting themselves from accountability.

"Backsliding"(Jeremiah 3):

Context: Israel worshiping other gods, breaking covenant relationship. Church use: Leaving a specific church building or disagreeing with leadership.

"Lukewarm"(Revelation 3:16):

Context: A specific church in Laodicea being materially wealthy but spiritually complacent. Church use: Anyone not meeting the church's activity and giving standards.

The pattern: Scripture taken out of context, twisted, and deployed as threat.

God's actual words become the church's weapon.

Churches discovered that fear is more effective than love for producing compliance.

Love-based motivation:

"God loves you. Respond to that love as you feel led." Result: Unpredictable behavior. Some give, some don't. Some serve, some don't. Some attend, some don't.

Fear-based motivation:

"God will curse you if you don't give/serve/attend." Result: Predictable compliance. People override their own judgment to avoid threatened consequences.

Churches need predictable compliance to function.

So they use fear. Systematically. Intentionally. Effectively. And they use God's name to do it.

Fear-based church systems are built on specific theological frameworks:

Framework 1: Transactional God

God as cosmic accountant keeping score. You obey, you get blessed. You disobey, you get cursed. Every action has a calculable divine consequence. This makes God predictable and controllable-if you do X, God must do Y. But it also makes God threatening. Every mistake could trigger divine punishment.

Framework 2: Angry God

God as perpetually disappointed parent just waiting for you to mess up so He can punish you. Grace is theoretical; wrath is practical. This makes people anxious, hypervigilant, desperate to perform correctly.

Framework 3: Distant God

God as remote authority figure who you can only access through proper channels (the church, the pastor, the rituals). Direct relationship is impossible or dangerous. This makes the church necessary. You need them to mediate between you and God.

Framework 4: Conditional God

God's love, acceptance, and blessing are conditional on your performance. Meet standards, God loves you. Fail standards, God rejects you. This makes people work desperately to earn what they're told is free.

None of these frameworks are biblical.

They're institutional inventions designed to produce fear that generates control.

What God Actually Said

Let's look at what God actually says vs. what churches claim:

On Giving:

Churches: "Give 10% or God will curse your finances." God: "Each of you should give what you have decided in your heart to give, not reluctantly or under compulsion, for God loves a cheerful giver."(2 Corinthians 9:7)

On Questioning:

Churches: "Don't question leadership. That's rebellion against God." God: "Test everything. Hold on to what is good."(1 Thessalonians 5:21)

On Fear:

Churches: "Fear God's judgment if you don't comply." God: "There is no fear in love. But perfect love drives out fear, because fear has to do with punishment."(1 John 4:18)

On Leaving:

Churches: "Leave this church and you'll backslide." God: "Neither height nor depth, nor anything else in all creation, will be able to separate us from the love of God."(Romans 8:39)

On Salvation:

Churches: "You need to keep proving you're saved or you'll lose it." God: "I give them eternal life, and they shall never perish; no one will snatch them out of my hand."(John 10:28)

The contrast is stark.

The contrast is stark: churches threaten while God assures; they create fear while God offers security.

Let's break down the most common threats:

THREAT: "God will curse your finances if you don't tithe." The Truth: God doesn't curse people for budget decisions. Financial consequences come from financial choices, not divine punishment for insufficient church giving. If not tithing caused curses, the majority of Christians throughout history (who didn't tithe) would have been financially destroyed. They weren't.

THREAT: "Leaving this church means backsliding from God." The Truth: Leaving a building or organization doesn't affect your relationship with God. If it did, every time you moved cities and changed churches, you'd lose salvation. Backsliding is turning away from God. Not turning away from a church.

THREAT: "God is keeping a record of your sins and will judge you." The Truth: If you're a believer, scripture says your sins are removed as far as east is from west. God isn't keeping score. Churches keep score. God offers forgiveness.

THREAT: "You need to be here every time the doors are open or you're lukewarm." The Truth: God doesn't measure devotion by attendance at a specific building. Lukewarm referred to spiritual complacency, not church attendance frequency.

THREAT: "If you question leadership, you're touching God's anointed and inviting judgment." The Truth: God never said leaders are above accountability. Biblical leaders were constantly challenged, questioned, and held accountable.

Every threat falls apart under scrutiny.

Because they're not from God. They're from institutions protecting themselves.

Churches conflate guilt and conviction. They're not the same.

Conviction (from God):

Specific to actual wrong

Leads to repentance and change

Resolves when addressed

Produces freedom after correction

Focuses on behavior, not identity

Guilt (from church):

Vague and pervasive

Leads to anxiety and shame

Never resolves (always inadequate)

Produces bondage and performance

Attacks identity and worth

Example:

Conviction: "I was unkind to that person. I should apologize." Guilt: "I'm a terrible Christian. God must be so disappointed in me. I'll never be good enough." Churches traffic in guilt, not conviction.

Because guilt produces compliance. Conviction produces transformation. Guilt keeps you dependent on the church. Conviction leads to actual growth.

Why do people stay in churches they know are harmful?

Fear of:

Divine punishment." If I leave, God will punish me." Losing salvation." If I walk away, I might not really be saved." Demonic attack." Outside the church, I'm vulnerable to Satan." Missing God's will." What if this is where God wants me and leaving means disobedience?" Proving doubters right." Everyone said

I'd fall away. If I leave, they were right." Abandoning God." Leaving the church feels like leaving God." None of these fears are from God.

What actually happened:

- Finances often improved *(10% returned to their budget)*
- No demonic attack followed
- Many felt God's presence more clearly — outside manipulation
- Most didn't backslide; they grew
- Peace increased without constant guilt
- Faith often deepened

The threats were false.
They were designed to keep people compliant — not based on actual divine consequences.

HOW TO RECOGNIZE INSTITUTIONAL THREAT VS. DIVINE TRUTH

Institutional threats:

- Create fear and anxiety
- Demand immediate compliance
- Benefit the institution
- Punish independence
- Can't be questioned
- Never resolve *(there's always more to do)*
- Make you dependent on the church

Divine truth:

- Creates conviction and clarity
- Invites response — doesn't demand it
- Benefits you and others
- Encourages growth
- Welcomes questions
- Resolves in grace
- Makes you dependent on God, not institutions

If we strip away church-imposed threats, what does God actually offer?

Acceptance — not based on performance.

"Therefore, there is now no condemnation for those who are in Christ Jesus."(Romans 8:1)

Security that can't be lost.

"No one will snatch them out of my hand."(John 10:28)

Love not dependent on compliance.

"But God demonstrates his own love for us in this: While we were still sinners, Christ died for us."(Romans 5:8)

Grace that covers failure.

"My grace is sufficient for you, for my power is made perfect in weakness."(2 Corinthians 12:9)

Freedom, not bondage.

"It is for freedom that Christ has set us free."(Galatians 5:1)

This is the opposite of what churches threaten.

God offers security. Churches offer anxiety. God offers acceptance. Churches offer conditional approval. God offers freedom. Churches offer control.

Living under constant threat causes real damage:

Psychological:

- Chronic anxiety
- Inability to trust own judgment
- Fear-based decision making
- Perfectionism and burnout

Spiritual:

- View of God as harsh judge, not loving father
- Inability to experience grace
- Performance-based faith
- Constant guilt and shame
- Difficulty trusting God

Relational:

- Using fear/guilt to control others
- Difficulty with healthy boundaries

- Inability to leave abusive relationships (if God wants me here, I must stay)

The threats don't just control behavior. They damage people.

And churches use God's name to inflict that damage.

Jesus didn't threaten people into following Him.

He let people walk away. Rich young ruler left. Jesus didn't chase him, threaten him, or manipulate him. Let him go.

He questioned religious authorities. Constantly challenged Pharisees, Sadducees, teachers of law. Didn't treat them as untouchable.

He welcomed doubters. Thomas doubted. Jesus didn't condemn him. Showed him evidence.

He prioritized people over institutions. Healed on Sabbath. Violated religious rules to help people. Put human need above religious compliance.

He offered rest, not burden." Come to me, all who are weary and burdened, and I will give you rest."(Matthew 11:28)

They chase people who try to leave. They protect authorities from questioning. They punish doubt. They prioritize institutional rules over human need. They add burdens rather than offering rest.

If Jesus is the model, modern church practice is the contradiction.

God never threatens to abandon you for leaving a building. Churches threaten that constantly. Because they need you to believe leaving them equals leaving God.

But consider:

Paul left Judaism. Didn't mean he left God.

Reformers left Catholic church. Didn't mean they left God.

Many churches change you've ever made. Didn't mean you left God.

Leaving a harmful institution isn't leaving God.

It's protecting yourself from people using religious framing to harm you. Being trapped in a specific building, under a specific pastor, participating in a specific institution. God is not that small. That limited. That dependent on human organizations.

HOW TO DISTINGUISH GOD'S VOICE FROM CHURCH MANIPULATION

God's voice:

- Brings peace, even when correcting
- Aligns with Scripture in context
- Produces freedom and growth
- Benefits you and others
- Can be questioned and tested
- Leads to love, joy, and peace

Church manipulation:

- Creates anxiety and fear
- Uses Scripture out of context
- Produces bondage and compliance
- Benefits the institution
- Cannot be questioned
- Leads to guilt, shame, and control

If a message collapses under scrutiny, it isn't divine — it's designed.

If you've been living under church threats, here's what you need to hear:

You have permission to:

Stop giving money you can't afford because you fear divine punishment. God doesn't curse your finances for budget decisions. Question leadership without believing you're rebelling against God. Testing everything is biblical. Blind obedience isn't. Leave a harmful church without losing your salvation.

Your relationship with God isn't dependent on membership at a specific institution. Miss services without guilt. God doesn't measure devotion by building attendance. Set boundaries without believing you're selfish. Self-protection isn't sin. Think for yourself without believing doubt is demonic. Questions are healthy.

Blind faith is dangerous. Prioritize your wellbeing and your family's wellbeing over institutional loyalty. God cares more about you than about the church's survival.

God never required you to stay in harm's way to prove faithfulness. Churches did. And they used God's name to do it.

God offers relationship, not threats. Security, not anxiety. Freedom, not control. Grace, not performance requirements.

Everything you've feared — the curses, the punishment, the judgment, the loss — didn't come from God. It came from churches that benefit from your fear.

God never threatened you. The church did.

And once you see that distinction clearly, you're finally free to have actual relationship with God without the church standing between you, using threats to extract compliance.

That's freedom. And it's what God wanted for you all along.

Chapter 22: The Offering Wasn't Voluntary

Multiple former members describe they call it an offering. That word implies choice. Voluntary. Optional. Given freely. It wasn't. You were told God required it.

You were told withholding it was robbing God. You were told your financial stability depended on it. You were told your spiritual health required it. You were told refusing it meant you lacked faith, invited curses, proved you didn't trust God.

That's not voluntary. That's coercion.

Voluntary means:

- No penalty for declining
- No pressure to participate
- No guilt for opting out
- No consequences for saying no
- Church offerings have all of those.

Penalty for declining: "God won't bless you." Pressure to participate: Public offering time. Everyone sees if you pass the plate without giving.

Guilt for opting out: "How can you take from the church without giving back?" Consequences for saying no: "You're robbing God. You're under a curse." That's not offering. That's extraction with religious packaging.

Watch what happens during offering time:

The sermon before the offering consistently emphasizes giving. Always. It's setup. Priming. Making you feel guilty if you don't give.

The music during the offering is strategic. Soft, worshipful, emotional. Making you feel like withholding money is withholding from God.

The public nature means most people can see who gives and who doesn't. Social pressure. Shame if you pass the plate empty-handed.

The announcements about budget needs, upcoming projects, staff salaries. Creating urgency." We need this. Will you step up?" The testimonies of people who gave and were blessed. Creating expectation that giving produces divine return. None of that is voluntary. It's manufactured pressure designed to extract compliance.

What Actual Voluntary Looks Like

Voluntary giving would be: A box in the back. Give if you want. No one watches. No one knows. No pressure. No announcements. No guilt. Take it or leave it.

Churches can't survive on truly voluntary giving.

Because when giving is actually voluntary-no pressure, no guilt, no consequences-most people give less. Or nothing. Churches know this.

So they create pressure while calling it "voluntary." Listen to how churches frame offerings: "We're going to receive the offering now." Not "offer an opportunity to give." Receive. Implies expectation. You're supposed to give.

They're receiving what you owe." Bring your tithes and offerings." Not "consider giving." Bring. Command. Expectation. Obligation." Honor God with your finances." Implies not giving dishonors God. That's guilt.

That's pressure." Sow your seed in faith." Implies if you don't give, you lack faith. That's manipulation.

Every phrase is designed to make giving feel mandatory while technically calling it voluntary.

Many churches require tithing for membership. Want to be a member? Prove you tithe. Want to serve in leadership? Show your giving records. Want the pastor to marry you? Demonstrate faithful giving first.

That's not voluntary. That's pay-to-play.

Your participation, your access, your standing in the community — all conditional on financial contribution. Call it what it is: dues. Membership fees. Required payments. Just don't call it voluntary.

Kids are taught to give their allowance, their birthday money, their earnings." God gets His 10% first." Children don't have the capacity to consent to financial obligations. They're being trained. Conditioned. Programmed. By the time they're adults, tithing feels automatic. Not voluntary. Just what you do.

That's not voluntary giving. That's childhood indoctrination creating adult compulsion.

What happens if you stop giving? In some churches, nothing visible. But people notice. Leadership notices. Your access to certain opportunities changes. Invitations decrease. Influence diminishes. In other churches, it's overt. You're approached. Questioned. Counseled. Your spiritual condition is diagnosed. Your commitment is questioned.

If there's a social cost to not giving, it's not voluntary.

It's compliance purchased through fear of social consequence.

The ultimate coercion: spiritual consequences." God will curse what you don't bless Him with." Your finances will be devoured if you rob God." The windows of heaven close when you're unfaithful." These are threats. Direct threats.

Give or face divine punishment. That's not an invitation. It's extortion with God's name attached.

WHAT THEY WON'T ADMIT

Churches won't say: "We need your money to pay salaries and mortgages. Giving is required for us to function. We've created financial obligations that demand your compliance. We can't operate on truly voluntary contributions. So we use guilt, pressure, and spiritual threats to extract what we need." That's the truth.

But they say: "This is worship. This is honoring God. This is voluntary giving from cheerful hearts." While applying every pressure tactic available to ensure compliance.

If you can't say no without consequences, it's not voluntary. If you feel guilt for declining, it's not voluntary. If there are spiritual threats attached, it's not voluntary. If children are programmed before they can consent, it's not voluntary. If social standing depends on participation, it's not voluntary.

The offering wasn't voluntary.

It was required. Pressured. Coerced. Manipulated. Extracted. And calling it an "offering" doesn't change what it actually was:

A mandatory payment disguised as worship.

Chapter 23: God Was Never for Sale – You Were

They sold you the idea that God required payment. Salvation through seed offerings. Blessings through tithes. Healing through faith gifts. Breakthrough through sacrificial giving.

But God was rarely for sale.

You were.

Churches presented God as transactional. Give money, receive blessing. Sow seed, reap harvest. Tithe faithfully, unlock favor.

But here's what actually happened:

You gave money. The church received it. You got nothing guaranteed. The church got everything. God wasn't part of the transaction. God's name was just the marketing.

They weren't selling God to you.

They were selling you to the system.

Your Labor Was the Product

Churches didn't need to sell God. God's free. They needed to sell you on the idea that God required your:

Once you believed that, you became the product.

Your unpaid volunteer hours: Product sold to the church as "ministry." Your financial contributions: Product sold to fund pastoral salaries and buildings.

Your recruiting efforts: Product sold as "evangelism" while you built their customer base.

You weren't buying God. You were being sold.

Look at what churches actually sell:

Access.

Pay for conferences. Pay for special events. Pay for premium seating. Pay for private meetings with leadership.

Influence.

Large donors get access to decision-making. Major givers become elders. Money buys voice.

Blessing.

Seed offerings purchase divine favor. Tithes unlock windows of heaven. Sacrificial giving releases breakthrough.

Community.

Membership requires financial participation. Full access costs money. Belonging has a price.

God isn't being sold. Access to the church is being sold.

And they used God's name to make you buy it.

How much does God cost in church? 10% of gross income minimum. That's the entry price. Building fund campaigns. Special offerings. Mission trips. Conference fees. Books. Merchandise. Average committed church member gives 15-20% of income annually when you count everything.

For a family earning $50,000:

Tithe: $5,000 Building fund: $1,200 Conferences/camps: $800 Offerings: $500 Resources: $300

Total: $7,800 annually

That's the price of access to God through the church.

But God was never charging that.

the church was. And keeping it.

What You Actually Bought

You thought you were buying:

- A relationship with God
- Spiritual growth
- Eternal security
- Divine blessing

What you actually bought:

- Membership in an organization
- Access to programs
- A seat in a building
- Participation in activities
- The privilege of working for free

God wasn't part of the purchase.

God wasn't what you received. God was what sold it.

They advertised God. They delivered institution. They promised divine encounter. They provided programs. They sold eternal blessing. They gave temporary access to facilities.

Classic bait and switch.

You came for God. You got sold church.

You Were the Commodity

In any marketplace, someone is the product. Chapter 2 laid this out in detail: your attention, labor, money, loyalty, and recruiting efforts were all harvested for the church's benefit. God wasn't for sale. You were being sold — to the system, for its benefit.

Watch who got rich. Not you. You gave 10-20% of income, worked for free, and stayed financially struggling. The church leadership collected guaranteed salaries, benefits, housing allowances, book royalties, and speaking fees.

They couldn't say: "We need your money to pay our salaries and maintain our buildings." That's too honest. So they said: "God requires your tithes. Honor Him with your finances." Same transaction. Different packaging.

What churches fear most: you realizing that God doesn't require payment. That grace is actually free. If you realize that, you stop paying them.

God is free. Always was. Always will be. The church costs money. Not God. And they used God's name to charge you for access they never controlled in the first place.

Final Thoughts

God invites. The church demands. God offers. The church extracts. God asks. The church takes.

Know the difference.

The patterns in this book aren't anomalies. They're systematic. The coercion isn't accidental. It's designed. And what's been taken from you — money, time, labor, autonomy, voice — wasn't offered freely. It was extracted through pressure dressed in spiritual language.

One respects autonomy. The other violates it.

What Happens Next

If you stay: Watch for the patterns documented in this book. Notice when manipulation happens. Protect your family. You don't have to leave to be aware.

If you leave: Expect grief. Expect anger. Expect relief mixed with guilt. Find community outside the church walls. Give yourself time — healing takes years, not weeks. You will survive this.

If you're rebuilding faith: God is not the church. Spirituality doesn't require institutions. You can have a relationship with the divine without paying for access. What's real will remain when the manipulation falls away.

A Final Word to Pastors

Not all of you are corrupt. Many of you entered ministry to serve people and found yourselves trapped in systems you didn't design. Some of you recognize your church in these pages and feel sick about it.

You can change. You can demand financial transparency. You can stop using manipulation tactics. You can pay volunteers fairly. You can welcome questions. You can build something healthy.

This book isn't asking you to close your church. It's asking you to stop running it like a con. The invitation to reform is genuine. The people in your pews deserve better. So do you.

References and Sources

This book draws on extensive research from multiple sources. Key references are organized by category below.

Financial Data and Statistics

Giving USA Foundation. Annual reports on charitable giving in America.

Empty Tomb, Inc. Research on church spending patterns and benevolence allocations.

Barna Group. Studies on Christian giving patterns and church engagement.

Pew Research Center. Studies on religion in America, church demographics, and giving patterns.

National Study of Congregations' Economic Practices (multiple years).

Biblical Scholarship on Tithing

Carson, D. A. Various writings on New Testament interpretation and church practices.

Blomberg, Craig. Neither Poverty Nor Riches: A Biblical Theology of Possessions. IVP Academic, 1999.

Köstenberger, Andreas J. Various writings on New Testament theology and church practice.

Prosperity Gospel Research

Bowler, Kate. Blessed: A History of the American Prosperity Gospel. Oxford University Press, 2013.

Walton, Jonathan L. Watch This! The Ethics and Aesthetics of Black Televangelism. NYU Press, 2009.

Harrison, Milmon F. Righteous Riches: The Word of Faith Movement in Contemporary African American Religion. Oxford University Press, 2005.

Religious Trauma and Psychology

Winell, Marlene. Leaving the Fold: A Guide for Former Fundamentalists and Others Leaving Their Religion. Apocryphile Press, 2006.

Johnson, David and VanVonderen, Jeff. The Subtle Power of Spiritual Abuse. Bethany House, 1991, 2005.

Hassan, Steven. Combating Cult Mind Control. Park Street Press, multiple editions.

Lalich, Janja and Tobias, Madeleine. Take Back Your Life: Recovering from Cults and Abusive Relationships. Bay Tree Publishing, 2006.

Investigative Journalism and Watchdog Organizations

Trinity Foundation. Investigative research and documentation on televangelism and religious financial practices.

GRACE (Godly Response to Abuse in the Christian Environment). Investigation reports.

Houston Chronicle. “Abuse of Faith” investigative series (2019).

Fort Worth Star-Telegram. Investigations into religious institutional abuse.

Christianity Today. Investigative reporting on church financial practices and abuse.

The Washington Post. Investigative journalism on religious organizations and leadership.

The New York Times. Reporting on religious institutions and financial practices.

Celebrity Pastor Net Worth

Forbes magazine. Wealth estimates and profiles.

Celebrity Net Worth. Publicly reported estimates (noted as such where cited).

Legal and Tax References

IRS Publication 1828: Tax Guide for Churches and Religious Organizations.

Colombo, John D. "Why Is Harvard Tax-Exempt?" Boston College Law Review, 2011.

Various state attorney general reports on religious organization finances.

Faith Healing Deaths

Swan, Rita. Research and documentation through Children's Healthcare Is a Legal Duty (CHILD).

Court records from prosecutions in Oregon, Idaho, and other states.

Medical journal case studies on religious refusal of medical care.

Note on Sources

Where specific statistics are cited, original sources were consulted. Where patterns are described, they reflect documented cases from multiple independent sources. All named individuals are public figures whose activities have been reported by mainstream journalism.

For additional reading recommendations, see Appendix A.

APPENDIX A: RESOURCES FOR RECOVERY

If you're leaving a high-control religious environment or processing religious trauma, you're not alone. The following resources may help.

Crisis Support

If you're in immediate crisis or having thoughts of self-harm:

- National Suicide Prevention Lifeline: 988 (call or text)
- Crisis Text Line: Text HOME to 741741
- International Association for Suicide Prevention: https://www.iasp.info/resources/Crisis_Centres/

Organizations and Support Communities

- Recovering from Religion Website: RecoveringFromReligion.org
- Free secular support groups
- Trained peer support volunteers
- Resources for those questioning or leaving religion
- Religious Trauma Institute Website: ReligiousTraumaInstitute.com
- Educational resources on religious trauma syndrome
- Therapist directory
- Certification programs for professionals
- Spiritual Abuse Resources Website: SpiritualAbuseResources.com
- Information for survivors
- Resources for those helping survivors
- Legal information
- The Clergy Project Website: ClergyProject.org
- Confidential support for current and former religious leaders who no longer believe
- Peer community

Finding a Therapist

Look for therapists who specialize in:

- Religious trauma

- Spiritual abuse recovery
- Cult recovery
- High-control group exit counseling

Directories:

- Psychology Today therapist finder (filter by specialty)
- Secular Therapy Project: SecularTherapy.org
- Religious Trauma Institute therapist directory
- Questions to ask potential therapists: >
- Do you have experience with religious trauma or spiritual abuse? >
- Are you familiar with high-control religious environments?
- Will you respect my current beliefs (or lack thereof) without pushing an agenda?
- How do you approach religious content in therapy?

Books for Recovery

Understanding What Happened: - Leaving the Fold by Marlene Winell — The foundational text on religious trauma syndrome - The Subtle Power of Spiritual Abuse by David Johnson and Jeff VanVonderen - Combating Cult Mind Control by Steven Hassan - Take Back Your Life by Janja Lalich and Madeleine Tobias

Processing and Healing: - Faith Shift by Kathy Escobar - Out of the Fog by Dana Morningstar - Complex PTSD: From Surviving to Thriving by Pete Walker

For Specific Issues: - Purity Culture: Pure by Linda Kay Klein - Prosperity Gospel Recovery: The Prosperity Gospel Exposed by Costi Hinn - Pastoral Abuse: Battered Sheep by Mary Alice Chrnalogar

Podcasts

- Life After — Stories and support for those leaving high-control religion
- The Deconstructionists — Interviews with people navigating faith transitions
- Exvangelical — Examining evangelical culture and recovery
- Born Again Again — Humor and healing for ex-evangelicals

- Straight White American Jesus — Academic analysis of American religious movements

Online Communities

- r/Exvangelical (Reddit)
- r/ExPentecostal (Reddit)
- Life After Facebook groups
- Recovering from Religion local support groups

Financial Recovery

If you've experienced financial exploitation in a religious context:

- Consult a fee-only financial advisor (not commission-based)
- Contact your state attorney general if you believe fraud occurred
- National Foundation for Credit Counseling: NFCC.org
- Consider speaking with a CPA about proper charitable deduction documentation

For Family Members

If someone you love is in a high-control religious environment:

- Take Back Your Life by Janja Lalich (has sections for families)
- International Cultic Studies Association: ICSAhome.com
- Avoid ultimatums; maintain relationship connection
- Educate yourself without lecturing

Important Reminders

- Healing is not linear. You will have good days and difficult days.
- Your experience was real. You're not "overreacting."
- You don't have to have everything figured out immediately.
- It's okay to grieve what you lost, even if leaving was the right decision.
- Finding community outside church is possible, though it takes time.
- Professional help is not a sign of weakness; it's wisdom.
- You are not alone.

About the Author

◆ ◆ ◆

Reuben Armstrong grew up in the church — not as a casual attendee, but as an insider. He served as choir director, Sunday school teacher, drill team captain, and dedicated member for over two decades. He witnessed firsthand the gap between what churches preach and what they practice.

After years of silence, Armstrong decided to document the patterns he observed: the financial extraction, the emotional manipulation, the accountability gaps, and the systems that make exploitation feel spiritual. This book is the result.

Armstrong remains a believer in God. He does not remain a believer in systems that use God's name to extract money from people who can't afford it.

He lives in the United States and can be reached at reubenarmstrong4907@gmail.com.

Thank you for reading.

APPENDIX B: HOW TO EVALUATE ANY CHURCH

◆ ◆ ◆

A Diagnostic Framework

This appendix provides practical tools for evaluating any church — whether you're currently attending, considering joining, or helping someone you love assess their situation. These are not opinion-based judgments. They are observable, verifiable criteria based on patterns documented throughout this book.

This framework is not a test of faith, sincerity, or spiritual maturity. It evaluates systems, not souls. Healthy churches may still score imperfectly. What matters is pattern, response to questions, and accountability over time.

Use this framework systematically. Score honestly. Trust what you observe, not what you're told to believe.

SECTION 1: THE 60-SECOND RED FLAG TEST

Before investing time in detailed evaluation, answer these five questions:

1. Can you find a detailed, line-item budget showing exactly where money goes?
2. Do you know the senior pastor's total compensation (salary + housing + benefits + outside income)?
3. Can members vote on major financial decisions?
4. Are questions about finances, leadership decisions, or doctrine welcomed without defensiveness?
5. Could you leave this church tomorrow without losing your primary friend group, support system, or social standing?

Scoring: 5 Yes = Healthy indicators. 3-4 Yes = Investigate further. 0-2 Yes = Significant red flags.

SECTION 2: FINANCIAL TRANSPARENCY DIAGNOSTIC

2.1 Budget Transparency Checklist

Request the church's annual budget. Mark each item as Available, Hidden, or N/A: Total annual revenue. Total annual expenses. Staff salaries (itemized by position). Senior pastor total compensation. Housing allowance details. Benefits packages. Building/facilities costs. Missions/outreach spending (with breakdown). Benevolence fund (actual disbursements). Administrative costs. Marketing/advertising expenses. Conference/travel expenses. Reserves/savings. Debt obligations.

Scoring: 0-3 hidden = Normal. 4-7 hidden = Concerning. 8+ hidden = Financial opacity.

2.2 Compensation Ratio Analysis

Senior Pastor Compensation Ratio = Senior Pastor Total Compensation ÷ Median Household Income of Congregation

Under 1.5x = Modest. 1.5x-2.5x = Reasonable. 2.5x-5x = Elevated. 5x-10x = Concerning. Over 10x = Extreme — extraction pattern likely.

Staff Compensation Equity = Senior Pastor Compensation ÷ Lowest Paid Full-Time Staff

Under 3x = Equitable. 3x-5x = Standard nonprofit range. 5x-10x = Corporate hierarchy. Over 10x = Executive extraction model.

2.3 Spending Allocation Analysis

Calculate percentage of budget for each category. Healthy ranges: Staff compensation (total): 40-55%. Senior pastor (of total budget): 5-15%. Facilities/mortgage: 15-30%. Missions/outreach: 10-25%. Direct benevolence: 5-15%. Programs/ministry: 10-20%. Administration: 5-10%.

Warning Signs: Staff over 60%. Senior pastor over 20%. Missions under 5%. Benevolence under 2%. "Pastoral discretion" categories over 5%.

2.4 Financial Accountability Structure

Answer Yes, No, or Unknown: Is there an independent finance committee? Do non-staff members have signing authority? Is there an annual independent audit? Are audit results shared with congregation? Can any single person authorize large expenditures alone? Are there written financial policies? Is the pastor's compensation set by independent board? Are related-party transactions disclosed?

Scoring: 6+ Yes = Healthy. 3-5 Yes = Concerning. Under 3 Yes = Dangerous.

SECTION 3: LEADERSHIP ACCOUNTABILITY DIAGNOSTIC

3.1 Governance Structure Assessment

Mark each as Present, Absent, or Unclear: Written constitution/bylaws. Elected board or elders. Term limits for leadership. Defined process for removing leaders. Regular congregational meetings. Voting rights for members. Grievance/complaint process. External denominational accountability. Independent board members (not staff/family). Conflict of interest policies.

Scoring: 8-10 Present = Strong accountability. 5-7 = Moderate. Under 5 = Weak — power concentrated.

3.2 Pastor's Family Employment Audit

List all family members receiving income from the church. For each: Position, Compensation, Qualifications Verified (Y/N). Assessment: 0-1 employed = Normal. 2-3 = Monitor for nepotism. 4+ = Family business model.

3.3 Decision-Making Transparency

For the last three major decisions, answer Y/N: Was congregation informed before decision? Was congregation input solicited? Was there a vote or formal approval process? Were dissenting views acknowledged? Was financial impact disclosed? Could members opt out without consequence?

Scoring: 5-6 Yes = Transparent. 3-4 Yes = Partial. 0-2 Yes = Top-down control.

SECTION 4: CONTROL PATTERN DIAGNOSTIC

4.1 Information Control Assessment

Rate each as Never, Sometimes, Often, or Always: Leadership discourages reading outside sources. Questions are deflected or treated as disloyalty. "Touch not God's anointed" is invoked to silence criticism. Members are discouraged from discussing concerns with each other. Information about problems is restricted to leadership. Past controversies are minimized or rewritten. Members who left are spoken of negatively. Outside perspectives are labeled as "worldly" or "dangerous."

Scoring: Mostly "Never" = Healthy. Any "Often" or "Always" = Control tactics present.

4.2 Social Control Assessment

Rate each as Never, Sometimes, Often, or Always: Friendships are primarily/exclusively with church members. Leaving would mean losing your social network. Members are encouraged to report concerns about others to leadership. There is pressure to attend multiple services/events weekly. Missing events requires explanation or causes concern. "Accountability partners" report to leadership. Dating/marriage outside the church is discouraged.

Business relationships are primarily within the church.

Scoring: 0-2 "Often/Always" = Normal. 3-4 = Enmeshment developing. 5+ = Social capture.

4.3 Spiritual Control Assessment

Rate each as Never, Sometimes, Often, or Always: Pastor claims direct revelation from God for specific decisions. Disagreeing with leadership is framed as sin or rebellion. Blessings are tied to obedience to church leadership. Curses or spiritual consequences are threatened for leaving. Pastor's interpretation of Scripture cannot be questioned. Prophetic words include specific financial amounts. Spiritual status is tied to giving levels.

Members are taught they need the church for spiritual safety.

Scoring: Any "Often" or "Always" = Spiritual manipulation present. 5+ = Cult-like dynamics.

SECTION 5: GIVING PRESSURE DIAGNOSTIC

5.1 Offering Tactics Checklist

During a typical service, mark which tactics are used: Extended offering time (over 5 minutes). Emotional music during offering. Testimonies of financial blessing tied to giving. Specific dollar amounts suggested or demanded. Countdown timers or urgency language. Public commitments or pledge cards. Consequences named for not giving (curses, closed heavens). Promises of financial return on giving. Guilt language ("robbing God," "unfaithfulness").

Special offerings beyond regular tithe. Pressure to give during financial hardship. "Seed faith" or "first fruits" language. Naming specific people to give specific amounts.

Scoring: 0-2 = Standard. 3-5 = Pressure tactics present. 6-9 = Manipulation-heavy. 10+ = Extraction system.

5.2 Giving Expectations Assessment

Answer Yes or No: Is 10% tithe taught as mandatory/biblical requirement? Are offerings expected beyond the tithe? Is giving tracked by leadership? Does giving level affect access to leadership or opportunities? Are non-tithers excluded from leadership positions? Is there pressure to give during personal financial crisis? Are specific campaigns presented as spiritual obligations? Is gross vs. net income debated from the pulpit? Are pledges tracked and followed up?

Is giving history reviewed during membership processes?

Scoring: 0-2 Yes = Voluntary model. 3-5 Yes = Obligation-based. 6+ Yes = Extraction-based.

5.3 Prosperity Gospel Indicators

Mark each as Taught, Not Taught, or Unclear: Giving produces guaranteed financial return. Poverty indicates lack of faith. Wealth indicates God's favor. Specific dollar amounts have spiritual significance. "Seed faith" produces "harvest." God wants believers to be rich. Financial breakthrough requires sacrificial giving. Pastor's wealth demonstrates anointing.

Scoring: Any "Taught" = Prosperity gospel elements. 3+ = Prosperity gospel church. 5+ = Full system.

SECTION 6: VOLUNTEER EXPLOITATION DIAGNOSTIC

6.1 Volunteer Expectations Assessment

Answer Yes or No: Are volunteers expected to serve multiple hours weekly? Is serving framed as spiritual obligation rather than choice? Do volunteers do work that staff should do? Are volunteer "commitments" tracked and enforced? Is stepping back from serving treated as spiritual problem? Do volunteers work in roles that require professional training? Are volunteers given adequate breaks and boundaries? Can volunteers decline requests without guilt?

Are volunteer contributions acknowledged and appreciated? Is there a clear process for volunteer concerns?

6.2 Volunteer Labor Calculation

Calculate your church's volunteer labor value: Number of regular volunteers × Average hours per week × Reasonable hourly rate ($15-25) × 52 weeks = Annual volunteer labor value. Compare to total staff compensation.

Assessment: Volunteer labor exceeds staff compensation by 3x+ = Exploitation likely.

SECTION 7: EXIT COST ASSESSMENT

7.1 Calculate Your Exit Costs

If you left tomorrow, what would you lose? Rate severity 1-10 for each.

Social Costs: Close friendships. Casual friendships. Children's friendships. Business relationships. Professional network. Support system. Social activities.

Practical Costs: Childcare arrangements. Children's programs. Counseling/support groups. Recovery programs. Educational programs. Community assistance.

Identity Costs: Leadership role. Ministry identity. Sense of purpose. Spiritual community. Family expectations.

Total severity score: Under 30 = Low exit costs. 30-60 = Moderate. 60-100 = High. Over 100 = Extreme.

7.2 Exit Barrier Identification

Mark which barriers you face: Fear of spiritual consequences. Loss of salvation concerns. Family pressure to stay. Financial entanglement. Employment connected to church. Housing connected to church. Children's social consequences. Spouse's resistance to leaving. Fear of being shunned. Uncertainty about beliefs. No alternative community identified. Guilt about "abandoning" commitments.

Scoring: 0-3 = Normal considerations. 4-6 = Concerning entanglement. 7+ = High-control characteristics.

SECTION 8: HEALTHY CHURCH INDICATORS

Mark each as Present, Absent, or Unsure:

Financial Health: Budget publicly available. Independent financial oversight. Reasonable pastoral compensation. Significant outreach/benevolence spending. No high-pressure giving tactics.

Leadership Health: Accountable governance structure. Term limits for leaders. Questions welcomed. Disagreement tolerated. Admission of mistakes.

Relational Health: Members have outside friendships. Leaving is treated with grace. No monitoring or reporting. Healthy boundaries respected. Diversity of thought allowed.

Spiritual Health: Focus on service over extraction. Humility in leadership. No manipulation tactics. Doubt and questions normalized. Grace over performance.

Scoring: 16-20 Present = Healthy. 11-15 = Mostly healthy. 6-10 = Significant concerns. Under 6 = Unhealthy.

SECTION 9: COMPARISON MATRIX

Healthy Church vs. Exploitative Church:

Finances: Transparent, accountable, modest leadership compensation vs. Opaque, unaccountable, excessive wealth.

Giving: Voluntary, no pressure, generosity celebrated vs. Obligatory, high pressure, amounts demanded.

Leadership: Servant leaders, accountable, admit mistakes vs. Celebrity leaders, unaccountable, infallible image.

Questions: Welcomed, explored, valued vs. Deflected, punished, labeled as sin.

Boundaries: Respected, encouraged vs. Violated, discouraged.

Exit: Graceful, relationships maintained vs. Shunned, relationships severed.

Identity: Supplement to life vs. Replacement for life.

Doubt: Normal, pastoral care offered vs. Dangerous, remediation required.

Service: Voluntary, appreciated vs. Expected, extracted.

Growth: Internal transformation vs. External metrics (attendance, giving).

SECTION 10: DECISION FRAMEWORK

10.1 If You're Considering Joining

Before committing: Request and review detailed budget. Ask about pastor's compensation. Attend for 3+ months before joining. Talk to former members if possible. Research online reviews and news coverage. Observe how questions are received. Notice giving pressure tactics. Assess your exit costs if you join.

Don't join if: Financial information is refused. Questions are treated with hostility. Pressure to commit quickly. Former members describe it negatively. High-pressure giving. Social isolation encouraged.

10.2 If You're Currently Attending

If your assessment shows concerns: Minor concerns = Raise questions with leadership; observe response. Moderate concerns = Document patterns; build outside support network; set boundaries. Significant concerns = Develop exit plan; reduce financial involvement; protect children. Severe concerns = Execute exit plan; prioritize safety; seek outside support.

Questions to ask leadership: "Can I see a detailed budget breakdown?" "How is the pastor's compensation determined?" "What is the process for raising concerns about leadership?" "How are major financial decisions made?" "What happens when someone decides to leave?"

Evaluate responses: Defensive, evasive, or hostile = Red flag. Open, transparent, welcoming = Healthy sign.

10.3 If You're Helping Someone Else

Do: Listen without judgment. Validate their experience. Provide information. Maintain relationship regardless of their choices. Offer practical support if they leave. Be patient.

Don't: Issue ultimatums. Attack their beliefs. Force confrontation. Cut off relationship if they stay. Underestimate exit costs. Rush their process.

SECTION 11: DOCUMENTATION TEMPLATE

If you're documenting concerning patterns, record: Date. Type of incident (Financial pressure / Spiritual manipulation / Leadership misconduct / Boundary violation / Retaliation for questions / Other). What happened. Who was involved. Witnesses. How it made you feel. Documentation saved (Yes/No). Location of documentation.

SECTION 12: RESOURCE QUICK REFERENCE

Questions Every Church Should Answer

1. What is the senior pastor's total annual compensation?
2. What percentage of the budget goes to outreach vs. operations?
3. Who has authority to spend church funds?
4. When was the last independent financial audit?
5. What is the process for removing a pastor?
6. How are major decisions made? 7. What happens when someone leaves?

Warning Phrases

"Touch not God's anointed" = Don't question leadership. "You need spiritual covering" = You can't leave safely. "God told me to tell you" = Manipulation incoming. "Sow a seed for your breakthrough" = Give money to get money. "Test God in your tithe" = Give despite financial hardship. "The enemy is attacking your giving" = Guilt for not giving more. "Robbing God" = Shame tactic. "This is just between us" = Secrecy/isolation tactic. "You're in rebellion" = Disagreement = sin.

"We'll pray for you" (dismissively) = Your concerns don't matter.

Healthy Phrases

"That's a great question" = Questions are valued. "Here's our complete budget" = Transparency is practiced. "We made a mistake" = Humility is present. "Take whatever time you need" = Boundaries are respected. "We'll miss you" (when leaving) = Grace is extended. "Give as you're able" = Generosity without pressure. "Let's look at the text together" = Teaching over dictating. "What do you think?" = Input is valued.

FINAL NOTE

This framework is a tool, not a verdict. No church is perfect. Healthy churches have flaws. The question is whether the church's systems, patterns, and responses indicate an environment of genuine care and accountability — or extraction and control.

Trust your observations. Document what you see. Seek outside perspective. And remember: questioning an institution is not the same as questioning God.

Your discernment is not disloyalty. It's wisdom.

If this framework raises concerns, revisit the chapters on control, extraction, and exit to better understand the patterns at work.

www.ingramcontent.com/pod-product-compliance
Ingram Content Group UK Ltd.
Pitfield, Milton Keynes, MK11 3LW, UK
UKHW041634190726
13854UKWH00006B/2496

9 780979 836022